ULRICH ZWINGLI: THE PATRIOTIC REFORMER

ULRICH ZWINGLI
THE PATRIOTIC REFORMER

A HISTORY

WILLIAM M. BLACKBURN

SOLID GROUND CHRISTIAN BOOKS
BIRMINGHAM, ALABAMA USA

Solid Ground Christian Books
6749 Remington Circle
Pelham AL 35124
205-443-0311
mike.sgcb@gmail.com
www.solid-ground-books.com

ULRICH ZWINGLI: *The Patriotic Reformer*
by William M. Blackburn (1828-1898)

First published in 1868 by the Presbyterian Board
of Publication, Philadelphia, PA

First Solid Ground Edition: March 2013

Cover design by Borgo Design, Tuscaloosa, AL

ISBN- 978-159925-231-5

PREFACE.

No other reformer struck out a more original and independent course than Ulrich Zwingli. No other man attempted to be, at the same time, a preacher, author, statesman, military patriot and reformer. Why he gave such varied direction to his noble energies, and how well he succeeded in his efforts, it is partly the design of the present volume to show. His personal history is full of interesting incidents; his character rich in admirable qualities; his public life conveys a lesson upon the mingling of religion and politics which it may be well to ponder in later times. The author has endeavoured to set forth the man and his friends as they grew in piety and laboured together in studying the Word of God, teaching and preaching the truth, and restoring the Church to the foundation of Christ and his Apostles. It may serve as a companion to "William Farel," thus making tolerably complete the publications of the Presbyterian Board upon the early history of the Reformation in both French and German Switzerland.

The authorities chiefly consulted are, The Life and Times of Ulrich Zwingli, by J. J. Hottinger—Zwingli, or the Rise of the Reformation in Switzerland, by R. Christoffel—Histoire de la Confederation Helvetique, par A. L. de Watteville—Histoire de la Reformation de la Suisse, par Abram Ruchat—D'Aubigne's History of the Reformation in the Sixteenth Century—Scott's Continuation of Milner—Stebbing's History of the Church of Christ from the Diet of Augsburg to the Eighteenth Century—Dupin's Ecclesiastical History—Gailard's History of the Reformation—Church Histories by Mosheim, Giesseler and Kurtz—Gerdesii Historia Reformationis—Sleidani, De statu religionis et reipublicæ, Carolo Quinto Cæsare, Commentarii—Biographie Universelle—Le Grand Dictionnaire Historique, par M. Louis Moreri—Bayle's Dictionary—Hertzog's Real-Encyclopaedie für Protestant. Theologie und Kirche.—Leben und Schriften der Väter und Begründer Reformirten Kirche—Zschokke's History of Switzerland—Ledderhose's Life of Melancthon—Cunningham's Reformers and the Theology of the Reformation—Calvin's Letters—The Zurich Letters (by Parker Society)—and Switzerland the Pioneer of the Reformation, by the "Countess Dora D'Istria" (Madame Ghika). Reference is had also to such articles in various Reviews as a full sketch of Zwingli in Blackwood's Magazine, 1828, and a life in the Bibliotheca Sacra, vols. viii. and ix. The field is not a new one, nor is it barren; and it is hoped that it may be profitably reaped again for the benefit of the patrons of the Presbyterian Board. To the harvest no denomination of Christians holds an exclusive title. If the good seed of divine truth shall be found in the sheaves of this gleaning, and there be a soil for it in the reader's heart, the Lord may bless the volume now committed to his care.

W. M. B.

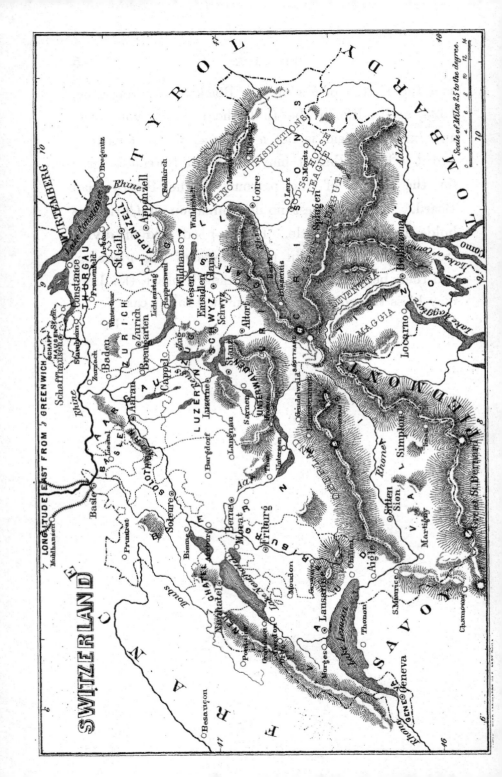

CONTENTS.

CHAPTER I.

THE AGE OF CONVENTS.

CHAPTER II.

ULRICH, THE SHEPHERD-BOY.

CHAPTER III.

THE YOUNG PASTOR OF GLARIS.

CHAPTER IV.

THE PARSON TEMPTED TO WAR.

7

CHAPTER V.

PREACHING TO PILGRIMS.

CHAPTER VI.

THE ROMISH SAMSON.

CHAPTER VII.

A NEW STYLE OF PREACHING.

CHAPTER VIII.

PATRIOTIC LABOURS.

CHAPTER IX.

THE SCHOOL OF THE CROSS.

CONTENTS.

CHAPTER X.

ANNA REINHARD AND HER HOME.

CHAPTER XI.

THE MONKS AND NUNS.

CHAPTER XII.

THE TWO PETITIONS.

CHAPTER XIII.

MYCONIUS IN TROUBLE.

CHAPTER XIV.

NEW TRIUMPHS.

CHAPTER XX.

ZWINGLI FACES LUTHER.

CHAPTER XXI.

TAKING THE SWORD.

CHAPTER XXII.

THE GOSPEL WEAPONS.

CHAPTER XXIII.

THE LAND BLOCKADE OF THE FIVE CANTONS.

CHAPTER XXIV.

PERISHING WITH THE SWORD.

12 CONTENTS.

CHAPTER XXV.

THE SURVIVORS.

ULRICH ZWINGLI.

CHAPTER I.

THE AGE OF CONVENTS.

I T is a long way from Bangor in Ireland to Lake Constance in Switzerland. It must have been a weary road to travel nine hundred and fifty years ago. Yet in the year of our Lord 610, there were two Irish missionaries journeying through the wild regions between the Swiss Lakes of Zurich and Constance, and seeking for a place where they might teach the Gospel to the heathen tribes that dwelt among the mountains. One of these was Columban,* brought up in the convent of Bangor. Suddenly taken with a desire for foreign travel, he went into Eastern France, founded several convents, and was at length obliged to flee. He started for Ireland, but his vessel was driven back by a storm. He then resolved to go to the wild tribes of Switzerland. The other missionary was Gallus, who had been the pupil and companion of Columban. He was a "Scotchman of noble

---

* Not Columba, who founded the great convent on the Scottish island of Iona, from which went forth so many missionaries into Europe. Iona was the seat of the Culdees, who went into heathen lands "like bees from their hive." O'Donnell says, with a pun on the name of the great founder, which means a dove, "From the nest of Columba these sacred doves took their flight to all quarters."

birth," for every Irishman was called a Scot in those days. There are many legends about these men, invented by the monks of later times; perhaps what we now write of them is true history. By following them a little we may get some idea of what Switzerland was when Zwingli was born.

Columban wished to bury himself in deeper solitudes than any he had yet found. He loved to wander in the woods and sit for days in a lonely place reading his book. He was not like an apostle, ever anxious to preach the gospel to as many pagans as he could reach. His idea was to be a hermit, and yet teach all who might gather about his lonely cell. He struck the Rhine at Mentz (Mayence), got a boat for himself and his followers, and set out up the river. Passing by the spot where Basle now stands, they worked their way into the river Aar, then into the Limmat, and halted not far from where Zurich is built. Then they went into Zug, and began their work. The natives gathered about them. Not far distant was a rude idol-temple. "You must not worship idols," they said to the ancient Suevi; "God is in heaven. God is everywhere. But your idols are not gods. Your temple is not God's house. You must destroy it."

"Nay," said the people, horrified at the idea. "We will not destroy it." They looked fiercely at the missionaries, asserting that they did not worship their rude idols, but their gods were Thor, Woden and the old Saxon deities. The religion of many of the ancient Swiss was doubtless that of the Druids. On some old houses is still seen the symbol called the "Druid's foot," but no one knows its meaning.

In a short time Columban found that the temple was in the way of the truth. He could not persuade the heathen Switzers that the true God was invisible. They would go to the idol-house, sing their wild songs, shout their doleful prayers, and engage in their rude sports. "The temple must come down," said he. Some of his companions or converts went and set it on fire, and threw the idols into the lake. The flames arose, and wrath burned in the hearts of the people. The missionaries had not been wise in their zeal ; they were obliged to flee.

Columban and his associates took their flight toward Lake Constance. It was a fearful journey over the mountains, through the deep forests, and among tribes of uncivilized men. They came at length to the castle of Arbon, near Lake Constance, where the ancients Romans once held their sway. They saw a man in the village, with a shorn head and a cross hanging upon his neck. "Who art thou?" inquired Gallus, who could speak ancient German better than the rest.

"I am Willimar, the pastor of this place. I see by your habit that you are Christians, and Christian brethren are very rare in these parts. Whither do ye go?"

"We know not whither: anywhere that our Lord may lead us to teach the Gospel to the perishing."

"Come in, ye blessed of the Lord," replied Willimar, who was overjoyed to have such brethren break his solitude and accept his hospitality. He led them to his humble convent, where they passed seven days of happy fellowship with the priest of Arbon.

"There is an ancient castle called Pregentia (Bregentz) at the head of the lake," said Willimar to his guests, who inquired for a place to dwell. "Go there; the country is fruitful, the lake will supply you with fish, and the people are as sheep having no shepherd."

"Farewell, good pastor," said the missionaries one morning; "we will build our Bethel in the desert." They went to Bregentz. They threw up a hut not far from the castle, where

16 ULRICH ZWINGLI.

there were the ruins of an old church; they made a garden; they cast their nets into the lake; they gave their fine fishes to the people, and the rude natives ceased to wonder and.began to love. Charity opened the way for Christianity. Gallus preached to them in their own language, and they began to believe. The missionaries built a church, and for three years there were promises of success. But persecution came; Columban was obliged to leave. He went to Italy, and founded the monastery of Bobbio, near Pavia.

Gallus was sick and could not follow his countryman and guide. With great grief he saw his father Columban depart; he lingered until he could walk, and then took his boat and his net and went to Arbon, where Willimar gave him a kindly welcome. No sooner was Gallus recovered from his sickness and the sad thoughts of his failure, than he begged the deacon Hiltibad to to conduct him into the vast forest, that he might find a suitable place for a new hermitage. Hiltibad knew the paths among the mountains, for his business was to hunt and fish and supply the convent with provisions. But the deacon said, "You will be in constant danger; the forest is full of bears and wolves."

"If the Lord be for us, who can be against us?" replied Gallus. "The God who delivered Daniel from the lions, is able to defend me."

The deacon prepared for the perilous journey. Gallus spent a day in prayer and fasting. Early in the morning they set out, scarcely knowing whither they went. They grew weary. At three o'clock the deacon said, "Let us rest a little and refresh ourselves. I have some bread here, and with my net I will catch fish from the brook."

"Nay," answered Gallus; "I will taste of nothing until a place of rest be found."

They wandered on until the sun was setting, when they came to a spot where the river Steinâch, falling from the mountain, had hollowed out the rock, and where plenty of fishes were seen swimming in the stream. The deacon could not resist the temptation, and casting in his net he drew out an abundance that would have gratified the fishermen of Galilee. He then took his flint, struck a fire and prepared an inviting supper. In the meantime—the story runs—Gallus was kneeling in prayer among the bushes. Hearing the call of the deacon, he attempted to rise, when a thorn caused him to fall. Hiltibad saw him, and ran to his assistance. But Gallus said, "Let me alone; here is my resting-place; here will I dwell." He consecrated the spot to God, arose, marked it by a cross made of a hazel-rod, and then yielded to the kindly attentions of the deacon.

On this spot Gallus founded the monastery which afterward became celebrated and bore his name being called St. Gall. He lived many years in seclusion, drawing to him a band of brother monks. The offer of a bishopric could not tempt him away; he secured the office for a native of the country whom he had trained at the convent. He laboured in his way for the conversion of the people until the year 640. Shortly before his death, he requested his old friend Willimar to meet him at the castle of Arbon. Feeble as he was, he summoned his last energies and preached to the people assembled at the castle. His strength failed him; he could not return to his convent, and he died at Arbon. He left behind him many followers who imitated his example, and who reared monasteries in those barbarous wilds. Other missionares followed, among whom were Thrudpert and Kilian, who preached to the Swiss and died martyrs to their faith. For nearly three centuries Ireland and Iona sent companies of learned and pious men into the countries along the Rhine. These men did not at first acknowledge the bishop of Rome as their pope. They believed nothing of the doctrines of purgatory, image-worship, adoration of the saints, the mass, nor transubstantiation. They were opposed and persecuted by the Romish clergy. The number of them who went into these foreign countries was so great that when the popish writers, long afterward, could not learn the origin of certain saints, they set them down as having come from the Irish and Scottish Church. Mosheim says, "That the Irish [Scotch as well] were lovers of learning; that they distinguished themselves, in these times of ignorance, by the culture of the sciences above all other nations, travelling through the most distant lands, is a fact with which I have been long acquainted. . . . The Irish were the first teachers of the scholastic theology in Europe." It may be claimed that Switzerland received the gospel mainly from the church of St. Patrick, who was anything but a Romanist. The authority of the pope was not acknowledged by him, nor by the ancient Church of the Scots. Nor was it by the ancient Church of the Swiss, until convents turned missionaries into monks, and monks turned the gospel into fables, and these fables led the people to believe that the pope was the Vicar of Christ, and that Mary should be adored as the Virgin and as the guardian of the Church.

It must be remembered that there were many errors in the teachings of such missionaries. At that time there was a passion for monkery. Christians built convents, and thought that they must become monks and nuns in order to serve God most faithfully. Scores of men, like Gallus, went into the German part of Switzerland and founded churches and convents. They did not introduce Christianity in the purest form. The errors they taught lived after them, growing worse and more numerous for centuries, until there was little else than a religion of papal ceremonies. The pioneer missionaries were remembered as great and holy men, and were exalted into "saints," whom the people worshipped. Among others were St. Columban and St. Gallus. Perhaps deacon Hiltibad had such honors paid to his name. Centuries passed away ; the ages became very dark ; the pope at Rome ruled the Church, and still the monks went about founding convents. Those which were long called the "Scottish Cloisters" were most celebrated for learning and piety.

There were two hermits at St. Gall about the year 1050 who wished to imitate the founder of their monastery. We do not know their names, nor whether they had any deacon to lead them into the Thurgovian forests. But St. Gall had grown too great and too much civilized for them, for the French kings had reared magnificent buildings, and princes had bestowed vast wealth upon the ancient abbey. Here was the asylum of learning during the Dark Ages, and this was the most celebrated school in Europe.* Perhaps the two hermits were ambitious to found another St. Gall. They went southward and entered the valley of the Tockenburg, through which flows the little river Thur. All around them was nothing but Alpine grandeur and solitude. How could they expect that narrow valley ever to be filled with people? They pushed on until they reached some of the springs

---

* "Here the authors of Rome and Greece were not only read but copied; the writing of the monks of St. Gall, that most invaluable accomplishment when printing had not yet enlightened the world, was exquisitely fine, and many possessed the sister art of embellishing their MSS. by illumination. . . . They reduced into the vulgar tongue many parts of the Bible, especially the Psalms, Canticles and Ecclesiastes. . . . Visitors from all countries, even England, Ireland and Scotland, brought their literature to this mart of erudition."—*Historical Pictures of the Middle Ages.*

of the river Thur, and there they built two cells and dwelt alone.
By degrees other monks joined them. Then came people, indus-
try and civilization. So wild had been their house that the
place was called *Wildhaus.* Two hamlets, Schonenboden and
Lisighaus (Elizabeth-house), now stand near the old convent. It
is a barren spot, too high up in the cold winds for the fruits of
the earth to grow. One may stand there and look upon the narrow green strip of a valley sloping down from his feet, or turn
and gaze upon enormous masses of rock that rise around him
"in savage grandeur to the skies."

Thus went the Word of God to Wildhaus along with much of
error and superstition. The Bible became less and less used,
and more secretly hidden within convent walls. Popery rested
like a cloud over Switzerland. The people needed to learn one
thing: that was not to look to the convents for holiness, nor to
Rome for light, but to the Word of the Lord and to Jesus
Christ. A reformation was needed. It would come as soon as
a native of Wildhaus should bring to light the hidden Bible.
Obscure towns have often been the birth-place of illustrious
men.

Two facts should be borne in mind as we enter upon the history of the Reformation under Zwingli. The first is the strength
of Romanism in Switzerland. It had a castle in every convent;
it had an army in every canton. The larger towns and the
cities were the first to yield; the wilder districts defended their
superstitions to the last. It was ignorance that fortified popery.

The second fact is the independence of the cantons. There
was a union among those in which the German language prevailed; they had their confederacy. But yet each canton had
a style of liberty peculiar to itself, and a fierce jealousy of its
own rights. Some of them claimed to be independent republics,

When the reformed teachers and preachers entered into a canton, it was easy for the priests to arouse the people by crying out that their liberties were in danger, and that the Protestants wished to destroy their confederacy, founded by the heroes of Grütli and William Tell.

CHAPTER II.

ULRICH, THE SHEPHERD-BOY.

(1484–1506.)

NOT far from the old church of Wildhaus, and still nearer to Lisighaus, on a path that leads to the pasture-grounds across the river, stands the cottage of a peasant. The story is that the trees of which it is built were felled on the very spot. It bears the marks of an ancient time. The timbers are black with age; the walls are thin; the windows are made of small, round panes of glass; the roof is weighed down by stones to protect the shingles from the grasp of the storm. Just in front is a bubbling spring, an emblem of the pure waters of eternal life.

It is claimed that this is the house in which dwelt a man named Zwingli,* during the latter half of the fifteenth century. He was more than "an humble peasant" in the eyes of his neighbours, for he was of an ancient family and was highly esteemed among the Alpine mountaineers. The parish of Wildhaus had long been under the control of St. Gall, whose abbot claimed it as his manor. But the people wrung their rights from his hands, and set up an independent community, having the power to elect their own parish officers. They at once made Zwingli their ammann (head-man or bailiff), and chose his

---

* Pronounced *Zwing-ly*.

brother Bartholomew as their parson; the latter was also dean of Wesen.

Margaret Meili, the bailiff's wife, had the respect of the villagers, reared her two sons, Henry and Nicholas, in the best way she knew, and often told them of their uncle John Meili, who became an abbot in Thurgovia.

On New Year's day, 1484, a third son was born in the quiet cottage, just seven weeks after Luther came wailing into the world. Parson Bartholomew came over from Wesen, baptized him, and fixed upon him the name of his father, Ulrich. One after another, five younger sons appeared in the family, and ninthly a daughter Anna ended the list. It was a happy household. No Alpine bailiff seemed more content than Ulrich the elder. His good character, his official dignity and his numerous children made him the patriarch of the mountains. He was a shepherd, having meadows and alps of his own, and considering himself a guardian of the rights and liberties of the people.

From time immemorial the dwellers at Wildhaus had been a simple, cheerful, song-loving race of shepherds. It was their custom in May to lead their flocks to the lower slopes of the mountains, and every lad that had his lamb went shouting after the herds of sheep and cattle, whose numberless bells were tinkling forth the mirth of the morning. Little Ulrich might go to these lower pastures, but when the flocks went higher up Mount Sentis, he must linger nearer home, and direct his busy mind to studies in natural history. If we may judge that in the writings of his manhood he inserted some of the memories of his youth, we may imagine the thoughtful child searching for illustrations of "The Providence of God." He saw that the field-mouse had been wise enough to take care of itself and lay up its winter stores. Hidden behind some rock, he perhaps watched the porcupine making a fork of his quills and carrying to his nest a supply for the future. Or he saw the marmots running about, gathering together the softest grass, one making a wagon of the other; this one lying on his back and throwing out his feet like a rack, while the others loaded him with hay, and then seizing his tail they dragged him and his load to their store-house. Meanwhile one marmot was posted on a high place as a sentinel, and if Ulrich laughed at their ingenuity or threatened them with danger, they made a hasty retreat to their homes.

In midsummer the shepherds went far up the mountains, and the herds cropped the tender grass by the side of the glaciers. The hardier sons would remain there for days and weeks tending the flocks, but not forgotten by their parents nor unvisited by the young villagers. On a clear day the youth would form parties, start early and wind their way up into the fresh breezes, to meet the shepherd-boys, and spend hours among the crags, taking with them baskets of provision for the herdsmen. As they went up they played their rustic instruments and sang the *ranz des vaches;* the shepherds welcomed them, from afar, with shouts and Alpine horns, and when the parties met they engaged in innocent glee, clambering the peaks and frightening the chamois that grazed in the gorges. We may imagine young Ulrich among them, watching a lamb that ventures upon more liberty, leaves the flock and strays away, hidden, at length, by some jutting crag. He sees the movement, hastes with nimble feet, climbs over the rocks, and drives back the wanderer, whose bell tinkles so fast that it inspires the company with new laughter. But the lad lingers out of sight. Is the child of nine years lost? He is watching the eagle that had an eye upon his lamb. He is gazing devoutly at the peaks that seem everlasting, and appear as the stepping-places into the skies, where God dwelleth. He is getting other illustrations for a work on "The Providence of God," which he will write at a future day. One of his friends said afterward: "I have often thought from these sublime heights, which stretch upward toward heaven, he took something heavenly and divine."

Thus passed the summers. The winter evenings were long in his father's house. Books were rare, and Ulrich could not often sit in the chimney-corner and read by the light of the fire. If the wiser men dropped in to talk of politics, he wished himself in some of the neighbouring hamlets, where the dreary time was lightened by the joyous voice of song or the merry tones of such instruments as were skilfully played in almost every cottage. But the lad did not always find the conversation dry and somnific. The leading men of the parish often rehearsed the legends of the ancient times, and St. Gall seemed a giant. They told how their forefathers groaned under the heavy yoke of counts and abbots who held rule over them. "But did not the Tockenburgers conquer the Zurichers and gain their independence?" little Ulrich would ask.

"Indeed they did," one of the elders would reply, in boastful tone. "They did it easily; there is no such a people as the Tockenburgers anywhere among the lakes. 1 remember the year—it was 1469—for I was wounded then. But I pushed on and laid low a Zurich captain, and that turned the tide of battle." The company smiled, for this hero was not usually mentioned with so much honour except when he was telling his own story.

Ulrich often heard such men tell how their native valley of the Tockenburg had gained more and more freedom, and the love of country was kindled in his heart. He felt patriotic for Switzerland; if any one of them dropped a word unfavourable to lib-

erty, he took up the cause and warmly defended it. The boy
also often hung upon the lips of his grandmother, as she repeated legendary tales and biblical stories. She had treasured
up some knowledge of the Holy Word, which had been so beautifully copied by the monks of St. Gall, and brought by the two
hermits to Wildhaus. Had she been free from all Romish
errors, she might have proved another grandmother Lois teaching a Swiss Timothy the Scriptures of truth.

The kind bailiff was delighted with the promising mind of his
third son. His two clerical uncles urged his parents to train up
little Ulrich for a priest, and they began to think that he might
do something better than tend herds on Mount Sentis. One
morning, when he was nine or ten years old, his father took him
by the hand and started for Wesen. They went panting up the
Gulmen, and from the green heights the lad might have looked
down on the valley of Glaris, the forests of Einsidlen and the
lake of Zurich, without dreaming that in those districts he was
some time to wage a warfare for the truth of God. But his eyes
were fixed upon the little silvery lake of Wallenstadt, and he
wished himself at the lower end of it, sitting at his uncle's din-
ner-table. After a journey of eight or ten hours they entered
the house of Bartholomew Zwingli, the dean of Wesen. "You
have put lofty ideas into Ulrich's head," said the father to his
brother, "and now I have brought him, so that you may try
what he can do."

"Right gladly will I measure him," answered the dean. "So,
Ulrich, you will be as a son to your uncle." Thus the lad was
left with one who loved him and took delight in his quick mind,
cheerful heart and firm adherence to truth. Ulrich was sent to
school, where he soon learned all that the village schoolmaster
could teach. This will not appear wonderful if we remember

that the common schoolmaster was anything but a prodigy in learning.

A class of poor and often lazy men roamed about teaching, for a pittance, the merest elements of an education. Two well-painted placards, of the olden time, preserved at Basle, show us what these strolling masters assumed to teach. Each represents a school-room. In one, the children are sitting or kneeling on the floor with their books, while the teacher is ready to administer the rod if the boy at his desk does not recite well. In the other are older scholars. The following advertisement is written under both:

"Whosoever wishes to learn to write and read in German, in the quickest way ever found out, though he does not know a single letter of the alphabet, can in a short time get enough here to cast up his own accounts and read; and if any one be too stupid to learn, as I have taught him nothing, so will I charge him nothing, be he who he may, burgher or apprentice, woman or girl. Whoever comes in he will be faithfully taught for a small sum, but the young boys and girls after the Ember weeks, as the custom is" (1516.)

Children and adults often sat upon the same bench. There was nothing like a division into classes; each did the best he could in his own way. The rod was one of the persuasives to study. In the better Latin schools one rule was, "The school-master shall beat the pupils with rods, and not with his fist or staff, and particularly not on the head, lest, on account of their youth, he might thereby do great damage to the memory." For a long time a yearly holiday was kept, under the name of "The Procession of the Rods." The pupils went out in summer to the woods, and came back with large bundles of birch-twigs, cracking jokes and singing—

Ye fathers and ye mothers good,
See us with the birchen wood
Loaded, coming home again :
Use it for our moral gain,
Not for injury or pain.
Your command and that of God
Prompt us now to bear the rod
On our bodies thus to-day ;
Not in angry, sullen mood,
But with spirits glad and gay.

Not unlike this were the common schools in the Swiss valleys. In larger towns a priest was usually the teacher, having a small salary and the gift of a coat once a year. Sometimes they were allowed what their pupils could beg for them. The poor scholars did the begging, going through the streets and singing under the windows. The school at Wesen was perhaps of this latter grade. It seems that Ulrich came in contact with boys who were guilty of deceptions and lies. He felt a great horror of falsehood. He tells us that one day the thought occurred to him "that lying ought to be more severely punished than theft. Hypocrisy is worse than stealing. Falsehood is the beginning of all evil. Man most resembles God by being true. Glorious is the truth, full of majesty, commanding even the respect of the wicked."

"Wesen can do no more for the lad," thought his uncle. "He must go to Basle." To this the father agreed. It seemed a long journey over the mountains, but the dean's friend, George Binzli, was at Basle, as the master of St. Theodore's school. This teacher took the child of the Tockenburg to his warm heart, and so helped him forward that the boy soon got beyond the man in knowledge. It was the fashion for the young students to imitate the learned doctors in holding disputations.

In these debating clubs young Zwingli excelled his classmates. He was the champion who won the victory. His older rivals grew jealous of him. On a small scale he was meeting with what would try his talents and temper at a later day. He outgrew the school at Basle, as he had that of Wesen.

"Send him to Berne," said his uncle Bartholomew, and thither he was sent, at the age of thirteen, to wonder at its fondness for petted bears and to find out that he was a poet. Henry Lupulus (Littlewolf) was there teaching the dead languages with great credit to himself. He had opened the first academy of learned languages in Switzerland. He had travelled in the East, had seen the Holy Sepulchre, had spoken Greek in Athens and witnessed the papal corruptions of Rome. History was at his tongue's end, and poetry dropped from his graceful pen. Ulrich found in his school a new world. He read the classics, admired the Roman orators and imitated the Latin poets. He came in contact with the monks and their style of religious life.

All Switzerland was talking of a man who had won the place of a saint in the minds of the people. He was Nicholas von der Flue, who had been a soldier in the field, an adviser in council, and at the age of fifty a hermit in the valley of Melchthal, where he dwelt in his lowly cell and passed his time in the exercises of piety. In 1481 the Swiss cantons were at strife, and war was threatened. The wise men assembled, but only made matters worse by angry debate. Some of them sought the advice of the hermit. He went to Stanz, suddenly appeared in the Diet, addressed the wrathful councillors as a father, and secured peace. The union of the cantons was preserved, and he was honoured throughout the whole land as one whose wisdom was almost superhuman. He died six years after, and Henry Lupulus sang the life of the pious hermit with enthusiasm. To this day crowds of pilgrims visit and pay their vows at his shrine.

But the monks of Berne were altogether different from the hermit Nicholas. The Franciscans were quarrelling with the Dominicans; each rivalled the other in tricks and delusions, and both sought to win young men into their convent. The Dominicans particularly noticed Zwingli. They were charmed with his fine appearance, his voice of song and his musical skill. They heard of his ready wit, his large mind, his noble spirit and his ardent love of knowledge. He might become a brilliant ornament of their order. They attracted him into their convent, and by their crafty arts almost persuaded him to live with them until he should become old enough to take the vows of a monk. But he was too honest to take any step without asking advice. It seems that he talked with his teacher and wrote to his father on the subject. They took alarm, and parson Bartholomew joined them in recalling Ulrich speedily from Berne, to send him to Vienna in Austria.

At the high school in Vienna were two young men, on whose brows the Emperor would one day place the poetic wreath, and whom all Switzerland would honour as eminent scholars. One of them was Joachim von Watt, or Vadian, the son of a rich merchant of St. Gall: the other was Henry Loreti, the son of a poor peasant of the canton of Glaris, and who took the name of Glarean. They gave a hearty welcome to young Zwingli, and these three Swiss students indulged in poetry, music, the classics and scientific studies, formed a lasting friendship, and prepared to work unitedly in a great reformation. They admitted to their circle two Swabian youths, who were to become the enemies of their doctrines at a future day. One of these was John Heigerlin, called Faber because he was the son of a smith; he was a man of pliant character, proud of honours, ambitious for renown, and fitted to become a courtier rather than a scholar. The other was John Meyer of Eck, a man who read much, forgot little, spoke with eloquence and won friends by the liveliness of his genius. He became the greatest theologian of the Roman Church in Germany, and entered the lists against Luther as Doctor Eck. With such students young Zwingli mingled during his two years' stay at Vienna. In 1502 he returned to Wildhaus, but his native mountains did not satisfy him. He had tasted the waters of learning, and he could not be content to live among the songs of his brothers and the lowing of their herds. God had another purpose concerning him.

He went again to Basle, taught in St. Martin's school and studied in the university, earning enough to pay his way, so that he drew no longer upon his father's slender purse or his uncle Bartholomew's generosity. Wolfgang Capito became his warmest friend, and was struck with the wit and music of the student of the Sentis mountains; for when Ulrich was weary of his studies in scholastic divinity, he took up one of his numerous musical instrments and made his room ring with the tunes of his native land or sang the songs of the Swiss warriors. In his love for music he was quite equal to Luther. If any think this a weakness, let him remember David and his Hebrew harp. There was not an instrument of which Zwingli could not soon make himself master. His enthusiasm for the art was contagious; he imparted a taste for it throughout the university. But he did not waste time upon it, for, having relaxed his mind, he returned to his studies with the greater zeal. The theology of the schools and the monks disgusted him: it was full of useless questions and trifling answers; a medley of confused ideas, empty babbling and barbarism, without one grain of sound doctrine. "It is a mere loss of time to study it," said he, and he waited for something better to appear. The Lord, who had led him hitherto, was bringing the right teacher.

In the town of Bienne, on a little lake at the base of the Jura Mountains, lived a burgomaster who had educated his son Thomas with great care. The young man had gone farther than most students of his time, and made himself familiar with the Holy Scriptures while he studied under the celebrated Reuchlin. The world was beginning to hear of Thomas Wittembach when he came to Basle, in 1505, and opened a course of lectures. The students flocked to his classes. He spoke with life, and some of his words were prophetic. "The time is not far distant," said he, "when the old scholastic theology will be swept away, and the ancient doctrines of the Church be revived. God's word is the foundation of all truth. Absolution by priests is a Romish cheat. Christ's death is the only ransom for our souls." The good seed fell into the soft heart of young Zwingli. A new path was pointed out as the true way of life; he and his friend Capito rushed into it.

Among the students was a young man of twenty-three, small in stature, pale and sickly, but gentle in his manners and intrepid in spirit. Zwingli found him to be Leo Juda, the son of a married parish priest in Alsace, and the nephew of a hero, who died at Rhodes fighting against the Turks. Leo was fond of music, had a fine voice and played the dulcimer with skill. Love of song and of truth united him and Zwingli in friendship for life. Often did they spend an hour in singing together, and no doubt rehearsing the new doctrines boldly proclaimed by Wittembach or recorded for their eyes in the Book of God. But they were not to be long in fellowship at Basle. Soon the hour was struck when they must part, until with stronger powers they should meet again to urge on the cause of the Reformation. Leo went to his native province and settled as the parson of St. Pilt.

In later years Leo wrote of Wittembach: "Zwingli and I enjoyed his instructions at Basle in 1505. Under his guidance we passed from polite literature, in which he was fully at home, over to the more earnest study of the Holy Scriptures. . . . Whatever of thorough knowledge we possess we owe it to him, and must remain his debtors as long as we live."

Zwingli had conferred upon him the title of Master of Arts, but he never made use of the degree. He used to say, "One is our Master, even Christ." A call was preparing for him.

CHAPTER III.

THE YOUNG PASTOR OF GLARIS.

(1506–1510.)

IT was known among the priests who sought fat livings that a pastor was wanted at Glaris,* a small town in a rich valley that in our day sends some of its celebrated cheese to America. Henry Goldli, one of the pope's young courtiers, and his Master of Horse, sought the living, that he might add it to several other benefices held by him, and thus, with all his offices, he might have revenues enough to enable him to live at Rome with greater comfort to himself. As for the Alpine people, he did not think of dwelling and preaching among them. The pope granted him the incumbency.

But the shepherds and cheese-makers of the valley had a will and a choice of their own. Proud of the antiquity of their race, and loving the freedom that had cost them so many struggles, they were not willing to receive a pastor who could show them nothing but a slip of parchment bearing the name of the pope. His aristocratic blood and lofty pretensions did not in-

---

* The use of slates in schools is one of the great discoveries. It is related that in the sixteenth century certain poor people of this canton gathered some of the smooth stones of their valley and sold them. One framed a piece and used it for keeping his accounts. Others began to write upon slates. A trade sprang up, and Swiss slates became known throughout the civilized world.

crease their respect. In some way they heard of young Zwingli. Perhaps Glarean told them of his fellow-student at Vienna, or parson Bartholomew may have met some of them at Wesen, where they went to market, and spoken of his truth-loving nephew. They chose Ulrich Zwingli, and he accepted their call. He had humble thoughts of himself. " God has granted me," said he, " from my boyhood to devote myself to the acquirement of knowledge, both human and divine. . . . I acknowledge myself to be a great sinner before God, though I have not lived an immoral life, and on no occasion has discipline been exercised upon me."

He went to Constance to be ordained a priest, preached his first sermon at Rapperswyl, on the lake of Zurich, read the mass for the first time at Wildhaus on St. Michael's day, in the presence of his relatives, and set out for Glaris. It was the year 1506, when he was twenty-two years of age. The people were waiting for their new parson. But lo! there was trouble. Henry Goldli showed his parchment, and insisted on being their priest and receiving all the revenues. The intruder would not yield until Zwingli paid him a sum of money for renouncing claims that were totally groundless. Such was one of the abuses under which the people groaned in that age, and which opened their eyes to the need of reform.

The young pastor applied himself with zeal to the duties of his large parish, visiting the cottages in the one rich valley and the poorer hamlets on the mountain slopes. He had charge of nearly one-third of the canton of Glaris. He was then a Romish priest, not much different from the best of the surrounding clergy. He was free from all those scandals which disgraced the Church of his day, and sought to hold firmly to one noble resolution: " I will be true and upright before God in every situation of life in which the hand of the Lord may place me." His later friend, Myconius, says of him: "He became a priest and devoted himself to the search after divine truth with all his heart, for he was well aware how much he must know to whom the flock of Christ is entrusted."

But he was pained to find such a contrast between the purity of the gospel and the corrupt lives of the people. They were grossly licentious in their manners, even with all their simplicity and good-nature. The Swiss in those days were reputed to have as little respect for the seventh commandment as the Italians in their most profligate cities. The brave soldiers, hired to fight for those who would pay them the most gold, learned bad habits abroad, and returned to lead an idle and dissipated life at home. The clergy could not always reprove them, for "like people, like priest." The monks and the nuns often illustrated and increased the depravity. No priest was allowed to marry, and yet it would have been difficult to find one who lived in a real state of celibacy. There were some priests in the Alpine regions who were secretly married, and reared families in the fear of God. Zwingli then had work enough to do in setting forth a holy example and in boldly correcting the sins of the people. When tempted, he turned to God with tears and prayers, and laid hold of the strength of the mighty Jehovah.

To get the truth he went directly to the sacred fountains of the Bible. He drank the "waters of Siloa that go softly." He knew the Scriptures only in the Latin version, for there was, as yet, no translation into German-Swiss, but his fellow-priests thought him profoundly learned in the Bible, of which they knew almost nothing. He paid great attention to the graces of public speaking. He studied the classics that he might acquire the elegancies of oratory. He read often the masterpieces of eloquence. But all this was in vain unless the love of Christ was shed abroad in his heart.

One of his labours in the parish was the training of the youth. He founded a Latin school at Glaris, and gathered into it a band of young men from the first families of the land. He taught them what he could, and then sent them to Basle, where his friend Glarean taught the high school, boarding the students in his own house, so that he might watch over their morals; or they were sent to Vienna, where Vadian was the rector of an academy. But wherever they went they bore engraved on their heart the memory of their first master, and kept with him an unbroken correspondence.

"Thou art to us like a guardian angel," wrote Peter Tschudi from Paris, whose brother Egidius also wrote, "Help, help me, that I may be recalled to thee, for nowhere do I like so well to live as near thyself." The Tschudis were a family of heroes, whose fathers had been warriors terrible to the hosts of Charles the Bold of Burgundy. Valentine, a cousin of the two just quoted, wrote to Zwingli: "You have offered me, not only books, but your very self. I have found no one who could explain the classic authors with such skill and clearness as yourself. Can I ever cease to be grateful to you for the great benefits you conferred upon me? On every occasion that I returned home, and lately, especially, when I was suffering four days from a fever, you were ready to do me any service. The whole benevolence of your soul overflowed to me." At Paris this young man compared the spirit that prevailed in its university with that which he had found in his own narrow valley, and he said, "In what frivolities do they educate the French youth! No poison can equal the sophistical art that they are taught. It dulls the senses, weakens the judgment, brutalizes the man and makes him a mere echo, an empty sound. Ten women could not make head against one of these rhetoricians. Even in their prayers, I am certain they bring their sophisms before God, and by their syllogisms presume to constrain the Holy Spirit to answer them."

Zwingli had reason to think that his school was doing some good in the world. He was elevating the standard of education. Erasmus, the sage of Rotterdam, who then was the monarch in the literary world, wrote to him saying, "All hail! say I to the Swiss people, whom I have always admired, whose intellectual and moral qualities you, and men like you, are training."

There was at Friburg a certain judge Falk, a strong papist and active politician of that period, who was a patron of the liberal studies. He offered to let Zwingli dwell in his country-seat near Pavia, Italy, enjoy all its revenues for two years, and have a charming retreat where he could indulge his literary tastes. But Zwingli declined the offer. Perhaps he suspected that the design was to win him over to the Romish cause. Temptations of this sort were frequent in his experience.

The young pastor still watched over the souls of men with fidelity. He wrote afterward of this period: "Young as I was, the office of the priesthood filled me with greater fear than joy, for this was ever present to me, that the blood of the sheep, who perished through any neglect or guilt of mine, would be required at my hands."

CHAPTER IV.

THE PARSON TEMPTED TO WAR.

(1510–1516.)

A POOR herd-boy, named Matthew Schinner, who attended the school at Sion in French Switzerland, was singing one day in the streets for his bread, when an old man called him by name. They talked a little, and the lad gave such wise answers that the aged man said to him, with that prophetic tone which those seem to have who are on the brink of the grave, "Thou shalt become a bishop and a prince."

The beggar-boy was pleased with the prophecy, and from that hour a boundless ambition entered his soul. He went to Zurich and to Como, spake the German and Italian of each place, and displayed such wonderful powers of mind that he astonished and outstripped his masters. He became the priest of a small parish in his native Valais, rose rapidly and dreamed of higher promotions. A man had been elected as the bishop of Sion, but some one must go to Rome and obtain the pope's confirmation. Matthew was sent, but with a tricky heart he asked the appointment for himself, and the pope granted it, so that the messenger went home as the bishop of Sion. When Louis XII. of France was at war with Pope Julius II., this bishop knew that each party would be glad to employ the Swiss in his service. He offered himself to Louis and named his price.

" It is too much for one man," said the king.

" I will show him," replied the exasperated bishop, "that I alone am worth many men." He then turned to Pope Julius, who heartily welcomed him. In 1510 the bishop succeeded in attaching the entire Swiss confederation to the side of the warlike pontiff. Schinner received a cardinal's hat, and smiled as he saw that there was but one step more between him and the papal throne.

The new cardinal cast his eyes over all the cantons of Switzerland, and wherever he saw a man of influence he hastened to win him to himself. The pastor of Glaris drew his attention, and he prepared the glittering bait. Zwingli had been too poor to buy the books he wanted: the money paid to Henry Goldli had made him still poorer, and besides he had been generous to his students. All at once he was informed that the pope had set apart an annual sum of fifty florins for him, so that he might freely pursue his studies. He accepted it without suspicion for a time, and devoted it entirely to the purchase of classical and theological books. The crafty cardinal softly told him that, in return for this favour, he could not do less than lend his talents and energies to the cause of the pope, whom Zwingli still regarded as the vicar of Christ.

Cardinal Schinner by his eloquence, the payment of a little gold and the promises of large plunder, raised eight thousand Swiss soldiers, and sent them over the Alps into Italy, but they soon found themseves out of rations and almost perishing. The French conquered them by arms and bought them with money, so that they returned ingloriously to their mountains. They carried back with them all the vices they had acquired—distrust, violence, party spirit and disorders of every kind. Citizens refused to obey their magistrates; children grew insolent to their parents; parishioners mocked their priests; shepherds neglected their flocks and herds; farmers let their lands run to weeds; luxury increased the vices of one class and beggary those of another; the holiest ties were broken and the confederation seemed upon the verge of ruin.

The young priest of Glaris opened his eyes and uttered his indignation. His silence could not be bought with golden bribes. He lifted his powerful voice to warn the people. In 1510 he wrote his poem entitled *The Labyrinth.* Within the mazes of a mysterious garden, Minos has concealed the Minotaur, that monster, half-man, half-bull, who feeds upon the bodies of the young people. Perhaps the garden was the alliance with Rome, and Minos was the pope. But he says plainly: "This Minotaur represents the sins, the vices, the irreligion, the foreign service of the Swiss, devouring the sons of the nation." A bold man, Theseus, appears and overcomes all enemies, slays the monster and saves his country.

"In like manner," says the poet-priest, "are men now wandering in a labyrinth, but as they have no clue to its mazes, they cannot regain the light nor find the way out of it. Nowhere do we find an imitation of Christ. A little glory leads us to risk our lives, torment our neighbour and rush into disputes, war and battle. One might imagine that the furies had broken loose from the abyss of hell." A Theseus in the person of a reformer was needed.

Such poems deserve notice simply as the effusions of a man whose pen could write nobler things. In his zeal to remove certain great political evils, he wrote " A poetic fable concerning an ox and other beasts." It winds up with the following:

"Where bribery can show its face,
There freedom has no dwelling-place. . . .

Freedom must stand by bravery,
Sheltered and guarded evermore.
Amid the bloody ranks of war,
Amid the fearful dance of death,
Let gleaming swords drawn from the sheath,
And spears and battle-axes, be
Thy guardians, golden Liberty!
But where a brutish heart is met
And by a tempting bribe beset,
There noble freedom, glorious boon!
And name and blood of friends too soon
Are cheaply prized; and rudely torn
Are oaths in holy covenant sworn."

In April, 1512, the Swiss confederates were again persuaded by Cardinal Schinner to enter the service of the pope for the defence of Italy and the Church. Glaris was in the foremost rank, eager to drive the French out of Lombardy. As the banner of his own canton was unfurled, Zwingli felt that his parishioners, who were in the army, needed a chaplain and guardian. Scarcely was there an able-bodied man in his parish who did not enlist. He felt compelled to march with them. According to an old custom, the magistrates appointed him to follow the army as a field-preacher. He must carry arms. Twenty thousand Swiss crossed the Alps wearing a white cross, and bearing a standard on which were the words, in letters of gold, "The tamers of princes, the lovers of justice and the defenders of the holy Roman Church." Cardinel Schinner sent them two rich presents from the pope: one was a red silk hat decorated with gold and pearls, so as to represent the descent of the Holy Ghost; the other was a golden sword adorned with costly gems. The pope said that these emblems signified the blessing of God upon their arms, but the soldiers were likely to interpret them as meaning that the "holy father" would pay them well. The Swiss scaled the walls of cities and fortresses, and before the eyes of their enemies swam rivers with their halberds in their hands. The French were defeated at every point, and swept out of Lombardy. The people crowded from all quarters to thank the victors; the nobles made them liberal gifts of fruits and wine; monks and priests mounted the pulpits and praised the Swiss as the people of God, and the pope conferred on them the title of the "Defenders of the liberty of the Church." It is stated by some writers that the red hat and golden sword were presented to them through Zwingli after their victory, with the papal promise, "Let them ask what they will—the holiest shall not be denied them."' Some of the more devout among them begged the permission to have painted on their banners the image of the crucified Redeemer; the men of Glaris wished to carry that of the risen Saviour.

On his return to Glaris, Zwingli applied himself to hard study. "I gave my labour to the Greek language, so that I might be able to draw the doctrines of Christ from the fountain of truth. I am resolved," he wrote to Vadian, "that no one shall turn me from it, except God; I do it not for glory, but for the love of sacred learning." He read the Fathers without any blinding reverence for them, but "just as one asks a friend what he means." But the ancient doctors did not satisfy him. He prayed for the Spirit to lead him into all truth. The New Testament in its original tongue became his study and his peculiar delight. He compared Scripture with Scripture, saying, "I must neglect all these matters [of mere human reason], and look for God's will in his word alone. I began earnestly to entreat the Lord to give me his light; and although I read the Scriptures only, they became clearer to me than if I had read all the commentators." The deeper he sank his shaft into this mine, the farther he got away from the doctrines of Rome, and he began to see their error. The study of the Greek Testament was at the basis of the Reformation.

"Zwingli's course was slow but progressive," says D'Aubigne. "He did not arrive at the truth, like Luther, by those storms which impel the soul to run hastily into its harbour of refuge: he reached it by the peaceful influence of Scripture, whose power expands gradually in the heart. Luther attained the wished-for shore through the storms of the wide ocean; Zwingli by gliding gently down the stream. These are the two principal ways by which men are led by the Almighty. Zwingli was not fully converted to God and to his gospel until the earlier years of his residence at Zürich; yet the moment when, in 1514 or 1515, this strong man bent the knee to God in prayer for the understanding of his word, was that in which appeared the first glimmering of the rays of the bright day that afterward beamed upon him."

About this time his eye fell upon a poem of Erasmus, in which Jesus Christ is represented as addressing mankind, perishing through their own fault, and complaining that men do not seek grace from Him who is the source of all that is good. "The *source* of *all good?*" repeated Zwingli, shut up in his room; "yes, ALL. Why then go elsewhere? are there any creatures or saints of whom to ask aid? No, Christ is our only treasury of grace."

Every book that came from the pen of Erasmus, Zwingli hastened to purchase. He was delighted when the "prince of letters" went to Basle in 1514, where the bishop received him with every mark of esteem, and all the friends of learning gathered around him. Zwingli felt that he must visit him. On arriving in the city, he found there a small man about forty years of age, of delicate frame and exceedingly amiable. It was Erasmus, not yet crossed by Luther and angered because the Reformation was going farther than he had intended. His polished manners soon won the priest of Glaris, who at first trembled with timidity in the presence of the great genius. "I give you myself," said the sage, and they talked of the times, the revival of learning and the restoration of the pure Scriptures to the Church.

As Zwingli mingled with the scholars who formed a literary court about Erasmus, and was introduced to them by his friend Glarean, he was charmed with a young man from Lucerne named Oswald Geisshausler, to whom Erasmus gave the softer Greek name of Myconius. He must be distinguished from Frederick Myconius, the disciple of Luther. Oswald was rector of St. Peter's school in Basle. He had married a wife of an admirable disposition, and he was living as hospitably as his scanty income could afford. The returned soldiers made an example of their rough campaigning habits at his house. On a dark wintry day some of these ruffians attacked his quiet dwelling in his absence. They knocked at the door, threw stones, used the most indecent language to his modest wife, dashed in the windows, entered the school-room, broke everything they could and then retired. Little Felix saw his father coming shortly after, ran to meet him with loud cries, and his wife, unable to speak from fright, made signs of the desolation. Oswald saw it all, and his blood boiled. Just then the soldiers were heard in the streets, and seizing a weapon the schoolmaster pursued the rioters to the cemetery. They took refuge within it and prepared to defend themselves. Three of them fell upon Myconius and wounded him. He went home, and while his

wound was being dressed, the wretches again broke into his
house with furious cries. Oswald says no more. Such scenes as
this were not rare in Switzerland before the Reformation sub-
dued the roughness of the people.

The schoolmaster of Basle and the parson of Glaris perceived
each other's abilities, but neither coveted praise. "I look upon
you schoolmasters as the peers of kings," said Erasmus. But
Oswald replied, "I do but crawl on the earth: from my childhood there has been something humble and mean about me."
All were ready to say of Zwingli, "He will yet be the glory of
Switzerland." But the many friends of the gospel at Basle did
not spend their time in studying and admiring each other. They
improved the privilege of hearing an eloquent preacher, whom
we must not pass with neglect.

A child was born the year before Zwingli, in Franconia, of
rich parents, and named John Hausshein, "the house-light."
His pious mother consecrated to learning and to God the only
child that Providence had left her. His father at first des-
tined him to business and then to law, sending him to the renowned university at Bologna. But when John returned the
Lord touched his heart and inclined him to study theology. He
entered the ministry, preached in his native town, and by the influence of Capito received the appointment of preacher at Basle.
Already had he translated his name into Œcolampadius, and
truly, as the name signifies, he was "the light of the house"
when he preached with an eloquence that filled his hearers with
admiration. His great theme was Christ; his object was to secure the salvation of sinners. Erasmus admitted him into his
circle of scholars, saying, to his delight, "There is but one thing
that we should look for in Holy Scripture, and that is Jesus
Christ." Would that the monarch of the schools had always

submitted to this excellent rule! He gave the young preacher, as a memorial of friendship, the first part of the gospel of John. Œcolampadius kept it suspended to his crucifix, "in order that he might remember Erasmus in his prayers."

Zwingli received a new impulse for study, for duty and for preaching. He returned to his native mountains with his soul full of what he had seen and heard. He poured out his heart to his students and his friends, and they were delighted to see that he had increased in wisdom and in zeal. The aged respected him for the consolations which he imparted; the young, for the interest he took in their welfare; the magistrates, for his courageous patriotism; and the faithful pastors more distant esteemed him as a true and bold minister of God. Nothing important was done in the country without first consulting him. Well had it been if his advice had been followed both in Church and State.

When Francis I. ascended the throne of France in 1515, he resolved to regain his footing in Italy and avenge the French name. A Romish king was at war with his pope. The pope again sought the help of the Swiss. Attracted by the offer of gold* and plunder, they were ready to drop their labours, quit

---

* "No money, no Swiss," has been a reproachful proverb for centuries. A Swiss journal has recently given this explanation of it: The duke of Sforza once said to the Swiss soldiers, who had helped him gain a victory, "Help yourselves like knights to the plunder, for I have no money." The answer was, "This we cannot do; where there is no money, there can be no Swiss;" meaning that if there was no just pay, they would not plunder the goods of the people. Yet the wonder is that Switzerland has not been completely ruined by the foreign service. From 1474 to 1774, eight hundred thousand men fought for the French kings, and three-fourths of them were slain. Fifteen millions of dollars were paid them.

their Alpine pastures and march to "defend the Church."
Zwingli could not stay the powerful influence of the tempting
Cardinal Schinner. The men of Glaris would enlist, and he
must join them. He took the sword and placed on his shoulder
the glittering halberd. A Swiss army was again on the plains of
Italy, and he was their armed chaplain. The battle was delayed.
The French had their secret agents at work among the Swiss
soldiers, offering bribes and sowing discord. Zwingli saw that
they were becoming "demoralized." It wrung his heart. Often
he stood in the camp haranguing them with energy, and appeal-
ing to them to avoid disgrace. Five days before the battle of
Marignan, he preached in the square of Monza, where all the
soldiers who had not deserted and who still remained true to
their colours were assembled. But he appealed to them almost
in vain, for he would not descend so low as to give the rein to
their passions and incite them to plunder and debauchery. "If
we had then and always followed his advice," said his friend
Steiner, "what evils would our country have been spared!"
The French bought off a large part of the army. The cardinal
Schinner appeared, spoke to the rest with his impetuous eloquence, appealed to their basest passions, promised them the
spoils of war, and so electrified them that they rushed down
upon the enemy like a torrent against the rocks. The flower of
the Swiss youth perished at Marignan. Zwingli threw himself
into danger, wielding the battle-axe and almost perishing by it.
The mountaineers were defeated; the French first conquered
them, and afterward bought them over to their interest, to the
great sorrow of their brave chaplain, who felt jealous for the
honour of his countrymen.

This second martial visit to Italy was not unprofitable to
Zwingli. Even amid the tumult of camps he indulged his

spirit of inquiry. When the Swiss forces were driven back to Milan, he did all that he could for his wounded companions, and then made researches in the old libraries and churches. He found a mass-book used in the time of Ambrose. At once he saw how very different it was from that which Rome had brought into use. It had nothing in it really about the mass. Which was the true one, the ancient or the modern? He solved that question by going farther back—to the word of God, in which there was not a shadow of foundation for the mass, for penance, or for any of the peculiar rites of the Romish Church.

After his return to Glaris, he was one day at Mollis, in the house of parson Adam, along with several other priests, when he happened to light upon an ancient liturgy. It was about two hundred years old. They compared it with the one which they used every week in their churches. Among other differences were these words, " After the child is baptized, let him partake of the sacrament of the Eucharist and likewise of the cup."

" In that day," said Zwingli, " you see that the sacrament was given in our churches under both kinds. But now the cup is withheld—only the bread is given." Here, then, was an important discovery. The Church had departed from the customs of the Fathers. They went to the Bible and found that the Lord intended both the bread and the wine to be administered in the Lord's Supper.

The parishioners of Glaris found Zwingli preaching with new energy. Four years before he had bent his head over his Bible; now he raised it and told them what he had discovered in the word of God. He did not attack Rome nor expose the errors of the clergy and the Church. "If the people understand what is true," said he, " they will soon discern what is false." This, however is not always the true rule, and he would yet depart from it. Sometimes, by pointing out error in the proper spirit, the truth is made the more manifest. "The spring is the time for sowing," said he, and he could not stop to root out the tares. "Let both grow together until the harvest."

We have not forgotten his book-money. We are anxious to know what he did with the annuity. So long as it was a mere pension he received it, but when it seemed to him as a bribe, he refused it. About the year 1516 he wrote, "I confess here, before God and all the world, my sin [in drawing the annual sum for books], for before the year 1516 I hung mightily on the Roman power, and thought it highly becoming in me to take money from it, although I told the Romish ambassadors, in clear and express terms, when they exhorted me to preach nothing against the pope, that they were not to fancy that I, for their money, should withhold one iota of the truth; so they might take back or give it as they pleased." They still urged it upon him as a pension.

His conscience was thus clear, and he boldly rebuked the men of Glaris for receiving bribes of the French party. Myconius wrote: "He began now to follow the example of Christ in denouncing from the pulpit certain base vices then very common, especially the taking of gifts from princes and engaging in baleful, mercenary wars; for he saw clearly that the divine truth would never find an entrance until these sources of iniquity were closed." With all his wise boldness he was touching the tender point in the hearts of some of his parishioners. They had sold themselves to France. The French interest gained the upper hand in Glaris, and from this time his residence there was made uncomfortable. God was stirring up the eagle's nest, that he might take his servant in his everlasting arms and bear him nearer to himself.

Zwingli dated the beginning of the Reformation in German

Switzerland with the year 1516, one year before Luther bravely posted his theses on the church door at Wittemberg. D'Aubigne says: "It has been erroneously concluded from these dates that Zwingli's reform preceded that of Luther. Perhaps Zwingli preached the gospel a year previous to the publication of Luther's theses, but Luther himself preached four years before those celebrated propositions. If Luther and Zwingli had strictly confined themselves to preaching, the Reformation would not so rapidly have overrun the Church. Luther and Zwingli were neither the first monk nor the first priest who had taught a purer doctrine than the schoolmen.* But Luther was the first to uplift, publicly and with indomitable courage, the standard of truth against the dominion of error; to direct general attention to the fundamental doctrine of the Gospel—salvation by grace; to lead his generation into that new way of knowledge, faith and life from which a new world has issued; in a word, to begin a salutary and real revolution."

Yet the priest of Glaris deserves all the credit of acting_independently of the monk of Wittemberg. God kindled many fires at different points about the same time. The fact that the same truths were brought to light by various scholars, without any knowledge of each other or any preconcerted plan, is a proof that the truth and the work were both of the Lord. The Reformation was wholly of God, lest any man should boast. Among the Alps there were many who were simultaneously searching

---

* Not to mention many others of that age, we refer to Lefevre in Paris, who taught Farel in 1510—1515 the doctrines of justification by faith and of regeneration by the Holy Ghost. Farel was the first great Reformer in French Switzerland, and altogether independent of Luther. See " *William Farel,*" *Presbyterian Board of Publication.*

the Scriptures, and broaching their new discoveries. "In Switzerland," says D'Aubigne, whose love for his mountain-land has made him familiar with its history, "the struggle begins in different cantons at the same time; there is a confederation of Reformers; their number surprises us; no doubt one head over-tops the others, but no one commands; it is a republican senate in which all appear with their original features and distinct influences. They are a host; Wittembach, Zwingli, Capito, Haller, Œcolampadius, Oswald Myconius, Leo Juda, Farel, Calvin." He might have added Glarean and Vadian. "In the German Reformation there is but one stage, flat and uniform as the country itself; in Switzerland the Reformation is divided, like the region itself, by its thousand mountains. Each valley, so to speak, has its own awakening, and each peak of the Alps its own light from heaven."

We know not whether Zwingli was at all sensitive on this point of priority, but he had a right to assert his just claim. In later years he was compelled to do it in self-defence. Luther had been proclaimed a heretic by the pope and excommunicated, to his eternal honour, be it remembered. It was thought that the speediest way of getting rid of Zwingli's influence was to stigmatize him as an imitator of Luther. His answer was: "I began to preach the gospel before a single individual in our part of the country ever heard the name of Luther. This was in 1516. Who called me a Lutheran then? When Luther's exposition of the Lord's prayer appeared, it so happened that I had shortly before preached from Matthew on the same prayer. Well, some good folks, who everywhere found my thoughts in Luther's work, would hardly let themselves be made to believe that I had not written this book myself; they fancied that, being afraid to put my own name to it, I had set that of Luther instead. Who then called me a follower of Luther? Then how comes it that the Romish cardinals and legates, who were at that very time in Zurich, never reproached me as a Lutheran until they had declared Luther a heretic, which, however, they could never make him? When they had branded him a heretic, they first exclaimed that I was a Lutheran, although Luther's name was entirely unknown to me during these two years-that I kept to the Bible alone. But it is part of their cunning policy to load me and others with this name. Do they say, You must be a Lutheran, for you preach as Luther; I answer, I preach too as Paul writes; why not call me a Paulian? Nay, I preach the word of Christ; why not much rather call me a Christian? In my opinion, Luther is one of God's chosen heralds and combatants, who searches the Scriptures with greater zeal than has been done by any man on earth for the last thousand years.

"Therefore, dear Christians, let not the name of Christ be changed into the name of Luther; for Luther has not died for us, but he teaches us to know him from whom alone our salvation comes. If Luther preaches Christ, he does it as I do; although, God be praised for it, an innumerable multitude, much more than by me and by others, have been converted to God through him, for God metes out to every man as he will. For my part, I shall bear no other name but that of my Captain Jesus Christ, whose soldier I am. No man can esteem Luther more highly than I do. Yet I testify before God and all men that I have never at any time written to him, nor has he to me. I have purposely abstained from all correspondence with him; not that I feared any man on this account, but because I would have it appear how uniform the Spirit of God is, in so far that we who are far distant from each other, and have held no communication, are yet of the same mind, and this without the slighest concert.

But I will not be so bold as to place myself by the side of Luther, for each of us works according to the ability given us of God."

Such was Zwingli's position. Beautifully does he also say, "Seeking for the touch-stone of truth, I found none other than the 'stone of stumbling and rock of offence.' I began to test every doctrine by this test. Did I see that the touch-stone gave back the same colour, or rather that the doctrine could bear the brightness of the stone, I accepted it; if not, I cast it away. At length I brought it so far that at the first touch of the stone I could tell what was false and adulterate, and from that time forward, no power, no threatening could bring me to place the like faith in the human as in the divine."

CHAPTER V.

THE legend runs that in the time of Charlemagne, a German monk, named Meinrad, of the noble house of Hohenzollern, resolved to end his days in solitude and prayer. He passed by St. Gall, to the south of Lake Zurich, and there on a little hill among the pines he built a cell. He was devoted to a little black image of the Virgin, which had been given him by St. Hildegarde, the abbess of Zurich. In 861 two robbers came and murdered him, without a thought of being detected. The monk had reared two pet ravens, which pursued the ruffians as far as Zurich, croaking and flapping their wings over hill and dale. So strange a pursuit gave trouble to the consciences of the murderers, and they betrayed themselves. They were arrested, convicted and put to death in Zurich on the spot where now stands the Raven Inn.

The reputation of the saint increased, and men sought his cell in the Finsterwald. It was in ruins, but was rebuilt in the tenth century, and a church founded there by the Benedictine hermits (*Einsiedlern*). The church was built in honour of the Virgin Mary, and to increase the reverence for it the story was invented that when the bishop was about to consecrate it, a voice was heard thrice, crying, "Stop! stop! God himself has consecrated it." The bishop ceased, and angels attended the Virgin

55

Mary as she dedicated the church to God. The pope declared this a true miracle, though the monks knew the trick. Pope Leo VIII. forbade the faithful to doubt the truth of the legend. It took the name of "Our Lady of the Hermits," and a plenary indulgence was declared to all pilgrims who should repair to the shrine, where were inscribed the words, "Here is a full remission of sins." Hence for nine centuries there has been an almost unbroken line of pilgrims to this sacred place. A town grew up, which is still called Einsidlen.* Wealth poured into the monastery. It gained extended power, having various parishes and convents-under its command. It was the rival of St. Gall. Its abbot came to be a prince of the "Holy Roman Empire," and had a seat in the Diet. Princes and nobleman became his chamberlains, marshals and cup-bearers. A reformation was needed. To its famous school many sons of the nobility were committed for several centuries.

Conrad of Rechberg was the abbot-prince of Einsidlen in the time of Zwingli. In his youth he had been forced to join the monks by selfish relatives, who now paid him visits since he had risen to such a height. If he wished to shun them, he mounted his horse, called his hounds and set out for the forests, for he was one of the most celebrated of huntsmen. On one of his farms he reared a breed of horses which became famous in Italy. With all his love for the chase, he was serious, frank, fearless, and seems to have been as upright and pious a man as could be found in a convent. A little rough sometimes, yet under his monk's cloak there beat as warm and generous a heart as ever throbbed under a coat of mail. There were two things that he equally detested—debates in scholastic theology and the preten-

---

* Einsiedlern, Einsiedeln, Einsiedlen.

sions of Rome. He did not believe in the infallibility of the
pope, and many papal ceremonies were nonsense to him.
Luther would have enjoyed him, even if Conrad had said, "No
arguments now upon justification."

But he did not always leave his fawning relatives when they
.came to wind themselves into his heart. He sometimes remained at home and sent them off in a hurry. He once said to
them, "You have stuck a cowl on my head at the peril of my
soul, and I must be a monk while you ride about as country
squires. But, my good people, don't come here begging anything
of me, but just return over the road by which you came."

When certain officials came to visit his order, and reproached
him for not reading mass and for making no great account of it,
he said, "Although I am master here in my own convent, and
could send you away with a very short answer, yet I will tell you
plainly what I think of the mass. If the Lord Jesus Christ be
really in the host (wafer), I know not how very highly you esteem yourselves, but I do know that I, a poor monk, am not
worthy to look upon him, to say nothing of daring to offer him
up in sacrifice to the eternal God. If, however, he be not present
there, woe's me if I hold up bread to the people before the
Lord our God, and call upon them to worship a wafer. Therefore let me alone. If God will, I shall so preside over God's
house that I may be able to give account to him. As I have no
need of you, please to go ; you are dismissed."

At another time Leo Juda was discussing some intricate question at the table with the superior of the convent, when the
abbot exclaimed, "What care I for your disputations? I say
now, and ever shall say with David, 'Have mercy upon me, O
Lord, according to thy loving-kindness, and enter not into judgment with thy servant.' I desire to know nothing more."

Conrad was old; and he retired altogether from the administration of the cloister, committing it to Baron Theobald of Geroldsek, a doctor of divinity. He was a man of mild character, sincere piety and great love for literature. His favourite plan was to gather about him a circle of learned and pious men, as teachers, chaplains and preachers, giving them leisure for study. He heard of Zwingli, and in 1516 invited him to be priest and preacher at the convent. The parson of Glaris did not hesitate, for he saw that his influence in the parish was disturbed because he did not hold French opinions in politics.

"It is neither ambition nor covetousness," said he, "that takes me there, but the intrigues of the French." There were also reasons of a higher kind. He would have more time for study, and he could preach the gospel to the thousands of pilgrims who resorted thither, and they might carry the good news of Jesus Christ into distant lands where they dwelt.

All who truly lovèd the gospel at Glaris loudly expressed their grief when losing their faithful pastor. They blamed the politicians for driving him away. "What can be more distressing," said Peter Tschudi, a chief man in the canton, "than to be deprived of so good a pastor?" His parishioners, seeing him determined to go, resolved to continue to him the title of pastor of Glaris, with a part of the salary, and the privilege of returning whenever he chose.

Zwingli was hailed with joy by Geroldsek and his select company. They were eager to learn from him what they did not yet know—that there was a complete salvation in Christ. He was soon regarded as the spiritual instructor in the convent. Geroldsek sat as an inquirer at his feet, begging for more light. "Study the Holy Scriptures," said Zwingli, "and that you may better understand them, read St. Jerome. However, the time will

come (and that soon, with God's help) when Christians will not
set great store either by St. Jerome or any other doctor, but
solely by the word of God."

"We will all read the Scriptures," answered the manager,
"and the nuns too shall have the Bible." He permitted the
nuns of the convent of which he had the charge to read it in
the German tongue, saying that this was better than to be daily
drawling over their Latin mass-songs in their usual heedless
manner, and that if any of them felt burdened by their vows,
they might return to their homes. One of the first effects of
the revived gospel was to dissolve the convents and particularly
the nunneries.

How Zwingli sang with Leo Juda we are not told, but doubtless the songs of the Tockenburg and the national airs were laid
aside. He grew more serious. At Glaris he had been known to
take part in worldly amusements, but now he sought to avoid
every appearance of evil. He drew to him Francis Zing, the
chaplain, and John Exlin (Oechslin), who renounced their errors
and yielded to the convictions of the truth and the Holy Spirit.
A studious circle of men sat together, far removed from the noise
of parties, reading the Bible, the Fathers, the masterpieces of
antiquity and the writings of the restorers of learning. Friends
often joined them from distant parts. Capito came. The two
old friends of Basle walked over the convent together, strolled
through the wild scenery of the neighbourhood, talked of the new
doctrines and sought to know God's will. "The pope must
fall," said Zwingli. "The sooner the better," answered Capito,
who was then a bolder man than afterward.

Amid such leisure, books and friends, Zwingli began a work
which was of great service to him. As in the ancient days the
wiser Hebrew kings transcribed the law of God with their own

hands, so he copied the Epistles of Paul in the Greek character. This copy is still preserved at Zurich. The editions of the New Testament were then voluminous, and Zwingli thus had one that he could carry with him wherever he went. He committed its chapters to memory, as he afterward did other books of Scripture. Thus he became thoroughly furnished for the work of preaching, for in proclaiming the gospel he was to show himself the Reformer at Einsidlen. He prepared his sermons with great care. He studied the passage on which he intended to speak in its original language, and when in the pulpit commented upon it. But how could he preach with any hope of success so long as he saw the abounding idolatry? It was quite equal to that of the natives of that region, who were once angry at Columban when they saw that some of his followers had burned their idol-temple to the ground. The objects of worship were different, but the superstitions were of the same spirit. Mary was adored instead of Christ and the Father. Her picture, said to be centuries old, was of more value in their eyes than the true cross.

In honour of the angels who were said to have filled the church when it was consecrated by a miracle, the festival of the angel-consecration had been appointed and long observed. Crowds of pilgrims wished to spend this day at "Our Lady of the Hermits." Zwingli felt as Paul did at Athens when he saw the city wholly given to idolatry. He must make every effort to correct it. He laid hold of two great truths—God is everywhere, and Christ alone saves. He went into the pulpit in 1517, on the day of the angel-consecration. He attacked boldly the superstitions of the crowds around him. The church, the abbey and the valley were filled with the devotees of Mary. They had come from all parts of Christendom. Troops of pilgrims were still pouring in, or in long files they were going up the slopes of the mountain to an oratory, singing their songs or counting their beads. But those who filled the church supposed that there they were nearer to God than in any other place.

"Do not imagine," said the preacher, "that God is in this temple more than in any other part of creation. Whatever be your country, he is there as well as at Einsidlen. There he can hear and help you. Can long pilgrimages, offerings, images, the invocation of saints or of the Virgin, secure to you the grace of God?" Some of his hearers began to rebuke themselves for having travelled so far for God's grace, when they could have received it at home. But they were hearing what they never knew before, and were thankful for new light. Others would have left the church if they could. The doors were thronged.

"Who is a hypocritical Christian but the pope, who exalts himself in the place of Christ, says he has his power, and so binds God to Rome and Romish sanctuaries? Men must come to the holy places, and bring money in enormous quantities to enrich them. And in just such places are more wantonness and vice than anywhere else. . . . He who ascribes to man the power to forgive sins, blasphemes God. Great evils have sprung from this source, so that some whose eyes have been blinded by the pope have fancied that their sins were forgiven by sinful men. Thus God has been hid from them." There were priests in the audience who shrugged their shoulders at these words, and might have risen to defend the pope and the confessional, had they not feared the indignation of the people.

"We do not dishonour Mary when we teach that she ought not to be worshipped. But we dishonour her, indeed, when we ascribe to her the majesty of God. She would not suffer such idolatry if she could speak to us. For she worships Christ and the Father, and she would abhor the reverence which should be paid only to God. He who puts his faith in her divine Son, honours her the highest, for her honour is her Son's. Yea, if ye will honour her, then imitate her pure life, her steadfast faith in Jesus, her adoration of the Christ. So strong was her trust in him that no wretchedness, no poverty, no conduct of the people who rejected him, no daily reproaches, were able to turn her from him, so as even once to doubt in him."

Thus Zwingli preached to thousands of pilgrims at the festival of the angel-consecration, and afterward at Pentecost. The impression was powerful. All were astonished, some enraged, some delighted. Not a few fled in horror from the scene; others lingered between the faith of their fathers and these new doctrines; many went to Jesus, who was set forth as meek, gentle, willing to receive them and forgive, retaining the gifts they had brought for the Virgin. A crowd of pilgrims returned homeward to various lands, declaring what they had heard at Einsidlen, that " *Christ alone saves, and he saves everywhere;* not Mary, but Christ is the Saviour; not men, but God forgives sins; not works, but faith is the way of justification and eternal life." Often did whole bands, belated in the journey to "Our Lady," meet the returning companies, hear the astounding reports, learn the simple lessons of faith, and turn back to their homes; or if they pressed on, many did so in order to hear with their own ears the words of the man who preached that Jesus could save them without pilgrimages, without confession to priests, without the invocation of saints and without any merits of their own. Mary's worshippers daily decreased in number. It was from their offerings that Zwingli and Geroldsek were to derive their incomes. It was to the preacher's pecuniary advantage that she should continue to attract deluded thousands. But he was supremely above such a base consideration. This bold witness to the truth felt happy in making himself poor if he could lead lost souls into the riches of grace and glory.

One man came all the way from Basle to hear Zwingli at Whitsuntide. He entered the church, but none knew him as Gaspard Hedio, doctor of divinity. He was struck with the text, "The Son of Man hath power on earth to forgive sins." He drank in every word. From that hour he loved Zwingli. He would have liked to call upon him and lay bare the convictions in his soul, but he was timid. He wandered round the abbey; his courage did not rise; he dare not advance. He remounted his horse and slowly rode away, often turning his eyes back toward the walls that enclosed so great a treasure, and bearing in in his heart the keenest regret that he had not ventured to meet, face to face, the man who had so touched his heart.

The famous Cardinal Schinner sought repose from weariness in politics and from the disturbances in his diocese, and spent some time at the convent. He may have heard Zwingli say, "The popedom rests on a bad foundation; apply yourselves to the work; reject all errors and abuses, or else you will see the whole edifice fall with a tremendous crash." But the cardinal was too fox-like to enter into a discussion, for that might drive the Reformer to a point from which no crafty arts could win him back to Romanism. Other men were coming as legates from Rome to try their force of persuasion upon the intrepid preacher.

There came to Eidsidlen two men who were intent upon saving Zwingli to the Romish Church and enlisting him in politics, so that he might win back the cantons to the papal service. Cardinal Puccius and the legate Ennius talked with him frequently, and offered him such pensions and honours as had tempted Erasmus and silenced the batteries which he had turned upon Rome. But they could not purchase his liberty of speech. " I am resolved," said he, " to preach the pure gospel to the people, whatever may occur and even if Rome totter."

" The pension need not compromise you," replied the shrewd legates. " It is a simple tribute to your scholarship. We entreat you to receive it."

" I will accept it for a short time, but do not imagine that for the love of money I will retract a single word of truth."

The legates had not gained their object, for the bold preacher would not enter the pope's service, although he then had no intention of setting himself in open hostility to Rome. Cardinal Puccius took alarm. He obtained for Zwingli a high but nominal appointment from the pope—a mere sinecure, with no work and no pay. He was given a parchment which informed him that " he deserves, in the eyes of the pope, a recognition of his great learning, and some distinguished marks of paternal approbation. Therefore he (the legate) raises him, by papal authority, to the honourable distinction of acolyte-chaplain of the holy father, whereby he may perceive the favour in which he is held." He was counselled to aspire after higher honours. The ladder was placed at his feet, with the livings of bishops, the red hats of cardinals, the privileges of the Roman court and a chance for the papal chair, all at the top of it. " All these will I give thee," said the tempter. Would he choose the way that led to these earthy glories, or prefer the crown of thorns and the cross of Christ? The same Rome that sought to frighten Luther offered her favours to Zwingli; in both cases she failed. Her cardinals had made proposal of relief to him; he would now make overtures of reform to her bishops. Why not, since he was acolyte-chaplain to the pope?—a mere title indeed, but titles are something in the eyes of those who judge others by them.

John Faber, the classmate at Vienna, and still the friend of the Reformer, had entered the service of the bishop of Constance, and risen to be his general-vicar. Perhaps he had given his bishop some new ideas; at any rate, Hugh von Landenberg had declared quite strongly against the corruptions in the Church, and urged some mild reforms in his diocese. Might he not be persuaded to go farther, and lift high and carry bravely the standard against error? Zwingli would try him. A letter on reformation went from Einsidlen to Constance. The bishop read it. Faber could tell him who Zwingli was. "Convent-preachers are not my advisers," we hear the bishop say: "when the holy father orders a reform it will be time enough to begin it." Such was his reply. A vicious woman may have softly whispered in his ear that a lax bishop should not meddle with repentance.

If Hugh von Landenberg were living to this day, he would not be able to remember a pope who set earnestly about a reform, beginning at the right point. In the sixteenth century almost every "holy father" had his chair beset with men urging him to correct the great abuses in the Church. If one of them called a council for reform, he contrived to have nothing done, for he knew that if the work was thoroughly begun the whole Romish system must be destroyed. There was one common mistake made by all the Reformers in their first efforts, unless we except William Farel. They sought to enlist prelates and princes in the work, and have them urge it forward by the power of their office and the weight of their names. But God did not intend that the mighty movement should be in their hands. They would not manage it well. He had other servants, who should teach the humblest of men that they might be the sons of God and co-workers with him in his kingdom. He chose feeble agents, that the power might be of God. Not the old prelacy, but the eternal word should work the reformation.

CHAPTER VI.

THE pope needed money. He proposed to raise it, as two former popes had done with success, by selling pardons to the people under the name of indulgences. In an Italian convent was a monk named Samson, ready to sell them to the "good Christians" of Switzerland, as Tetzel had done in Germany. He received his commission, and was joined by men who would act as skilful auctioneers, puff the empty wares. and push on the scandalous traffic. He set out barefoot, and led his greedy train over the heights of St. Gotthard, whose glaciers are as old as the world. The band looked like wretched adventurers in search of plunder, bearing with them loads of paper signed in the name of the pope. In August, 1518, they reached Uri, and there opened their trade. The poor mountaineers gathered about the hawker as he cried, "I can forgive all sins; heaven and hell are under my dominion; I sell the merits of Jesus Christ to every one who will pay cash for absolution."

"What cheap forgiveness!" thought the deluded people. They handed up their money and took the paper which pretended to bear the signature of Pope Leo X. They imagined the wily impostor to be a messenger of peace to their troubled consciences, and vied with each other in grasping the proffered indulgence. Samson knew how poor these peasants were; he drew from them all they could give; he wanted a richer harvest, and after gaining some skill in his arts, he set out for a wealthier region, in the canton of Schwytz, from which comes the name of Switzerland.* Richer citizens came at his call, and he asked from them a larger price. The higher the rank, the more costly the pardon. But when he had negotiated for aristocratic sins, he turned again to the peasants and they laid their scanty earnings at his feet.

Zwingli heard of him, for he lived in the same canton. His soul was roused by the unblushing effrontery of Romanism and the blasphemies of the indulgence-seller. If the Dominican Tetzel made himself vile in the eyes of Luther, the Franciscan Samson was viler still in the eyes of Zwingli. A bold voice was lifted up at Einsidlen. The preacher took the pulpit, saying, "Jesus Christ the Son of God has said, *Come unto me, all ye that labour and are heavy laden, and I will give you rest.* Is it not audacious folly and shameless impudence for a man to say, 'Buy a ticket of absolution; give money to the monks; make sacrifices to the priests, and I will pronounce you free from all sin?' Can your gifts save you? No; Jesus Christ is the only sacrifice, the only gift, the only way. Those who sell the remis-

---

* The legend is that a colony of Swedes, long ago, was on the way to Rome, intending to dwell in a warmer climate. A storm blocked up the pass of the St. Gotthard, and robbers assailed them. Beaten back, they settled in the valley of Brunnen. The question arose, what name they should give to the new land. Two brothers wished to baptize it, each with his own name. They resolved to decide the matter by a single combat. Schioit conquered Scheiz, and was crowned the victor. By a little change, his name became Schwytz, the title given afterward to all Switzerland. This canton, with Uri and Unterwalden, gave origin to the Swiss confederation in the days of William Tell.

sion of sins for money are the companions of Simon the Magician, the friends of Balaam, the ambassadors of Satan."

The effect of this preaching was soon felt in the canton. The people began to say, "Samson is a cheat, a robber." He feared an uproar, dreaded to meet Zwingli, and turned aside to find more superstitious customers in the canton of Zug. Shortly after he had gone, a citizen of distinguished character, named Stapfer, was suddenly reduced to great distress. He had given his all for indulgences. He probably learned his error through the preaching of Zwingli, to whom he went, saying, "Alas! I know not how to satisfy my hunger and that of my poor children." The man who had attacked Rome had mercy on the victims whom Rome had fleeced. Every day he carried supplies to Stapfer. "It is God," said he, "who prompts us to charity; the giver deserves no praise. Every good thought and resolve comes from God. Whatever good work the righteous man doeth, it is God who doeth it by his own power."

"Since you provide for my temporal wants," said Stapfer, with noble candour, "how much more may I now expect from you the food that will satisfy my soul!" He said this four years after his losses, when he was secretary of state. He remained attached to Zwingli all his life.

On a September day Samson drew an immense crowd around him. The poorest were the most eager to buy indulgences, preventing the richer ones from getting near him, which did not suit his views. "Good folks," he cried, "do not crowd so much! make way for those who have more money. We will afterward endeavour to satisfy those who have none." Three days after he set out for other towns, where he befooled the people. He went to Berne. At first he was forbidden to enter the city, but through some friends he was finally allowed to set up his stall in St. Vincent's Church, where he bawled out to the crowds more lustily than before. To the rich he said, "Here are indulgences on parchment for a crown." Turning to the poor he said, "There are absolutions on common paper for three half-pence." The crowd once gave way to a celebrated knight, riding on a prancing dapple-gray horse, which the monk greatly admired. "Give me," said Jacques de Stein, "an indulgence for myself, for my troop, five hundred strong, for all my vassals at Belp, and for all my ancestors, and you shall have my charger in exchange."

"A high price for a horse!" thought the monk, but they soon came to terms : the steed was led to the stable, the knight took his parchment, and all those souls were declared exempt from hell. So much respect was felt for Samson that the aged and enlightened councillor De May, who had spoken irreverently of him, was compelled to fall on his knees and beg pardon of the haughty Franciscan. Even Henry Lupulus (Littlewolf), Zwingli's former teacher, was so carried away that he stood on the altar steps and interpreted the words of the Italian monk.

"When the wolf and the fox prowl about together," said the canon Anselm to the school director De Watville, "your safest plan is to shut up your sheep and your geese." Had the fox heard the witticism, he would not have felt disturbed.

The papal mountebank kept his best trick to the last. On the day before he left Berne, he cried out to the people, "Kneel down, recite three *Paters* and three *Aves*, and your souls will at once become as pure as at the moment of your baptism." The multitude fell on their knees, when Samson shouted aloud, "I deliver from the torments of purgatory and of hell all the souls of the Bernese who are dead, whatever may have been the manner and place of their death." He could ill afford to be so generous unless he had reaped a large harvest from the citizens.

But he was sometimes outwitted. The bishop of Constance, who had been heedless of Zwingli's letter, was angry because Samson had not brought his papers to be legalized by him, and he forbade the priests of his diocese to open their churches to the trafficker. At Baden, however, the parson dared not resist him. He put on airs of haughtiness and splendour. He formed a procession to march around the cemetery. Leading the wondering people, his attendants chanted the hymn for the dead. Suddenly he stopped, and pretending to see the souls escaping from earth to heaven, he exclaimed, "*Ecce volant!* Behold they fly!" This was too much to be endured. The eyes of the deluded must be opened. One man went into the belfry, poured upon the wind a sack of white feathers, exclaiming, "*Ecce volant!*" Many burst into laughter. The people, dead to reason, were alive to ridicule. Samson flew into a passion; his wares would not sell so readily. His wrath was somewhat appeased when he was told that the wag was not quite sane in his mind. The weak sometimes are wisest. The monk left Baden quite abashed and disgusted. He was about to arouse a man who would meet him with reason and argument.

No man in Bremgarten was more respected than Dean Bullinger. The greater errors in the Church were quite unknown to him in his quiet retreat, and yet he had little knowledge of the truths of the Bible. He was frank, zealous, eloquent, kind to the poor and ever ready to help the feeble ones of his flock. In his youth he united himself conscientiously with Anna, the daughter of a councillor in the town, and was a married priest, in spite of the laws of the Romish Church. In all Switzerland there was not a more hospitable house. His table was free to all comers; none of his guests was more cheerful than himself. Members of the Diet, going that way, often lodged with him for a night. "Bullinger holds a court," said they, "like the most powerful lord." They perhaps were feasted on the best game, for the dean was fond of hunting, and he might often be seen with the abbot of Mury and the lords of Hallwyl, followed by a pack of ten or twelve hounds, scouring the neighbouring fields and forests. This hunting clergymen had a son Henry, who became an eminent Reformer, and whom we shall meet hereafter.

On a February day, in 1519, the dean learned that Samson and his Italian troop were at the inn of Bremgarten. Bullinger was not be taken by storm. He boldly went to the inn and forbade the monk to sell his trash in his deanery. This was a thunderbolt not expected, for the junior priest and a school director had invited Samson to the town. No matter for all such invitations, thought the dean, who said, "I will not allow the purses of my parishioners to be drained by paying for letters which the bishop has not legalized."

"The pope is above the bishop," replied the monk, more solemnly and respectfully than usual. "I forbid you to deprive your flock of so signal a favour."

"Should it cost me my life, I will not open my church to you."

"Rebellious priest!" exclaimed Samson, with his accustomed pomposity. "In the name of our most holy lord, the pope, I pronounce against you the greater excommunication, and will not absolve you until you have redeemed yourself from such unprecedented rashness by paying three hundred ducats."

"I shall know how to reply to my lawful judges," said the

dean, leaving the room. "As for you and your excommunication, I care not for either."

"Impudent brute!" shouted Samson. "I am going to Zurich, and there I will lay my complaint before the Diet of Switzerland."

"I can appear there as readily as you," answered Bullinger, "and I will go thither immediately." A champion had just settled at Zurich, and we gladly turn from Samson to a better man.

CHAPTER VII.

A NEW STYLE OF PREACHING.

(1518–1519.)

FOR five centuries the minster or cathedral of Zurich had echoed the voice of papal Rome. The college of canons had been careful to choose a preacher who would bow to the will Romish Church. The last man of this stamp whom they were to hear left them at the time when the Reformation was threatening to disturb their indolent life. Who would succeed him?

These canons invited Oswald Myconius to take charge of the minster school. He at once thought of his friend and named Zwingli to them. Felix Frey, their provost, was prepossessed in his favour, inasmuch as the preacher at Einsidlen was a man of fine appearance, graceful manners and pleasing conversation, celebrated for eloquence and for the splendour of his genius. His brother canons were nearly all of the same mind. Other Zurichers had listened with delight to his sermons in the convent, and returned full of admiration. Everybody was soon in motion about the election of a preacher for the cathedral.

Myconius informed his friend of the movement: "Many are working night and day to have you chosen. Come and visit me."

"Wednesday next," replied Zwingli, "I will go and dine with you, when we will talk the matter over."

He went, dined, talked, looked about the city, thought well

of it, and saw that the cathedral pulpit offered a commanding position for one who would preach that "Christ saves everywhere." One of the canons met him and asked, "Are you willing to come and preach among us?"

"Yes: I have the desire to come, for there is reason to hope that if the grace of God be proclaimed from so renowned a place, and accepted there, the rest of Switzerland will follow the example." He returned to his abbey.

The visit caused alarm in the camp of his enemies. They urged several priests to offer themselves as candidates for the vacancy. Lawrence Fable, a Swabian, preached a sermon as a candidate, and a report got abroad that he was elected. "It is very true, then," remarked Zwingli on hearing it, "that no man is a prophet in his own country, since a Swabian is preferred to a Swiss. I know what the applause of the people is worth." But the secretary of Cardinal Schinner notified him that the election had not been made. The chaplain of Einsidlen secretly felt that if so unworthy a priest as Fable had pleased the people, it was time for some better man to be among them and cultivate their tastes. He was all the more eager for the place, and wrote to Myconius, who replied the next day: "Fable will always be a fable : our gentlemen have learned that he is the father of six boys, and already holds I know not how many livings." Sober reformers had their little pleasantries.

The foes of the gospel busily whispered their stories about Zwingli. Some said, "He is too fond of music;" some, "He is too lively in company;" others, "He was once too intimate with persons of light conduct, and was led astray." True, he had once fallen somewhat in his younger days at Glaris, but he had never gone so far as most priests of his day, and they had poisoned the very air that he breathed. But he had repented of all youthful wanderings, and a man of purer moral life could not be found in the land. The stories of his opposers fell to the ground.

"Hope on," wrote Oswald, "for I hope." It was really a contest between Romanism and Reform. Oswald was intent upon winning the day. He visited the burgomaster Roust, a veteran warrior, who had known Zwingli at Marignan, and at the shake of whose gray head many a council was yet to be brought to order. Zwingli was his man. The election was held on the eleventh of December, 1518. Out of twenty-four votes, seventeen were for the Reformer. There was hope for Zurich and for Switzerland.

A good work had been done at Einsidlen, not only in Zwingli's heart, but in the whole country. The people of Winterthur had sent him a call to be their pastor. The parishioners of Glaris objected, for they still hoped to win him back to them. He sent a good man to the people of Wintherthur. He visited Glaris, and in the town hall before the magistrates he resigned the pastorate, to their deep regret. They chose his former scholar, Valentine Tschudi as his successor.

Valentine was still a Romanist of the better type. After he inclined to the Reformation, he still remained the pastor, performing mass in the morning and preaching to a Protestant congregation in the evening. He avoided every subject of controversy. The burden of his sermons was, "Live like brethren, the disciples of one Lord and Master." When certain persons rebuked his tolerance, he replied, "Do you think it impossible to be a Catholic in the morning, a Reformer in the evening, and yet a Christian all the day?" But he at length became an entire Protestant. He wrote a history of the Reformation, and died in

1555. One of this family has recently been, and may still be, the pastor at Glaris.

It was a day of mingled joy and sorrow at Einsidlen when its inmates were told that their chaplain was going to Zurich. His removal would break up the brotherhood of scholars, and what prophet could say but that superstition would regain its stronghold, and make it the resort of pilgrims, who would hear only of Mary and bow to the black image? The state council of Schwytz presented him with an official mark of respect, styling him "their reverend, most learned, very gracious lord and good friend." They said, "Although grieved to lose you, yet we rejoice to have you go to Zurich."

"Give us at least a successor worthy of yourself," were the the words of the broken-hearted Geroldsek.

"I have a little *lion* for you," was the reply; "one who is simple-minded, prudent and deep in the mysteries of Scripture." This was Leo Juda, of the fine treble voice, and intrepid spirit. Leo went to Einsidlen, when Zwingli left its solitude for the busy city of Zurich, the centre of all the political interests of German Switzerland, where the most influential men dwelt among its seven thousand inhabitants.

There were many Swiss students at Paris, listening to Lefevre and reading the writings of Luther. They were thrilled with joy at the news of Zwingli's election. "All the youth of Switzerland," wrote Glarean, "rejoice, throw their caps into air, especially the Zurichers. . . . I foresee that your learning will excite great hatred, but be of good cheer, and, like Hercules, you will subdue the monsters."

The provost Felix Frey sat in the council-room, with the canons around him, to give Zwingli a reception. It may be well to look at these canons, and see what manner of men they were.

A few of them were honest men, sincere in their popery; but most of them were easy livers, who thought more of their stipends than of their duties. They would fall under the description given by a layman shortly before the Reformation, when he said, "The popes and the priests have completely oppressed us. Firstly, they have discovered the way to fish out all our secrets, namely, by the confessional. They next compel us to go to church, but it is only that we may sacrifice our money, But *they* never go to church themselves, except when they hope to get money. Their duty is to come to church and sing; yet, in order to have less singing to do, they have set up organs to do their work. They fail but in one thing, and for that they work day and night, and that is that we may go to hell for them." One of the Zurich precentors also had said of these same canons, "From a number of old horse-shoes a blacksmith can pick out one and turn it to good use, but I know of no smith who can, out of all these ecclesiastics, make one good canon."

It was an hour of unusual excitement—all felt how serious was the beginning of his ministry. Most of them feared innovation, and the young priest should fairly understand what was expected of him. "You will make every exertion," said they, "to collect the revenues of the chapter, without overlooking the least. You will exhort the faithful, both from the pulpit and in the confessional, to pay all tithes and dues, and to show by their offerings their affection to the Church. You will be diligent in increasing the income arising from the sick, from masses and from every church ordinance. As for the administration of the sacraments, preaching and caring for the flock, you may employ a substitute, particularly in preaching. You should administer the sacraments to none but persons of note, and then only when requested."

Money! money! That was first—the preaching of the gospel was of the last importance. So Zwingli was called to be a rent-collector for the canons! Fleecing the flock, and not feeding them, was to be his main business! But he had a very different idea. Thanking them for their call, but saying nothing about their advice, he gave them his plan: "The life of Christ has been too long hidden from the people. I shall preach upon the whole gospel of Matthew, chapter after chapter, without human commentaries, drawing solely from the fountains of Scripture, and seeking understanding by constant and earnest prayer. It is to God's glory, to the praise of his only Son, to the real salvation of souls and to their edification in the true faith that I shall devote my ministry." Preaching was first in his view; the instruction of the people was his great object; as for money, he said nothing about it.

This was new language; it was that of one who thought of reform. Some testified their joy, others their grief. "This way of preaching is an innovation," said they. "One new plan will lead to another, and where shall we stop?" Canon Hoffman, who had been zealous for the election, wished to prevent too great changes. Said he, "This explanation of Scripture will be more injurious than useful to the people."

"It is not a new manner," replied the young preacher. "It is the old custom. Call to mind the homilies of Chrysostom on Matthew, and of Augustine on John. Besides, I will speak with moderation, and give no person just cause to complain of it." Thus Zwingli proposed to restore the Scriptures to their ancient and rightful place.

Hoffman having failed in the chapter, wrote a request to the provost, asking him to prevent Zwingli from disturbing the faith of the people. The provost called Zwingli before him and addressed him very affectionately. But no human power could close his lips. He adhered firmly and resolutely to his purpose.

On New Year's day, 1519, the thirty-fifth birthday of the preacher, Zwingli went into the cathedral pulpit. A great crowd, eager to hear the celebrated man, was before him. "It is to Christ that I desire to lead you," said he—"to Christ the true source of salvation. His divine word is the only food that I wish to set before your souls." This was the theme of his inaugural on Saturday. He then announced that on the following day he would begin to expound Matthew's gospel. The next morning the preacher and a still larger audience were at their posts. He opened the long-sealed book and read the first page. He caused his hearers to marvel at that chapter of names. But it was the human genealogy of the Lord Jesus Christ—patriarchs, prophets, kings were mentioned in it—Jewish history was summed up therein—and how forcibly did it teach that all the preceding ages had existed for the sake of him who was born of Mary, and named Immanuel! And there was the name Jesus—"He shall save his people from their sins." The enraptured auditors went home saying, "We never heard the like of this before!"

On every Sabbath the people heard what they knew not before, as the preacher went on explaining Matthew, with a Greek Testament before him. He applied the gospel to the nature, the wants, the sins, the sorrows and the joys of man, with an eloquence that flowed through the channel of prayer. With courage he spared no one—neither pope, nor emperor, kings, dukes, princes, patriots, bishops, priests, laity. With uplifted voice he entreated all to repent, amend their lives, show charity, walk humbly and live in prayer and holiness. He extolled the infinite mercies of God and the completeness of Christ's atonement. "Let all Zurich place its trust in God."

The poor and unlearned—peasants, vine-dressers, smiths, weavers and shop-keepers—flocked to hear one whom they could understand. He respected them. One day a boy came to him and told him of a slip of the tongue which caused a wrong expression. He was pleased, and said, "We can learn much from boys when they are sharp and attentive." In such ways he won the hearts of the common people. To reach them he went to the market-places on Fridays, and drew multitudes. Myconius reports that more than two thousand people were soon hungering for the "strong meat" of the Scriptures. He was often seen in the halls where tradesmen met, conversing with them familiarly. Peasant and patrician found in him the same cordiality. One of his most violent enemies complimented him by trying to abuse him, when he said, "He invited the country people to dine with him, walked with them, talked to them of God, put the devil in their hearts and his books in their pockets. He succeeded so well that the notables of Zurich used to visit the peasants, drink with them, show them about the city, and pay them every mark of attention."

Poets, orators, statesmen and scholars were equally delighted. Many of them had ceased to attend church. "I derive no instruction from the sermons of these priests," Fuesslin, the poet, historian and councillor of state, had said. "They do not preach the things belonging to salvation, because they know them not." He and other distinguished men now listened to one who knew the things of God. "Glory be to God!" said they, after his first sermon, "this man is a preacher of the truth. He will be our Moses, leading us forth from this Egyptian darkness." From that day they upheld the hands of Zwingli. "Ye mighty

ones of the world, cease to proscribe the doctrine of Christ!"
wrote the poet Fuesslin. "When Christ, the Son of God, had been
put to death, fishermen rose up to fill his place. And now if
you destroy the preachers of the truth, you will see glaziers, millers, potters, founders, shoemakers and tailors teaching in their
stead."

Let us look at the man. He had a powerful frame, a majestic
countenance, a dignified manner, "Only look at his portrait,"
says Hagenbach. "Observe this energetic, well-compacted
head, this marked physiognomy, as if stone carved; this expan-
sive forehead, this full clear eye, this compressed mouth, with
the well-rounded lips." In all this God gave him power.
"Never," writes Myconius, somewhat extravagantly, "had there
been seen a priest in the pulpit with such an imposing appearance and commanding power, so that you were irresistibly led to
believe that a man from the apostolic times was standing before
you." But we could tell our good Oswald that Paul was probably a small man, with no very powerful presence.

"He is too fond of music," certain ones had said at the outset, and if they had lingered about his room they might have
had some slanderous stories to report on this score. Some did
call him "the evangelical lute-player and fifer." The vicar John
Faber of Constance, came over to see him, and found that his
old musical habits had not been entirely given up. He censured
Zwingli for this taste. "My dear Faber," was the frank reply,
"you do not know what music is. True, I have learned to play
on the lute, the violin, and other instruments, and they serve me
to quiet little children; but you are too holy for music! . . . Do
you not know that David was a skilful player on the harp, and
how by this means he drove the evil spirit out of Saul? Ah! if
you did but know the sounds of the heavenly lyre, the wicked

spirit of ambition and the love of riches, which possess you, would soon depart from you likewise." Let all who will, regard this as a weakness in Zwingli. He set to music some of his Christian poems, that others might partake of his joy.

And perhaps some said, "He studies too much." Often he was reading, writing or translating almost from day-break until noon. To Hebrew he gave some of his best hours. When dining he asked the news or gave kindly advice; he then walked with his friends or visited his flock. At two he resumed his studies. In the evening he wrote letters. He always stood up at his literary labour, and when engaged would allow none to disturb him, except for some very important cause.

A man named Lucian called on him one day and showed him some works of Luther. He wished to go about and sell them to the people. Rhenanus of Basle had sent him, saying, "Ascertain whether this man possesses sufficient prudence and skill: if so, let him carry from city to city, from town to town, and even from house to house, among the Swiss, the works of Luther, especially his exposition of the Lord's Prayer written for the laity. The more they are known, the more purchasers they will find. But take care not to let him hawk about any other books; for if he has only Luther's, he will sell them so much the faster." Lucian had travelled over almost all Switzerland, and he knew nearly everybody. Zwingli set him to work. He ought to have put into his basket copies of the New Testament. Thus the truth went far and wide into families dwelling distant from churches, or in parishes where there were no preachers of the gospel tidings.

On another day Dean Bullinger came riding into town on a panting horse, to out-distance the monk Samson, who might be making good time on the dapple gray that he had swindled from the rich knight. The dean laid before the Diet his complaints against the indulgence-seller, who had excommunicated him. He found there some messengers from the bishop, who came on the like errand, and he made common cause with them. All promised to support him. The spirit of Zwingli animated the city. The Reformer had seen the enemy gradually approaching, and preached against the indulgences. John Faber had encouraged him, promising him the bishop's support. "I am aware," said the pompous Italian, "that Zwingli will speak against me, but I will stop his mouth." The dean would see to that. The council of state resolved to oppose his entry in Zurich. Samson had already put up at an inn in the suburbs, and laid his plans. He would ride into the city and take it. He had one foot in the stirrup, when deputies came from the council, offered him the honorary cup of wine usually given to the pope's envoy, and informed him that he might dispense with entering Zurich. The inhabitants did not particularly need him nor his wares.

"I have something to communicate to the Diet in the name of his holiness," replied the monk. This was a mere trick. It was agreed that he should appear. He was cautious; his craftiness did not fail him. He spoke of nothing but the papal indulgences. The councillors reminded him of the affair at Bremgarten, and compelled him to withdraw the sentence of excommunication pronounced against the dean. He left the hall fuming with anger, and shook the dust of Zurich off his feet as he turned to other quarters, where deans were not so plenty nor councils so authoritative. The pope soon recalled him to Italy. "A wagon drawn by three horses, and laden with the money that his falsehoods had wrung from the poor, preceded him on those steep paths of the St. Gotthard that he had crossed eight months before, without money or parade, and burdened with only a few papers."

Zwingli had not the fierce spiritual conflicts that Luther first experienced. He turned more speedily to the great Deliverer. "When my heart is troubled because of my helplessness and the weakness of my nature, my spirit is revived at the sound of these glad tidings: Christ is thy righteousness; Christ is thy salvation; thou art nothing, thou canst do nothing; Christ is the Alpha and Omega; Christ is all things; he can do all things." Thus he gained the victory over himself.

The gospel had its victory over the people. The preaching of the Word had such an effect upon the town-council that, as early as 1520, they issued a decree to all parish priests, curates and exhorters, in town and country, "that they should freely and everywhere preach the holy gospels and the apostolic epistles, and all speak the same language as the Spirit of God should direct them, and only teach what they could prove by the word of God. As for the doctrines and commandments that were of man's institution, they should let them alone." This ordinance was a proof of the first great victory which the followers of the gospel publicly celebrated at Zurich. It was won by Zwingli on the plan of expounding the Scriptures.

CHAPTER VIII.

PATRIOTIC LABOURS.

(1519–1520.)

"THE great love that from my childhood I have borne to my native country compels me to make known my cares in regard to its state, lest greater mischief befall us. There is ground to fear that the lords, whom we beat with iron and halberd, will vanquish us with the touch of gold." Thus spake Zwingli, who hoped to reform the evils that had grown out of politics and mercenary wars. He felt it a duty to lift up his voice against everything that would destroy the union of the cantons. "Next to my concern for the word of God," he wrote, "the interests of the confederation lie nearest my heart. For the longing desire of my heart, and the great object of my teaching, have been to preserve the confederation, that it might remain as handed down to us from our fathers, true to itself and free from service under foreign masters, and that the members of it might live together in peace and friendship."

In ancient times the Swiss began their battles with prayer,*

---

* When kneeling in prayer on the plain of Grandson, the enemy rushed upon the army of the Swiss, it being supposed that the posture was a token of submission. But the kneeling soldiers were able to use their lances to a better advantage against the cavalry, and they gained the victory. Thus the Christian bowed in prayer has an advantage over his spiritual foes.

and when they gained a victory they fell on their knees and thanked God for his help. The monuments which they raised to commemorate battle-fields were chapels or houses of prayer. As the patriotic peacher pointed to these memorials of purer times, he said, "The Almighty granted to our ancestors favour in his sight, so that they freed themselves from a tyrannous nobility, and lived in concord with one another. They prospered; while right and justice were so well administered in this land that all who were oppressed in foreign countries fled hither, as to an asylum, for safety." But now the Swiss were going into battle for gold, and the monuments of their victories were riches with those who took bribes, and poverty with those who ran into extravagance and dissipation; loss of patriotism, national weakness, dissensions, idleness, immortality and the want of God's favour.

"Behold! how unlike we are to our ancestors!" exclaimed the patriot from his pulpit. "They would not suffer foreign masters in their land, but now we lead them in among us by the hand, if they only have money, that a few may get the purse while the many get the stripes. And when a pious man has brought up a well-doing son, then come the captains and steal him away, and he must expose himself to the danger of dying by hunger, disease, shot, wounds or murder. And if he reckon up his money, he will find that he could have won more at home by threshing the harvests which he might have raised, not to speak of his being run through with a spear ere the account comes to be paid: and at last of all, his poor old father, who has brought him up, and whom he should have supported in his old age, is reduced to the beggar's staff. But those who get the money want for nothing. And when the loss comes, your neighbour or your neighbour's son must bear it, while they go scot free. Although no one can be forced (to enter the foreign service), yet recruiting parties spread themselves over the whole land; then it is seen what young blood will do when it is up. In this way we lose our best sons, who for vile money are consumed in a foreign land. . . . A few become rich, but these so rich that they buy off the rest, getting hold of their vineyards, fields and meadows, and leaving them to poverty, or forcing them to sell themselves to foreign masters for wretched pay.

"Now no one will work to gain a living; the lands lie waste in many places; the people are degraded by poverty or unmanned by luxury. And yet to work is noble: it saves from wantonness and vice; it yields good fruit, so that a man can richly nourish his body without care, and without the fear of sullying himself with the blood of the innocent. It makes him hale and strong, dissipates diseases engendered by idleness; and increase follows the hand of the worker, as creation came at the first from the the hand of the all-working God. Thus there is nothing in the universe so like God as the worker."

Still farther let us hear the patriotic preacher, as he stood like a Hebrew prophet to warn the people against such evils as Micah and Jeremiah deplored:* "Let each one for himself reflect on the evils of war, and think how it would be with him if he were treated as we use our fellow-Christians. Think now that a foreign mercenary came into thy land with violence, laid waste thy meadows, thy fields, thy vineyards, drove off thy cattle, seized thy house furniture and carted it away; in the attack slew thy son while defending himself and thee, insulted thy daughters, kicked the dear wife of thy bosom when she went before thee and fell at the feet of the foreign soldier, begging for mercy toward thee and herself; dragged out thyself, a poor

---

* Mic. ii.; Jer. ii., v., xxiii.

worthy old man, from the place where thou wert crouching in fear in thine own house and home, knocked thee down in the presence of thy wife, despite her cries and despite thine own trembling, venerable, pleading gray hairs, and then at last set fire to thy dwelling and burnt it to the ground; wouldst thou not think within thyself that if the heaven did not open and rain fire on such villainy, if the earth did not yawn and swallow up such monsters, there were no God? And yet thou doest all this to another, and callest it, forsooth, *the right of war!**

"Those who, for truth, religion, justice and native country, venture their lives in war are true men, and their cause is sacred. But as for those bloodthirsty, mercenary soldiers, I am of opinion that they deserve to be branded as highway robbers, and that they are unworthy of the name of Christians. One danger is, that by serving in these foreign wars we thereby draw down upon us the wrath of God. Another danger is, that justice between man and man will be stopped, as an old proverb says, 'When arms are up in the hands, laws are under the feet.' The term *right of war* means nothing but violence [with such mercenaries], turn it over as you will. You say, Force must be employed to reduce the disobedient. Yea, verily, it were good that it went no farther, and that the thunderbolt of war struck only those who were disobedient in things lawful. But what do you say of the man who sells himself to a foreign master, to rob and desolate those who have done him no injury at all? The gifts of these foreign lords (be they bishops or popes, who ought not to go to war) blind the eyes of every man, however wise he may be,

---

* Zwingli probably drew this vivid picture from his own observation when in the Italian campaigns, and there heard soldiers plead "the right of war" as their apology for violence and plunder.

and deprive him of reason as well as piety: as Moses teaches 'A gift doth blind the eyes of the wise, and pervert the words of the righteous.' (Deut. xvi. 19.)

"And if one should inquire, How are we to deliver ourselves from these evils, and return again to union? I answer, By abstaining from *selfishness*. For if this base passion did not reign among us, the confederation were a union of brothers, rather than a mere league. If one rejoins to this, 'Selfishness is implanted in the human heart, from whence it cannot be eradicated, for God alone can know and change the heart,' then I answer, Do earnestly that which lies in your power. Where you find it punishable punish it, and let it not grow. And that it may be rooted out of the very hearts of men, give heed that the divine word be faithfully preached. For when God is not in the heart, there is nothing but the man himself, and he cares for nothing but that which serves his interests, pleasures and lusts. But when God possesses the heart, then man has regard to that which pleases God, seeks the honour of God and the welfare of his fellow-men. Now to have God you must have the knowledge of him. The knowledge of God can come to us in no way clearer than from the word of God. Will you then have this knowledge spread among you, so that you may live in peace and in the fear of God? Then see to it that the word of God is purely preached according to its natural sense, unadulterated by the glosses and inventions of man."

Thus Zwingli preached that the gospel was the only remedy for the evils under which his country groaned. He applied Christianity to politics. He wished patriotism to be tempered with piety. He sought to draw his countrymen from the love of gold to the love of God and of father-land. Let the foreign kings fight their own battles, but let the Swiss stay at home, cul-

tivate their lands, tend their flocks, toil in their shops, rear
their families in the fear of God, obey their laws, cherish
brotherhood, preserve peace in their cantons, strengthen
their confederation, reform the abuses in the Church, and
in all things be governed by the Word that came down from
heaven.

Francis I. was seeking again to enlist the Swiss youth
against the pope and form a treaty with the confederation. The
treaty was presented to the Swiss people in the usual corrupt
fashion, by bribing the leading men in each canton. One canton after another signed it. All of them joined the French
alliance except Zurich : she stood aloof, to the surprise of her
neighbours. What strange spell had fallen upon her statesmen?
What power had baffled French intrigue and resisted French
bribery? It was the spirit and power of the gospel. Zwingli's
sermons had awakened the conscience and inspired a new kind
of patriotism. They had led most of the bailiffs and burgomasters to say, " We must adopt a new policy, and have nothing
to do with foreign politics. We must triumph over selfishness
and profligacy—save our young men from vice and our country
from ruin."

Glorious was the victory which the word of God achieved on
the field of patriotism. Zwingli had won the day in the city;
but what would the men of the canton say? The council addressed them a letter, probably written by Zwingli, asking them
to give their views on the question of foreign service. One voice
came from the entire canton : the government should act on the
principles of their forefathers and have nothing to do with foreign masters, whether they were kings or cardinals, the emperor
or the pope.

" Zwingli is interfering in politics; he is intermeddling with the affairs of the confederation," cried his enemies, especially in the other cantons.

"Not at all," replied his friends. "He would have us keep clear of all foreign politics, and devote our attention to religion and to reform."

Cardinal Schinner appeared in 1521, urging that the men of the Swiss cantons had bound themselves in 1515 to aid the pope and defend the Church. Would Zurich abide by this former treaty? Zwingli's advice was asked. Said he, "What a people have once promised to do they are bound to perform, unless God shows them a fair method of escape from the alliance. But let them take care never to enter into such a treaty again. I believe there is an escape. The cardinal has employed intrigue and bribery to gain his end, which were expressly forbidden by the treaty. He has broken the conditions; we are not bound to the alliance. I would that the papal treaty had a hole burnt in it, and that the papal legate were bound on a board with his back to it and carried home. If a wolf comes into a land every one is up to kill the beast or drive it away; but against the wolves that devour the people no one will fight. They [the cardinals] are very properly dressed in red caps and cloaks; for if they be shaken, then out drop ducats and crowns: but if they be wrung, then out flows the blood of thy son, brother, father and friend."

"Hasten on the affair before the parson gets into his pulpit," said the crafty legate of the pope. The council confessed themselves bound by the papal treaty. The Zurichers marched to the help of the pope. The other confederates marched to the aid of the king of France, and were beaten along with the French. Zurich was thus arrayed against the other cantons, although her men were not in the battle. Thus a new ground of enmity was laid between Zurich and the other confederates.

The blame was charged upon Zwingli, who had spoken against the foreign service to either party. The patriotic preacher rallied the men of his canton. At his instance the clergy, laity, magistrates and citizens were brought to take an oath that henceforth they would no longer accept gifts, pensions or annuities from foreign princes. He had already ceased to draw the pension which had been urged upon him, although at that very time his income was too small to support him in comfort. When conscience regulates a man's money affairs, it is of some account.

In all this the Bible was the great power, as it was brought to bear upon the people through the sermons of Zwingli. "Whatever lies may be told," said he, "the sole cause of the abolition of the mercenary service under foreign princes, in the canton of Zurich, in town and country, was *the word of God.*" We see that one motive which urged Zwingli to labour for a Reformation was the love of his country. Not yet did he feel the strong enthusiasm for justification by faith which Luther manifested; not yet was he moved forward by the powerful affection for the Church which Calvin afterward exhibited; but he burned with love for his father-land, and to remedy the evils which were destroying his countrymen he faithfully applied the word of God. In this respect he was a true Swiss, with his native country on his heart. God gives to men different motives: Zwingli was first moved by true patriotism. No two great men are alike; each has "his proper gift of God;" each has his own individuality.

CHAPTER IX.

THE SCHOOL OF THE CROSS.

(1519—1520.)

BEFORE the Jamina pours into the Rhine it meets with a tremendous fall, making a frightful gorge, where is one of the most extraordinary scenes in all Switzerland. So deep and narrow is it that the sun shines into it only about five hours a day. The visitor seems to be at the bottom of a well or a mine. It was once the custom to let invalids down into it with ropes from the brink of the cliffs, to gain health from the mineral springs. It became a watering-place of great resort. Thousands sought relief at the baths of Pfeffers. Down into this "infernal gulf," as Daniel the hermit called it, our Reformer must go and learn how low he must descend into the valley of humiliation.

Zwingli did not spare himself, and in the toils and anxieties of his first year at Zurich he lost his health. He was advised to repair to the baths of Pfeffers. Many were sorry to be deprived of his genial visits and his sermons on Matthew, the canon Hoffman not being among them. One young student, Herus, who lived at his house, vented his feelings by saying, "Oh! had I a hundred tongues, a hundred mouths and a voice of iron, as Virgil says, or rather had I the eloquence of Cicero, how could I express all that I owe to you and the pain this separation causes me?" The pastor departed, perhaps took Wesen on his way,

94

and descended to the old baths in Eastern Switzerland. In the house where he lodged it was necessary to burn the lamps at midday. The superstitious were ever seeing ghosts and "mountain spirits" in the spray and the gloom. The fire of truth was still burning in Zwingli's heart. He let his light shine and served his Master, a thing said to be not always true of professing Christians at a watering-place. His affable spirit won the hearts of many of the invalids, as he pointed them to the Great Physician who healed the infirm at the pool of Bethesda. Among them was Philip Egentius, the poet and professor at Friburg in Brisgau, who from that time declared himself for the Reformation.

In a few days painful news came to him. The *great death* had appeared in Zurich. Travelling from the east, it had passed over him, hidden down in the shadow of the rocks. It was proving "the scourge of God," the terror of Europe, and where could he be safer from it than amid the spray of the Jamina? But the unselfish pastor thought chiefly of his flock. He must hasten home, likely as he was to be the victim of the plague. If Châteaubriand had known of this and thousands of similar cases, he would have given a better turn to his eloquent period than to say, "The Protestant pastor abandons the necessitous on the bed of death, and never risks his life in the midst of the pestilence."

Zwingli found his house deserted by all the young men who had lived and studied with him, except his youngest brother Andrew, who had waited for his return. He sent Andrew immediately to Wildhaus, that he might escape "the death." With heroic courage he went from house to house, devoting himself entirely to the victims of the frightful scourge. Every day he proclaimed the messages and consolations of Christ to the sick and the dying. In the pulpit he so preached that he raised the hearts of the terrified congregation with the invitations of Jesus to the heavy-laden and the promises treasured up in the Word of life. His faithful parishioners trembled for their pastor, as they saw him moving about among the shafts of death and bearing to them the cup of salvation. His devotion was talked of by friends at a distance. Two thousand five hundred people were swept away in a short time, and they were alarmed for him. Conrad Brunner of Wesen, soon to die of the plague, wrote to him from Basle, saying, "Do your duty, but at the same time remember to take care of your own life."

The caution came too late: Zwingli was attacked by "the great death." Switzerland seemed about to lose her mightiest preacher, Zurich her patriotic Reformer, his flock their best earthly friend. Dr. Hedio of Basle was thinking sadly of the possible result of "the murderous disease; for who would not grieve if the saviour of his country, if the trumpet of the gospel, if the courageous herald of the truth should be stricken down in the prime of life, high in hope and in the midst of his usefulness." The thoughts of Zwingli were turned inward; his eyes upward to heaven. His meditations and prayers were afterward recorded in poetry, whose rhythm and quaintness D'Aubigne has preserved in his version :

> Lo ! at the door
> I hear death's knock !
> Shield me, O Lord,
> My strength and rock.
> Thy hand once nailed
> Upon the tree,
> Jesus, uplift,
> And shelter me.

Willest thou then,
Death conquer me,
In my own noon-day?
So let it be!
Oh! may I die,
Since I am thine:
Thy home is made
For faith like mine.

Canon Hoffman was so bound to his creed that he could not bear the idea of seeing Zwingli die in the errors which he had preached. He said to Felix Frey, the provost of the chapter, "Think of the danger to which his soul is exposed. Has he not called all the doctors of the last three hundred and eighty years and more, innovators—such men as Albertus Magnus, Bonaventure, Aquinas and all the canonists? Does he not maintain that their doctrines are mere visions which they dreamt in their cowls within the walls of their cloisters? Alas! it would have been better for the city of Zurich had Zwingli ruined our vintage and our harvest for many years! Now he is at the door of death. . . . I entreat you to save his poor soul!" The provost does not seem to have thought that Zwingli's soul would be endangered by any of the opinions which so alarmed his brother canon, and he made no effort to induce him to recant.

Day and night were prayers ascending to God from the distressed believers for their pastor's recovery. No letter went from him to Wildhaus, where several persons had died in the village, and among them a servant of his brother Nicholas. The pestilence was threatening the valley of the Tockenburg. Andrew Zwingli wrote: "Tell me in what state you are, my dear brother. The abbot and all our brothers salute thee." As no mention is made of his parents, it is presumed that they were

dead. The report went abroad, far and near, that the Zurich
Reformer had fallen in death. The city of Basle was full of lamentations. The university felt the deepest sorrow. "Whom
the gods love, die young," said they in classic not in gospel
phrase. But the Lord heard the prayers of his people, the
plague forsook its victim, and at one time he could write with
emotions of gratitude :

> My God, my Sire,
>   Healed by thy hand,
> Upon the earth
>   Once more I stand.
> From guilt and sin
>   May I be free !
> My mouth shall sing
>   Alone of thee.
>
> The uncertain hour
>   For me will come,
> O'erwhelmed perchance
>   With deeper gloom.
> It matters not !
>   With joy I'll bear
> My yoke until
>   I reach heaven's sphere.

A letter went to Wildhaus with the joyful tidings. Young
Collin bore the news to Basle, and Hedio wrote : "Like a suddenly appearing angel of consolation came Rudolph Collin, as-
suring us that we had no cause to be cast down, for you were
safe." Wilibald Pirkheimer, of Nurnburg, wrote: "Let us sing
praises to God, who strikes and heals again the wounds, who kills
and makes alive, and who has called back your soul from the
grave." His unmusical fellow-student, John Faber, still his

friend, wrote from Constance, expressing his joy and love: "Nothing in this world would pain me more than the tidings that any calamity had befallen you, which God, in his mercy, avert. And this love you well deserve, for you work with such zeal in the vineyard of the Lord that when you are in danger a calamity impends the community. The Lord himself knows, however, whom he will stir up by bitter trials to a more earnest striving and a better and more enduring inheritance. Such a trial you have experienced from your heavenly Father." From regions more remote came such letters, refreshing to his spirit.

Zwingli went into his pulpit still feeble and scarcely able to preach. "The plague has so weakened my memory and intellect," he wrote to Myconius, "that in preaching I sometimes altogether lose the thread of my discourse. All my members are oppressed with a languor that I cannot describe." This was not all; his salary was so small that he was under a burden of embarrassments. He could not support himself and his two assistants. Gifts might have poured in, but he would not accept them. He half resolved to resign his position, which would have delighted Canon Hoffman, and retire to Einsidlen. A noble act on the part of a friend saved him to Zurich. Doctor Englehard, a canon, resigned his place and income in favour of the Reformer, making him a canon as well as cathedral preacher. Thus Zwingli gained a support and greater influence among the canons, which was the more desirable, since certain of these clerical gentlemen kept a suspicious eye upon him. They had made a noise because he did not act more zealously as a revenue collector, a sort of publican in the service of those Pharisees. "Indeed," said they, "instead of urging his hearers to pay their tithes as a religious duty, he denies their divine origin altogether, and represents their strict exaction as a tyranny. He thereby seeks to gain the confidence of the people in the same measure that he makes the monks hated and despised as mere cap-divines.'' Since death had not taken him from them, they and their sympathizers began to prepare thorns for his discomfort.

The Lord had led his servant nearer to himself that he might have the privileges of a son. D'Aubigne says: ''This pestilence of 1519, which committed such frightful ravages in the north of Switzerland, was, in the hands of God, a powerful means of converting many souls. But on no one did it exercise so powerful an influence as on Zwingli. The gospel, which had hitherto been too much regarded by him as a mere doctrine, now became a great reality. He arose from the darkness of the sepulchre with a new heart. His zeal became more active, his life more holy, his preaching more free, more Christian, more powerful. This was the epoch of Zwingli's complete emancipation; henceforward he consecrated himself entirely to God. But the Reformation of Switzerland received a new life at the same time as the Reformer. The scourge, *the great death,* as it swept over these mountains and descended into the valleys, gave a holier character to the movement that was taking place. The Reformation, as well as Zwingli, was baptized in the waters of affliction and of grace, and came forth purer and more vigorous. It was a memorable day in the counsels of God for the regeneration of this people.''

One of the happiest men in Zurich was Oswald Myconius, and one of the least likely to remove. True, he had embarrassments; but his cheerful wife was a helper meet for all trying circumstances, and to be near to Zwingli was a privilege worth no little endurance. They were bound together in strongest fellowship, walking in reliance on each other, like Luther and Melancthon. Yet there was a finger often pointing him to a new field. It was that of the Canon Xyloctect, who invited Oswald to return to his native place. "Zurich is not your country," said the canon; "it is Lucerne. You tell me that the Zurichers are your friends: I do not deny it. But do you know what will be the end of it? Serve your own country: this I would advise you, entreat you, and, if I may, command you."

It is said that more than a thousand years ago the boatmen used to see a lantern (*lucerna*) hanging by the water's edge to show them the landing, and hence the town was called Lucerne. Oswald saw a light inviting him to set foot in the city and there plant the gospel. But would it ever become other than the dark lantern of popery?

Soon Oswald was informed that he was appointed head-master of the collegiate school at Lucerne. It was the canon's work. Oswald no longer hesitated, for he saw in it the finger of God. Perhaps a schoolmaster might be the humble means of introducing the gospel doctrines of peace into the warlike city of Lucerne. Sad and tearful was the parting of Zwingli and his friend. It was just when the Reformer was weak and almost worn out, and after Oswald had gone, that he wrote to him saying, "Your departure has inflicted a blow on the cause I am defending, like that suffered by an army in battle array when one of its wings is destroyed. Alas! I now feel all the value of my Myconius, and how often, without my knowing it, he has upheld the cause of Christ!"

"What is your opinion of Luther's cause?" inquired Myconius of his friend. "As for me, I have no fear, either for the gospel or for him. If God does not protect his truth, who shall defend it? All that I ask of the Lord is, that he will not withdraw his hand from those who hold nothing dearer than his gospel. Continue as you have begun, and an abundant reward shall be conferred upon you."

The Reformer must travel through the country if he was to advance the Reformation. One day his former teacher, George Bingli, came over from Wesen, where he succeeded the good parson Bartholomew. It was the first week in 1520. "Let us go to Basle," said the visitor, "and see how the brethren do." They went and were welcomed. Zwingli electrified his friends by his powerful language. Capito learned how Zwingli had expounded the Scriptures; he began a similar work, took up Matthew's gospel and had an increasing audience. The hearers hailed the revival of Christianity. But his zeal and popularity roused opposition. A conspiracy of monks and priests was soon formed against Capito in Basle. They might drive him thence, but they could not destroy him.

At Mentz [Mayence] the young Albert, cardinal-archbishop was desirous of attaching to himself so great a scholar, and he invited Capito to his court. The learned man, seeing great hindrances at Basle, resolved to accept the invitation. The matter got abroad; the people were excited; they protested against losing their preacher; their indignation was roused against the priests, and a violent commotion broke out in the city. "Let him go," said some. "We can have Hedio."

"He is too young," certain ones replied. "He is Capito's disciple," said others. But this arrangement was effected. The new preacher began his work.

"The truth stings; it is not safe to wound tender ears by preaching it," said Hedio. "But it matters not. Nothing shall make me swerve from the right road."

The monks redoubled their efforts, saying, from the pulpit, "Do not believe those who tell you that the sum of Christian doctrine is found in the gospel and in St. Paul. Scotus has been of more service to Christianity than St. Paul himself. All the learned things that have ever been said or printed were stolen from Scotus. All that these hunters after glory have been able to do is merely to add a few Greek and Hebrew words to obscure the whole matter.''

Zwingli did much to strengthen the hands and hearts of these two assistant Reformers, not only by his visit, but afterward by letters. On his return, John Glother, of Basle, thanked him for the good he had received, saying: ''Never can I forget you. You came to see me—me a poor schoolmaster, an obscure man, without learning or merit and of low estate.'' Andrew Zwingli died of the plague in 1520; and the Reformer wept ''the tears of a woman'' over his beloved brother.

The Reformer needed both rest and help; he was to find each at Baden. The priest at this watering-place had once been one of the pope's guards, and had purchased his benefice by carrying the battle-axe. He was a kind-hearted man, but so fond of jovial company that he used to spend most of his time in jesting and revelling with bad men. His curate Stahel performed faithfully all the duties of the parish-priest. Zwingli was pleased with him, and said: ''I have need of Swiss helpers.'' Stahel became his fellow-labourer, dwelling in his house, and soon having reason to watch night and day in defence of the Reformer.

''Since the plague did not carry off Zwingli, we must see what we can do to crush him,'' thought some of his enemies. The worst foes were the monks and the mercenaries. The monks had been ordered by the council to preach only the word of God. They were confounded; most of them had never read it and all of them hated it. The mercenaries were angry because Zwingli had made the foreign service so unpopular, and induced the citizens to take an oath not to have aught more to do with bribes and pensions. Certain men were bent upon having these orders and these oaths repealed or creating a revolution. But to others there seemed to be a shorter method: remove Zwingli, and the old style of affairs would be restored. Plots began to be formed. The basest slanders were invented and circulated, in order to blast Zwingli's character, check the preaching of the gospel and drive him from the city. Several barons and noblemen, who had heard him at Einsidlen and supported his cause at Zurich, were turned against him by the calumnies of the priests. What he thought may be learned from his own words: "I have for some time past heard incredible lies told about me, but this has not grieved me, for I have always kept in mind that 'the disciple is not greater than the Master.' If they lied against Christ, it is no wonder that they lie against thee, Ulrich Zwingli." These slanders recoiled upon the monks like arrows turned back by an invisible hand. His death was now resolved upon. Poison or the poniard must free them from the witness of the truth. Myconius says: "After the temporary defeat of the priests and monks in Zurich, and the passing of the resolutions against pensions, it was by artifice that they schemed to get rid of their hated opponent."

An anonymous letter came from Swabia to him, and Zwingli read the warning: "If ever thou caredst for thy life, care for it now, for traps and snares are laid for thee; they encompass thee on every side; *death by poison* lies ready to take thee out of the way. . . . Be on thy guard, then. Out of thy house thou canst not safely eat anything. The priest who told me this dare not assert it plainly nor write it with impunity. Thy shrewd mind will lead thee to guess whence this warning comes. Whoever I am, I am thine: thou shalt afterward know me." It was afterward known that the writer was Michael Hummelberger of Ravensburg.

On the next day after this letter was received, just as Stahel was entering the Water church, a chaplain stopped him, saying: "Leave Zwingli's house forthwith; a catastrophe is at hand." The faithful assistant was not to be thus driven from his work. Assassins are likely to appear whenever a great movement is shaking human society, overthrowing old customs, changing old opinions and bringing in a new order of things. But the leaders are in God's hands, and he gives them courage for the crisis.

"We often had such alarms as these," said Stahel, "but we were well armed, and a patrol was stationed in the street to protect us." It was the habit of Zwingli at this time to sup with a friend or in the guild-hall, and some of the trustworthy citizens attended him home without telling him their fears. The council took measures to guard his house. Yet more than all these, was the eye of the sleepless Lord and the good hand of God upon him.

"There was not an hour," wrote Myconius, "that did not give birth to some deep-laid plot among the laity and priests against the life of the apostle of truth and righteousness. I pass over those not known to the world, though well known to myself. Once there came a man at midnight, calling him to visit a person dying. The assistant answered that Zwingli could not be roused from his sleep, for he was greatly fatigued by the previous day's labours: he himself [Stahel no doubt] would go instead. The man would not permit this on any account. The suspicion of the assistant was aroused; the door was shut in the face of the stranger. Next day it was found that Zwingli was to have been seized, gagged, thrown into a boat and carried away. Not long after a horse was kept for a like purpose. . . . Two drunken

Zurichers, whom I do not name, once attacked his house in the night, dashed in the windows and took possession, making such a noise that not one of the neighbours dared to enter. The burgomaster quelled the uproar, but the two men were not to be found. Search was made in the morning, the city gates were shut, every corner was spied into, but all seemed in vain until some women betrayed one of them. He was drawn out of the wine-cask of a certain priest, and led to prison amid the loud reproaches of the people. He would have been imprisoned for life, had not the Bernese interceded for him."

It was amid such scenes that Zwingli wrote to Myconius: "Let not your courage sink. There will not fail in our days men who will preach Christ fully, even though they know beforehand that, as it happened long ago, they will be blasphemed after death as heretics, traitors and villains. As for me, I expect for myself, as a victim devoted to death, the worst from all clergy as well as laity; and I pray to Christ for grace to meet whatever may befal me with manly courage, and that he may either uphold me or break me in pieces, as may seem good to him. . . . If I held it allowable to boast, I should rejoice to suffer shame for the name of Christ. Yet let him that thinketh he standeth take heed lest he fall."

CHAPTER X.

ANNA REINHARD AND HER HOME.

(1520–1524.)

THE true story of Anna Reinhard is full of romantic interest. A poor child of plebeian family, she never expected to outrival the rich daughter of a nobleman. A certain noble damsel in Thurgau was pointed out as worthy of the hand of John Meyer von Knonau, a young man of aristocratic birth who had been brought up at the court of his relative, the bishop of Constance. His father, who dwelt in his castle not far from Zurich, insisted upon the match. But he had a choice of his own. The surpassing beauty, the amiable spirit, the spotless character and the winning excellence of Anna Reinhard were all that he wished in a wife. In these was true nobility. Unknown to his father and against his will, they were married in the rustic parish church where she lived. At this step the old gentleman was so enraged that he forbade his son his house, refused him all support, and, as far as the laws of Zurich would permit, disinherited him.

John Meyer struggled on at Zurich, full of heart and happy at home, in due time enrolling the name of little Gerold and his two sisters on his family record. The gold of some agent, probably Cardinal Schinner, tempted him in his poverty, and he entered the mercenary service. For aught we know, he marched with the army in which Zwingli was chaplain, and he died in 1515, perhaps at Marignan.

Anna regarded her three little children as the priceless memorials of her husband, and lived solely for their education. Grandfather Meyer would have nothing to do with them, for he seemed pitiless, heartless, inexorable.

But one day the young widow's servant went with Gerold, a sprightly boy of three years, to the fish-market. At an inn sat the grandfather talking with some friends and looking out of the window. Seeing the child sitting in a basket, and acting in such good-humour as to draw all eyes upon him, the old gentleman inquired: "Whose handsome child is that?"

"It is your son's," was the reply.

"Bring him to me," said the grandfather, whose heart was touched, and all its ice melted in a moment. He kissed the boy, went home with him, greeted Anna as a daughter, and from that hour behaved as a good grandfather. Unhappily, the old man died soon after; yet happily for the widow and her children he did not leave them so large a legacy as to divert them from the path along which God was leading them to the riches of the gospel. It seems that they had a comfortable home in Zurich.

Gerold Meyer soon attracted the attention of Zwingli, when he became the kind pastor in the city. The Reformer became very fond of him, directed him in his education, and in 1521 sent him to Basle. There Gerold studied under teachers who loved the gospel, and sat under the preaching of men who proclaimed it. But he did not find Gaspar Hedio, whom we left as the successor of Capito. The archbishop Albert had taken Capito with him to attend the coronation of Charles V., and Hedio had gone to fill his place at Mentz. Basle thus lost her most faithful preachers. But William Rubli drew four thousand people to hear him, and young Gerold may have been among them. The preacher attacked the doctrines of the mass, purgatory and the invocation of saints, yet he did not so boldly preach the way of salvation. He was fond of making a parade of his boldness. On the festival of Corpus Christi he joined the great procession, but instead of carrying the usual relics he had borne before him a copy of the Holy Scriptures, handsomely bound, and inscribed in large letters with the words, "THE BIBLE: this is the true relic. All others are but dead men's bones."

The enraged priests accused Rubli before the council. A vast crowd was gathered at the spot. "Protect our preacher," said the citizens to the council. Fifty ladies of influence interposed in his favour: he was released, but was compelled to leave Basle. About this time he sought to attract attention and exhibit his contempt for the priests by taking to himself a wife, which the council of Zurich allowed him to do. Zwingli had persuaded the council to grant such permissions. Rubli was the first who ventured to accept the opportunity, but others soon followed his example. This was an important step in the Reformation; and although Zwingli did not intend thus to pave the way for himself, yet there was a force in circumstances under the hands of a wise Providence.

Anna Reinhard had been one of his first and most attentive hearers. She lived near him, and he could not fail to notice her modest worth, her piety and her affection for her children. No woman in Zurich had been more respected. Her boy Gerold had become Zwingli's son in the faith. The Reformer regarded marriage "as a most holy alliance;" but the usual public displays and ceremonies in confirming it were all folly to him, and were not required by the word of God. He may have felt that the Romish Church was wrong in making marriage a sacrament, but he was fearful of reproach and of the fierce enmity of the priests. He resolved to marry Anna, but he would not have it publicly celebrated. This private marriage occurred about the first of the year 1522. It was no secret among either-his friends or foes. Myconius, in July, 1522, salutes him and his wife. He lived in the house of Anna, who regarded it as his own. His enemies did not reproach him, nor accuse him of any wrong, nor cite him before the council and the church courts. They were ready to catch at the most absurd stories to vilify him, but on this occasion they were silent—a proof that he did not deserve their censure. Thus the Reformer gave no offence at the time; and Anna, who was yet "to be more cruelly tried than any woman recorded in history," was spared the sword of the slanderous tongue. It was reserved for later enemies to make their sacred union a subject of reproach and misrepresentation. But a public acknowledgment of their marriage vows was certainly very desirable. When he felt that such a step would give no offence to his parishioners, and would serve to confirm the principles that he had preached, he at once had the marriage publicly celebrated in the cathedral. It was on the 2d of April, 1524. The event gave great joy to his friends, at home and abroad.

Anna was devoted to the work of reform. She laid aside her silks and jewels, or disposed of them in aid of the poor, and attired herself as an ordinary burgher's or tradesman's wife. While Zwingli was such an economist of time, she was prudent in the management of their scanty income. Yet there was no lack of the most open-hearted hospitality and of attention to the sick and the needy. She proved what Capito had wished at the wedding: "That she might be a fellow-servant in the Word, a helpmeet of an apostle." By her sympathies and her activity she greatly lightened the heavy burden of cares that was laid upon the heart of the Reformer.

In the family circle Zwingli was not the thinker with the gown

of a scholar upon him.   He was all heart and tenderness toward
his family, and as fond as ever of music.   For the benefit of his
step-son, Gerold, he wrote and had printed a work on education,
in which he says : " The human mind is like a garden, which is
soon overgrown with weeds if it be not cultivated.   From youth
up it must be tilled with care.   If this be done, a rich harvest is
reaped ; but where this is not done, neither hand, nor eye, nor
tongue is put under control, and the man is an ill-regulated
being.   Orphans often turn out badly because they have no one
to train and educate them. . . .

" Satan desires to nestle in the hearts of the young, and to
defile these as yet pure vessels.   Wherefore the greatest care is
required in training them in the fear of the Lord, that these
new vessels may be filled with good habits and principles. . . .

" Many busy themselves in hanging their likenesses everywhere, that their names may be made famous and their family
become illustrious, while they, at the same time, neglect and des-
pise God's image and the true living images of themselves. . . .

" The peasant has an eye to order, and he takes care to plant
in one place trees, in another vines, here willows, there corn, so
that his grounds may yield all sorts of fruits.   If parents and
teachers bestowed the same care upon the training of the youthful mind, we should see it in a better state in our day. . . . The
vine, like every other training plant, lays hold of everything
that comes in its way, fastens to it and winds itself about it.
Thus it finds a support.   The father is such a support to his
children—the tree about which they grow.   Parents, then, should
be careful in their education."

The house of Anna Zwingli, left her, probably, by the repent-
ant grandfather Meyer, was the general resort and gathering-
place of the friends of the Reformation.   There they had their

genial hours, their fragrant wit, their literary conversations, their confidential disclosures, their serious discussions, their fervent prayers, their social happiness. The gray-headed veteran, Roust, came in to talk over the Italian campaigns, to refresh his courage in the work of reform and to give an impulse to young Gerold, who began to devote to the service of the State the fine talents which gave the brightest promise of future distinction. Werner Steiner, who was forced to leave his native canton of Zug, found a new home among friends that were dear to him. Leo Juda and his bride, Catharine, who had been a nun at Einsidlen, and perhaps one of those whom the good manager Geroldsek had allowed to go home, were frequent visitors. Zwingli was always glad to sing again with the lovable, courageous man whom he jocularly called "his little lion," and who was uttering a powerful voice in Zurich.

Musical entertainments were set on foot by Zwingli. He taught select circles of his friends to manage both the voice and the instrument, and parties met in each other's houses for song. As citizens and peasants took their domestic habits from Ulrich and Anna Zwingli, they formed musical circles in their houses. Thus arose the fine quartette in the Swiss cottages and the choir in the Swiss churches, and these became the leaders of Christian song among the Reformed. Where so much attention was given to sacred music at their homes, the people could not fail to become good singers in the congregation.

From the far distance certain exiles and friends of the gospel were coming as pilgrims to this sanctuary. "What a piebald host of men from the various countries of Europe received liberal supplies for body and soul in the simple house of the parish priest at the Great Minster!" The poor were fed, the oppressed cheered; all were pointed to the source of truth and urged on to noble endeavours. Ulrich, the duke of Wirtemburg, a cruel prince, had been expelled from his dominions; he sojourned for a time in Zurich, attended Zwingli's preaching and became a guest at his board. The hard heart grew tender, and in its mellow soil the good word took root. This man, whose family excited the interest of all Europe, went to Montbeliard in France, and opened the way for Farel to proclaim the gospel there with heroic energy.* One Reformer was thus ever helping another. Let us trace the steps of a valiant knight—the bitterest enemy of the duke Ulrich.

A lad of eleven years entered the convent of Foulda to become a monk. He was Ulrich von Hutten, descended from an ancient family in Franconia. He became disgusted with monkery, ran away from the convent at the age of sixteen and went to the university of Cologne, where he devoted himself to the study of languages and poetry. Somewhat later he led a wandering life, and was present as a common soldier at the siege of Padua in 1513. He saw Rome, noticed her scandalous abuses, and there sharpened those arrows which he afterward shot into her ranks. On his return to Germany he wrote a book against Rome, entitled "The Roman Trinity." In it he says: "There are three things that are usually brought away from Rome: a bad conscience, a disordered stomach and an empty purse. There are three things in which Rome does not believe: the immortality of the soul, the resurrection of the dead and hell. There are three things in which Rome traffics: the grace of Christ, ecclesiastical dignities and women." The publication of this work compelled him to leave the court of the archbishop of Mentz, where he had composed it.

But the knight of the pen was not to be silenced. He and

* Of this we have treated in "William Farel."

several literary gentlemen formed a learned league, and published the famous satire called "The Letters of Obscure Men."
It poured forth a terrible fire of ridicule upon the pope and all
his clergy.   No work dealt them more severe blows.   But satire
was not to be the sword of the gospel.   Luther boldly disapproved of the "Letters," although he still retained Hutten and
his band in the cause of reform.   They were a sort of skirmishing corps, who did valiant service against the grosser errors.

The knight Ulrich went to Brussels and sought to enlist under
the emperor, Charles V., then at variance with the pope.   But
Charles was no friend of gospel soldiers.   He had orders to seize
Ulrich and send him, bound hand and foot, to Rome.   The
inquisitor, Hochstraten, was to have charge of the business.
Hutten learned of the plot and escaped.   A little way out of
Brussels he met the inquisitor on the high road.   The terrified
papist fell on his knees and commended his soul to God and the
saints.   "No," said the knight, "I will not soil my sword with
thy blood."   He gave him a few light strokes and allowed him
to proceed on his way.

Ulrich found refuge in the castle of Ebernburg, where Francis
of Sickingen offered an asylum to all the persecuted.   There he
addressed to the crowned princes some of the ablest letters ever
penned against error.   There he wrote appeals to the people,
which inspired the German states with a horror of Rome and
with the love of liberty.   In his ardour for the Reformation he
imagined that the sword could accomplish quite as much as the
Bible.   Papal Rome used power; why not resist her with arms?
In this great mistake was his weakness.   Yet we are pleased to
find in him certain mild and delicate sentiments.   When his
parents died, he made over to his brothers all the family property, although he was the eldest son and heir to the estates.

He begged them not to write to him nor send him any money, lest, being detected and misunderstood, they should suffer the malice which his foes wished to expend upon him.

The castle of Ebernburg was called "The resting-place of the righteous." Martin Bucer was there. Œcolampadius was there, preaching daily to the warriors who wished to put down popery with the sword. They went daily to the church, but wanted a more fiery gospel, and at length grew weary of hearing sermons upon the gentle virtues of Christianity. "Alas!" said the preacher, "the Word is here sown upon stony ground!" Before long, Sickingen was bent upon serving the cause after his own fashion, despite the protests of Luther. He had written to Luther, saying, "My services, my goods and my body, all that I possess, are at your disposal. You desire to maintain the Christian truth: I am ready to aid you in the work." He marched against Treves, but failed. He retreated into his own castle of Landstein. The enemies whom he had roused up attacked him; he was forced to surrender, for he was mortally wounded. The leaders of the assault entered the castle, searched it, and at last found the stout-hearted knight in a vault, dying on his couch. He stretched out his hand to the elector Palatine, whose companions hurled upon him their reproaches. "Leave me alone," said he, "for I must now prepare to answer a more powerful Lord than you." When Luther heard of his death he said, "It is not by the sword that the Lord will have his gospel advanced."

Yet the dauntless Ulrich persisted in his wild schemes. He wrote to Luther, whom he loved because the young Reformer hated the monks: "It is with swords and with bows, with javelins and bombs that we must crush the fury of the devil."

"I will not have recourse to arms and bloodshed in defence of the gospel," was the reply. "By the Word the Church must be saved."

"As for me," answered Hutten, who saw the difference between their plans, "I am busied with the affairs of men; but you soar far higher and are occupied solely with those of God."

The pen of Ulrich was still busy, and its power was felt among the most eminent men in Germany. To an Italian legate he said: "I tell you, and repeat it, Marino [Caraccioli], the darkness with which you had covered our eyes is dispersed; the gospel is preached; the absurdities of Rome are overwhelmed in contempt; your decrees languish and die; liberty is beginning to dawn upon us." Hutten found that his lashing satires, his rhymes for the common people and his vigorous appeals to the emperor and the princes, did not call forth the powerful aid to Luther that he had expected. He thought of the fall of Landstein and the death of its hero in despair. Broken in heart and in health, he sought repose with Erasmus at Basle. "These two men," says D'Aubigne, "had long been friends; but the unpolished and turbulent knight, braving the opinions of others, ever ready to lay his hand upon his sword, dealing his blows right and left on all whom he met, could scarcely live in harmony with the squeamish and timid Dutchman, with his refined manners, his mild and polished language, his love of approbation and his readiness to sacrifice everything for its sake, and fearing nothing in the world so much as a dispute. On arriving at Basle, Hutten, poor, sick and a fugitive, immediately inquired for his old friend. But Erasmus trembled at the thought of receiving at his table a person under the ban of the pope and the emperor, who would spare no one, who would borrow money of him, and who would no doubt be dragging after him a crowd of those Gospellers, whom Erasmus dreaded more and more. He refused to see him;

and shortly after the magistrates of Basle desired Hutten to leave the city."

The young knight, wounded to the quick, wandered about, thinking the severest things against Erasmus, and with his pen he caused the timid sage to wince. But from their war of words nothing good resulted. It appears also that Duke Ulrich of Wirtemberg did not escape his trenchant pen. But there was another Ulrich of whom he had heard, and to whom he directed his weary steps. On coming to Zurich he met with a generous reception from the noble-minded Zwingli. Anna was ever ready to administer her best bread, her cordials and her consolations. Foes soon appeared in Zurich against the invalid knight, and he must leave the city, Zwingli procured means for him to visit the mineral baths of Pfeffers. But these could not relieve him. The Reformer then gave him a letter to John Schnepp, the pastor upon the small island of Ufnau, in the Lake of Zurich. This poor minister had some skill in the healing art, and entertained the sick exile with the most touching charity, vainly lavishing upon him all his care. In this peaceful and obscure retreat he felt once more the joyful hope which he had expressed to Zwingli : "That God would again muster the scattered friends of truth and humble their adversaries." It seems that he lamented the warlike spirit that he had manifested, and perceived that by a milder and yet as courageous a method he might have gained some of the most brilliant victories for the truth. The ark of God must not be touched by an iron hand. At the end of August, 1523, died Ulrich Hütten, "one of the most remarkable men of the sixteenth century." He had been expelled by one party, persecuted by another, deserted by nearly all, and having fought against superstition, he had scarcely possessed the truth. He was a fine specimen of a certain class of men who were frank, ardent, noble soldiers against the papacy, but who failed in time to prevent mischief to the cause of the Reformation. With him such chivalry expired. The French knight, Anemund, who assisted William Farel in Dauphiny, at first indulged some wild dreams, but he turned his impulsive energy to publishing the gospel. Ulrich left neither money nor books behind him—nothing but a pen.

CHAPTER XI.

THERE were three monasteries in Zurich, and no lack of monks. It was easy for the council to order them to preach nothing contrary to the gospel, but it was difficult to make them do it. How could they preach a gospel of which they knew almost nothing? How give up the legends and fables which were the sources of their greatest gains? They felt that their old liberties were to be taken from them: one, notoriously bad one among them, thus wrote to Henry Goldli, at Rome : " I hear that you intend to bring a falcon with you. My advice to you is to let it alone, for there is such a spirit prevalent here that we priests can scarcely walk safely about the town, not to speak of going a falcon-hunting or springing over boors' hedges. We are decried as useless, good-for-nothing persons, that for three hundred years, until the time of Luther and Zwingli, have deceived the people. Every common man hopes that the number of priests in Zurich will be reduced to six, or ten at most." They need not have been alarmed for their persons—only for their principles.

Immoral and ignorant as they were, they had powerful connections and influence. Several councilmen, who were loose in morals or fond of foreign gold, and who disliked the bold and faithful preacher at the great minster, went morning and evening to visit the cloisters and there hold their carousals. There they stirred up opposition, and hatched the darkest designs against the Reformer. They and the monks sent abroad the rumour that only strife and disunion would result from his preaching. They talked, busied themselves in every way, made a great noise, and at last got a hearing before the "little council." It was decided by the majority that in future there should be no more preaching against the monks.

"Thereupon the council hall gave a loud crash," says Bullinger. Many councillors were horror struck, and the meeting was suddenly dissolved. The preachers and the friars were now contesting with each other. A committee from the council met at the house of the provost, where many high words were passed, and the burgomaster finally advised each party to preach nothing that would disturb peace and unity. Zwingli replied, "I cannot accept this command. I will preach the gospel free and unrestrained, as was formerly agreed upon. I am parson and bishop in Zurich; I, and not the monks, have taken the oath. They must yield and not I. If they preach falsehood, I will come up to their very pulpits in their cloisters and contradict them. For my part, if I preach anything contrary to the Holy Gospel, I am willing to be censured by the chapter, by the council, every citizen, and be punished for it."

This was clear and decided, certainly. It had its effect. The monks began to speak of Thomas Aquinas and Scotus, the great scholastic writers, but the council decreed that the gospel should be preached, for Thomas and Scotus were of no weight. Nay, they went further; they granted permission to Zwingli and his friends to go into the chapels of the nunneries and preach, where only the monks had hitherto been permitted to hold forth. The truth thus won another victory.

Very soon John Faber, the vicar of the bishop, attracted the attention of the monks and mercenaries, who wished to secure him as the champion of their cause. This former friend of Zwingli now began to develop his real character. He had taken a lesson from Rome. John Eck, whom we remember as a fellow-student of Zwingli at Vienna, had gone to Rome to operate against Luther, and the pope had given him seven hundred ducats for travelling expenses. Rather expensive travelling, honest men said, but the knowing ones understood it. Faber at first ridiculed Eck, but soon he too coveted the wages of such service, and set out for Rome and the travelling expenses. Professor Egentius of Friburg wrote: "I begin to suspect Faber: he has many wants just now, and it said that he visits Rome to dedicate to the pope a book against Luther, for he has caught a hint of the pope's liberality to Eck. If he should come back from the seat of all evil, we shall all doubtless have to fall down and worship the golden image."

Zwingli said: "It appears to me that Faber has unlearned at Rome all the Christianity that he ever knew." The vicar was putting some bad thoughts into the head of the bishop of Constance. The monks dared not be too fast, for they knew the Reformer's popularity and his power over the citizens. They watched their chance. At length, in the early part of 1522, they found something heretical to lay before the bishop. He began to show the difference between the precepts of the gospel and those of men. During Lent he preached with vigour against certain papal customs. "For four years," said he, "you have eagerly received the holy doctrine of the gospel. Glowing with the fire of charity, fed with the heavenly manna, it is impossible that you can now find any savour in the wretched nutriment of human traditions. . . . There are some who maintain that to eat

meat in Lent is a fault, and even a great sin, though God has
never forbidden it, and yet they think it no crime to sell human
flesh to the foreigners and drag it to the slaughter." The mercenaries shuddered with wrath and vowed never to forget this
thrust.

Still Zwingli had not yet ceased to say mass, and he abstained
from meat on the appointed days. But there were some turbulent men who were not so careful to avoid offence. William
Rubli, the pompous priest, and others met at the house of coun-
cilman Huber on Fridays to eat meat, and thus show their
contempt for the Church. It was a matter of pride and not of
principle with them. A citizen of Lucerne came to Zurich and
said to some of this party : " You worthy confederates of Zurich
are wrong in eating meat during Lent."

"You gentlemen of Lucerne do the same," replied a Zuricher.
" We have purchased our liberty from the pope."
" And we from the butcher. If it be an affair of money, one
is certainly as good as the other." A printer, named Christoffel
Froschauer, ate meat to give him strength for labour, thinking
it to be no sin, but he made no pompous display of the matter.
The council brought him before them. He defended himself,
and was dismissed with a simple reproof. "That is the result of
Zwingli's doctrines," said his enemies. "Zwingli is the de-
stroyer and not the keeper of the Lord's fold." They besought
the bishop to interfere. He chose his deputies and sent them to
Zurich.

On a dark evening, Luti, an assistant of Zwingli, ran to him,
saying, " The bishop's commissioners have arrived ; all the par-
tisans of the old customs are stirring. A notary is sent to
summon all the priests for an early meeting in the hall of the
chapter."

At an early hour Zwingli went to meet them. Two of the deputies had a severe, angry look; they were Melchior Bottli, the suffragan, or bishop's assistant, and Doctor Brendli. The third was a milder man, John Vanner, the cathedral preacher at Constance, who was evangelical in his views and who kept silence during the whole of the business. The entire clergy of Zurich were present. The suffragan spoke in a haughty, excited manner, bearing hard upon Zwingli, but not naming him. Certain priests, who had timidly begun to take the side of the gospel, looked pale and drew heavy sighs. How Zwingli replied we learn from his own words: "Pithily and bluntly I answered the suffragan; in what sense and spirit let the worthy men who heard me judge. The suffragan let go this wing as if he had been beaten and put to flight, and he hastened to another battle-field, namely, to the town hall, where he, as I heard from some of the councillors, gave vent to the very same language against me, saying that he had nothing to do with me. This he said that I might not be brought before them."

Never was the Swiss Reformation in greater danger. It might be stifled in the cradle. The little council was composed of enemies to the gospel—the great council of two hundred of its friends. At first Zwingli appealed for admission to the latter in vain. "I was obliged to give up," he says, "and lay the matter before Him who hears the groaning of the prisoner, and pray him to defend his own gospel. Patient waiting has never disappointed the servants of the Lord." The gospel seemed about to be condemned without its defender being heard.

At last the cathedral preachers were admitted before the two hundred. They were Zwingli, Englehard and the aged Rœschli. The suffragan began his speech in a voice so soft and winning that one might have fancied him the mildest of all living men.

"The civil constitution," said this champion, "and the Christian faith are endangered. Men have recently appeared who teach novel, revolting and seditious doctrines." After a long speech about fasting and the like, he wound up by fixing his eyes on the senators, and saying: "Remain in the Church! remain in the Church! Out of it no one can be saved! Its ceremonies alone are capable of bringing the simple to a knowledge of salvation, and the shepherds of the flock have nothing more to do than to explain their meaning to the people." He prepared to leave the room.

"Most worthy suffragan," said Zwingli, earnestly, "and you, his companions, stay, I entreat you, until I have vindicated myself." But they were anxious to get away.

The venerable burgomaster Roust arose, saying: "I beseech you to listen to the reply of the pastor."

"I know too well the man I have to deal with," said the suffragan. "Ulrich Zwingli is too violent a man for any discussion to be held with him."

"How long since has it been customary to accuse an innocent man with such violence, and then refuse to hear his defence?" inquired Zwingli. "In the name of our common faith, of the baptism we have both received, of Christ the author of salvation and of life, listen to me. If you cannot as deputies, then at least do so as Christians."

A general murmur arose against the conduct of the papal party. They found that they could not fire their guns and then run away from the field. Abashed and speechless, they sat down. Zwingli then said:

"The reverend suffragan speaks of doctrines that are seditious and subversive of the civil laws. Let him learn that Zurich is more quiet and peaceful than any other city of the confederacy—

a fact which all good citizens ascribe to the gospel. Is not Christianity the strongest defence of a nation? What is the result of all mere ceremonies but shamefully to disguise the features of Christ and his disciples? There is a better way to bring the unlearned people to the truth. It is the way that Christ and his disciples followed. It is to give them the pure gospel. The people can understand and believe it, for the Holy Ghost will teach them. As to fasts, if one does not find forty days enough, let him fast all the year if he chooses; it is a matter of indifference to me. All I ask is that no one be compelled to fast. It is my duty to preach Christ faithfully, as I have done hitherto. As for the ceremonies, let those who live upon them undertake to explain them.''

There was a meaning in this last remark which the monks and deputies well understood, as their blushes and winces proved. It was touching the suffragan on a tender spot. Zwingli says in one of his writings : '' Is it not notorious that the suffragans fill their purses by the mummeries performed at their consecrations?'' The council broke up. The mission had failed. Certain questions were left to the pope and the cardinals, and the people were required to abstain from meat during Lent. But in this first skirmish between the two great parties the Reformation gained ground. The people saw that Zwingli had the best of the argument, for he had the word of God for his foundation. He felt stronger than before. Of the combat, he said : '' I hear that they intend to renew it. Let them come ; with God I fear them as little as the beetling cliff fears the waves that thunder at its base.''

Doctor John Vanner was so convinced of the truth of Zwingli's doctrine that he became a faithful preacher of the gospel. He went home, and began to lift up the true standard in Constance. The bishop poured out a vial of wrath upon him, but he was unmoved. "I prefer," said he, "to be a Christian with the hatred of many rather than forsake Christ for the friendship of the world." Zwingli took his pen to write a tract on "Abstaining from Meats, Offence-giving and Strife."

Four new attacks were now preparing for our valiant Reformer. We briefly sketch them, for through such battles our Christian liberties were restored to the Church. The first came from the aged canon Hoffman, who handed to the chapter of canons a long writing, in which he said: "Even should the parson be able to prove what crimes or disorders are committed by the clergy in certain convents, streets or taverns, it is no business of his, nor of any other one. He ought not to name anybody. Why does he give it to be understood (for my part I have rarely heard him myself) that he alone derives his doctrine from the fountain-head, and that others seek it only in pools and ditches? It is not to be expected that all priests will preach alike.' Zwingli met the onslaught, and Hoffman was obliged to yield. With sharpened wit the Reformer wrote to Myconius: "I gave him a shaking, as when an ox with his horns tosses a heap of straw into the air."

The second attack was made by the bishop of Constance. Faber was his agent, and he wrote a letter against Zwingli, without naming him. Its purport was: "The Turks are falling upon us Christians. It is no time for men to be preaching heresies and persuading the people to cease paying their tithes. Give the Church money to keep off the Turks." The letter was sent abroad to injure Zwingli's reputation, to alarm the people with dread of the Turks, and to secure a harvest of money. The monks of Berne read it and formed this resolution: If any persons read the books of Luther or Zwingli, or speak anywhere against the holy rites and customs of the Church, we will refuse them the holy sacraments in the hour of death, we will exclude them from Christian burial, and we will deny to them the prayers of Christendom.'' But Zwingli need not take up the pen against all this, for a Bernese monk took the field. Sebastian Meyer wrote a commentary on the bishop's pastoral letter, the spirit of which was, '' Behold, dear reader, the Turk is again at the door. Ye papists must needs sell indulgences and drive him off. Ah! for many years he has been to you a good Turk! He has brought you a great deal of money. How are you to get more? This is where the shoe pinches. When the Turk was near us in Hungary you gave yourselves no concern about him; but now, when he is farther away, marching on Italy, you are alarmed. Now as the papists have been for long years cheating the world by indulgences and a thousand other impostures, they must have heaped up an immense treasure, and yet they did not fight the Turk. Where is this treasure? Of what use are troopers to the bishops? It is to ride about on the highways and terrify the merchants, so that the money drops out of their purses, from sheer fright, into the hands of those to whom it does not belong. Let all this treasure be employed against the Turk. Send the bishops, cardinals, priests and cowardly monks to fight the Turk. Off with them, and no longer torment honest folks and terrify simple Christians.'' Zwingli had this caustic document republished in Zurich, and really won the day.

A third attack came from the same quarter before the second was fully ended. Faber wrote to the Zurich canons to '' guard against the poison of the new doctrines, and contend for the old rites. Stop such preaching. Remove the preachers.'' This letter was read in the chapter. Zwingli heard it and resolved to answer it.   He published a little book entitled *Archeteles*—"The Beginning and the End"—hoping that this would be the first and last defence necessary to make.   In this he said: "What have I done?   I have called all men to a knowledge of their infirmities; I have endeavoured to lead them to the only true God and to Jesus Christ his Son.   Hence I have spoken in such simple language that all the children of Switzerland can understand it. . . . When Julius Caesar felt the mortal wound, he folded his garments around him that he might fall with dignity.   The downfall of your ceremonies is at hand; see at least that they fall decently, and that light be everywhere substituted for darkness."

His book was widely scattered and read, and many must have been touched by the prayer with which it was winged: "O blessed Jesus, thou seest that ears of thy people are stopped by whisperers, traitors, self-seekers.   Thou knowest that from a child I have shunned all dispute, and yet thou hast led me to the conflict.   I call upon thee to complete what thou hast begun.   If I have built up anything wrongly, do thou overthrow it with thy hand.   If I lay any other foundation than thyself, tear it down.   O sweet Vine! whose husbandman is the Father, whose branches we are, do not abandon thy members; for thou hast promised to be with us to the end of the world."

The fourth attack was already being made from Constance. The general Diet of the Swiss confederacy was in session at Lucerne.   Most of its members were mercenaries, and of course enemies of the gospel.   They intensely hated the patriotic Zwingli for spoiling many a golden game.   Faber and his bishop looked to them for power to crush the Reformer.   They sent deputies post-haste to Lucerne, where the monks were entertaining the members of the Diet on the fat of the land, and saying, "If Zwingli will not hold his tongue, we will bawl louder than he." They did their best at bawling. The Diet sided with the oppressors, and the gospel preachers were threatened with silence. Zwingli felt annoyed by this decision, but bravely went on as the "pastor and bishop in Zurich." All these attacks, made almost at the same time by the strength of the papal clergy, who were backed up by the Diet, only roused him to fresh exertions. He heard in the muttering storm the voice of God, and had a sublime faith that the truth would prevail. He called his co-labourers into council at Einsidlen, where we will shortly look in upon them and read the petitions which they are preparing. Now we inquire for the nuns.

The council had a tender care over the sisterhood of nuns. Zwingli and Leo Juda were ordered to preach to them, while the monks were positively shut out from the convents. The light had not even glimmered in these cloisters, so careful had the Dominicans been to keep them in darkness. In the nunnery of Œtenbach were many veiled daughters of the first families in the city. Zwingli went thither, entered the pulpit and preached on "the clearness and certainty of the word of God"—a sermon afterward published and which bore good fruit in the convent. The Bible was read; believers avowed their new faith. Several nuns asked the council for permission to leave the cloister, and take with them the little property they had brought to it. Their request was granted. Others wished to dwell and die in the convent. They were allowed to live in a convent, on condition that the nuns of the various cloisters should lay aside the dress of their order, dwell together in one house, and attend the preaching of the gospel.

The ancient abbey or Frauen Minster (women's cathedral) was said to have been founded in the ninth century, and placed under its first abbess, St. Hildegarde. In this office was now Catharine von Zimmern. The breath of reform expelled the old air of superstition. The gospel displaced the missal. The true cross rose above the crucifix. Dr. Englehard preached to the inmates along with his evangelical brethren. They had large revenues from ancient legacies, but were convinced that their wealth might serve a better purpose than in purchasing their indolence and comfort. Catharine, the abbess, in 1524 handed over to the council all their revenues and lands, to be used "for the glory of God, the salvation of souls and the comfort and help of the poor." The nuns had enough allowed them for life, and all the rest of their income was applied to the benefit of the churches, the school and the destitute.

The monks were harder to manage. "To snore behind the walls of a cloister is not to worship God," said Zwingli, as he laid bare their vices and proved that monasteries were contrary to the divine Word. " But to visit widows and orphans in their affliction, and to keep oneself unspotted from the world, this is truly to worship God. The world, in this text from St. James, does not mean hill and valley, field and forest, rivers and lakes, towns and villages, but the lusts of the world, as avarice, pride, uncleanness, intemperance. More of these vices are met with in cloisters than in the world abroad, not to speak of envy and hatred. Let the monks lay aside their badges and cowls, and put themselves on a level with the rest of Christendom." The council ordered the monasteries to be emptied. On a certain Saturday afternoon a body of citizens, councilmen and soldiers proceeded to the work, taking with them the gospel ministers. They assembled the friars and gave them a piece of astounding news. "This gentry must leave their various convents, and live together decently in the convent of the Barefoot Friars." It was of no use to howl about it, for the militia were at hand. The monks gathered up their wares and entered upon a new mode of life. The younger friars of talent were made to study; the others to learn a trade; the strangers were given money to take them home or to enter a cloister in their own country; the feeble and the aged were supported, on condition that they would behave themselves and attend church when they were able. Thus in a quiet way the death-blow was struck to the monkish establishments in Zurich. Friars grew scarce in Zurich: most of them removed to the papal cantons.

The wealth of the convents was applied to the relief of the needy, since these institutions pretended to be asylums for the poor. It had been the custom for their poor scholars to beg for their living, as Luther had done in his youth. All this was forbidden by the council. The worthy poor were placed beyond the need of wandering about for alms. Vagrants were allowed a meal or a night's lodging and sent on their way, with the command not to return within six months. Zurich became a poor field for beggars and pilgrims. The city was regularly visited by men who sought out the cases of destitution and supplied them, watched over poor children and placed them where they could be educated. The gospel thus bore the good fruit of charity. Nor was her benevolence limited to her own people. If any cry of distress came from abroad she was ever ready to respond. It is so still. If there is an avalanche or landslide in any canton or village, a flood, famine or fire, the appeal to Zurich to "come over and help us" is never made in vain. It is almost a proverb, and heard everywhere, "Had it not been for Zurich, we should have starved." Such a spirit has been a blessing to her people, for God never fails to reward liberality.

A traveller at this very time (1866) writes: "We visited a

splendid building erected by the kindness of Miss Welcher, a maiden daughter of an iron merchant of Zurich. She seems to be about sixty years of age, and presides over the institution with dignity and piety, reminding one of Anna, who pitched her tent under the shadow of the house of God. (Luke ii. 37.) She spent about one hundred and twenty thousand dollars on the edifice. She pays the salary of an evangelical pastor, who is a native and student of Wirtemburg. He preaches on Sabbath afternoon at five, after all other churches are closed, and on Wednesday evening. It is also an almshouse, where a home is provided for such indigent persons as she thinks worthy her princely charity."

CHAPTER XII.

THE TWO PETITIONS..

(1522.)

ONE by one the men of truth were making a journey to Ein-sidlen, the ancient resort of thousands of pilgrims. It was the June of 1522, and they enjoyed the air of mountain liberty. They had left their homes at the call of Zwingli to hold their first synod or conference. *Their chief thought was: "We will see if there is righteousness in the bishop and any justice in the confederate Diet. They must repeal the act forbidding us to preach the pure word of God." Leo Juda* received them with joy into the old abbey, glad to remind them that their great leader, Zwingli, had there begun his work of reform. "What a change!" thought the noble abbot Geroldsek as he greeted the company. "Not five years ago, my good Zwingli, you stood up here alone, preaching to the pilgrims that *Christ alone saves and he saves everywhere.* But now what a host has gathered to your standard! Truly Christ is at work everywhere. Be true and firm in the cause, and stand up for your rights."

Next to the home of Zwingli, this renowned abbey had become a dwelling-place for the righteous, a stronghold of truth, a refuge for the tried and the troubled. The thirty-three patriots who

---

* We have anticipated events somewhat in a foregoing chapter, in order to arrange our materials according to subjects. Leo Juda went to Zurich at the end of 1522.

had met on the solitary plain of Grutli more than two hundred years before, to break the yoke of Austria, were not braver men than the ten or twelve preachers who met at Einsidlen to sunder the chains which the Swiss Diet had placed upon them. Among them we see Stahel, Werner Steiner, the canon Kilchmeyer of Lucerne, and the canon Fabricius of Zurich.* Zwingli leads them into the old chapel, and with devout prayer their conference begins. On it depend the mighty interests of the Swiss Reformation.

In the hand of Zwingli are two petitions written by himself. He moves that they be addressed, respectively, to the bishop of Constance and to the confederate Diet. The petition to the bishop is read first. It declares, "That heaven-taught truth which God the Creator has revealed through his Son to the sinful race of men, has been long veiled from our eyes by the ignorance, not to say wickedness, of a few men. God has resolved to give it to mankind in its original purity. Unite yourselves, then, to those who desire that all Christendom may return to Christ their common head. . . . On our part we are resolved to preach his gospel unceasingly, perseveringly, and without giving any just cause for complaint. Favour this, perhaps, strange, but not rash design. Be like Moses at the head of the people when they went out of Egypt, and with your own hands overthrow all that opposes the advance of the truth." The address then asks the bishop to restrain the gross immorality of the priests, and "to permit what has been rashly enacted to be wisely repealed, for fear the majestic edifice of the Church

* "There were many others who sympathized with the men who had met at Einsidlen; such were Haller, Myconius, Hedio, Capito, Œcolampadius, Sebastian Meyer, Hoffmeister and Vanner."—*D'Aubigne.*

should fall with a frightful crash, and spread destruction far and wide."

The petition to the Swiss confederation is still longer. Like the other, it asks that " the preaching of the gospel may not be forbidden, and that the priests be allowed to marry." It protests against giving the Lord's flock to a man " who preaches nothing but the payment of tithes and dues to the Church, who daily finds out new saints to whom offerings shall be made, who extols indulgences, and who fills his sermons with laudations of the pope." In it the petitioners say : " We are all Swiss, and you are our fathers. Many of us have proved ourselves to be true men in battle, in pestilence and in other calamities. We speak in the name of true chastity, but the scandals in the Christian Church must cease. If Romish tyranny oppress us, fear nothing, brave heroes ! The word of God, the rights of Christian liberty and divine grace will protect us. We have all the same country, the same faith : we are Swiss, and the virtue of our illustrious ancestors was ever displayed in the invincible defence of all the oppressed."

Such was the spirit of the two petitions. They were signed by those present, and then sent to be signed by other friends of the truth in other places. The appeal was thus made to the heads of both Church and State. "It was something really sublime for those times," says Henry Bullinger, "that these men should have thus dared to stand forth, and, rallying round the gospel, expose themselves to every danger. But God preserved them all, so that no harm befel them ; for God always preserves his own." It was indeed the sublimest act done on one of the darkest days of the Swiss Reformation. It made Einsidlen to the Reformed Church what Morgarten had been to the freed nation. It secured a holy confederation of Reformers. These

two petitions became to the Swiss Protestants almost what the
Solemn League and Covenant afterward was to the Scottish defenders of the gospel.

We shall often meet with these petitions as we advance, and
see their effect, particularly at Berne and Lucerne. The wrath
of the confederates was aroused. Such an unheard-of appeal
from a few teachers, priests and "gospellers" must not be tolerated by their dignities! Threats were uttered everywhere; in
some places blows were struck. Even Zwingli began to fear that
he had gone too far, and that his brethren must suffer for his
own words. Nothing for long years had so roused all Switzerland. Were the enemies of the Lord about to rise in their might
and drive the gospel from that land of mountain fastnesses?
Unto God he committed his cause, resolved, through him, to win
the victory. "We must obey God rather than men," became
the watchword in Zurich, and it was adopted by most of the true
Swiss clergy.

In Friburg there was a canon, named John Hollard, a native
of Orbe, where he had a brother who afterward aided William
Farel in introducing the gospel in that town. Canon John wrote
a letter to Haller and Sebastian Meyer; the magistrates of Friburg intercepted it, and learned something, probably, of Zwingli's
intentions. They deprived Hollard of his office, thrust him into
prison and finally banished him. But in this war when one soldier fell, his place was at once filled by another. John Vannius,
a chorister of the cathedral, soon declared himself in favour of
the new and the true doctrines. "How can the muddy waters
of the papal Tiber," said he, "compare with the pure streams
of the word of God?" But the chorister was not allowed to
chant in this strain. He was silenced. Friburg would not tol-
erate the gospel. She closed her gates, refused to receive the

new doctrines, held to popery, and has remained papal to this day.

It was in the convents that the most fury was expressed. The monks had little to do but ventilate their wrath. On the day of a great feast at the convent of Faubrunn, when the wine had got well into the heads of the guests, they began to hurl their darts against the late movements of Zwingli and his co-labourers. One thing particularly enraged the friars. It was that there was no priestly rank acknowledged among the Reformers, who held that the ministers were on an equality. The *parity of the clergy* had been advocated from the Scriptures. Indeed the elder of a church in many respects held an equal rank with the pastor. This was especially offensive to the monks, who could not abide hearing Zwingli called a bishop in Zurich. Only one friend of the Reformation was present, and he a layman named Macrinus, the master of the school at Soleure.* At first he avoided the discussion, passing from one end of the table to the other. But at last, unable to endure the violent language of the guests, he rose boldly and said: "Yes, all true Christians are priests and sacrificers, as St. Peter says: 'Ye are priests and kings!'"

"So then, you Greeklings and pedagogues are the royal priesthood?" cried out the dean of Burgdorf, one of the loudest brawlers. "A pretty priesthood, forsooth! beggarly kings! . . .

---

* Soleure is celebrated partly for the good-nature of its people. Three hundred years ago, two guild-brothers had a quarrel. The council ordered them to meet and drink wine together, and "my gracious lords" would condescend to come and drink with them. At a later day two women, who came to blows, were put into a small room and made to eat from the same dish with the same spoon. The home of Kosciusko was in this canton after his exile from Poland and his noble service to American independence.

priests without living!" At this the monks and priests fell upon him and illustrated their method of argument. The layman seemed vanquished for the time, but his cause acquired strength.

" So rude are the blows by which men strive to overthrow the house of God," writes Zwingli to Myconius, after hearing of such attacks, "that not only does the storm beat upon it, but also the hail and the thunder. If I did not see that the Lord watches over the ship, I should abandon the helm; but I see him through the storm, strengthening the tackling, hoisting the yards, spreading the sail, and even commanding the winds. Should I not be a coward if I abandoned my post and took to flight? I will not be impatient; I will confide all to his sovereign goodness. Let him govern; let him carry us forward; let him hasten or delay; let him even plunge us to the bottom of the deep; we will fear nothimg. *I still hold the opinion that the Christian Church, originally purchased by the blood of Christ, can be renewed alone by the blood of the witnesses for the truth, and in no other way.*"

The Reformers had sought the liberty of the gospel; they ought to have gone farther and sought for the freedom of the Church. They should have drawn the lines between the government of the Church and that of the State. In all their churches the town-council wielded too much power of discipline. The pastor was too much under the direction of the council. If a man committed an ecclesiastical offence, the council tried and punished him. The burgomaster was almost in the place of a bishop. The magistrates made laws for the ministers and parishes. As a specimen of those laws, we cite some rules concerning the keeping of the Sabbath. "We ordain," said the council, "that every man, be he noble-born or a commoner, be he of high or low estate, man or woman, child or servant, shall attend the church-service every Sunday at least, at the set time of public worship, except he be prevented by sickness or other sufficient cause." Also every one must not disturb the services, nor leave until they were finished. All inns must be closed before and during church-hours. Gambling, cursing, all excess in eating, drinking and dress were forbidden; small public houses were to be closed after nine o'clock every evening. Many holidays were declared to be "vain pastimes of popish extraction," and no longer tolerated. The ministers must enforce these laws with the aid of the magistrates. This board of moral discipline had power over the church members, summoning, trying, reprimanding, suspending or excommunicating offenders.

In thus giving up the ecclesiastical into the hands of the civil power, it was understood that the magistrates were to take the word of God as their sole directory. Zwingli watched the council with all jealousy, lest it should not abide by the divine Word in all cases. He wished to elevate the magistracy. It is stated by historians that this mode of discipline produced good results. "Under its protecting and sheltering influence there grew up and flourished those manly and hardy virtues which so richly adorned the Church of the Reformation at its commencement."

We have a body of church officers which sits in judgment upon certain cases and is called the *Session;* they had a body which stood and was called the *Stillstand.* After the pastor had preached and closed the services, he and the members remained, *still standing,* and if any case of discipline was brought up it received attention. The Stillstand could reprove and suspend temporarily, but no further punishment could be inflicted unless the case were carried before the magistrates. It should not be inferred that the form of church government was congregational. Affairs were in a state of transition from prelacy to a modified

Presbyterianism. Zwingli did not live long enough to perfectly establish his own system of doctrine and policy. It is worthy of notice that while the zealous Reformer was threatened at Zurich, he exerted a powerful influence in other quarters. In tracing it we may glance at the good work at Berne.

Berthold Haller was born at Aldingen in Wirtemburg, in the year that Columbus discovered America. He went to Rotwyl in Switzerland and studied under Rubellus, in whose school he met Oswald Myconius. They were of the same age, and were yet to devote their lives to the same cause of God. Haller next studied at Pforzheim under Simmler, with Melancthon as a fellow-student. The Bernese were attracting literary men to their warlike republic; Rubellus went thither, and was soon joined by Haller, then twenty-one years of age. He was named a canon, and soon became the cathedral preacher.

When Zwingli unbound the word of God and offered it to the Swiss, Haller was one of the first to accept the glad tidings. He eagerly wished to see the mighty man whom he respected as a father. He went to Zurich, where Myconius had spoken in his praise. The meek preacher of Berne told Zwingli all his trials; the strong man inspired him with courage. Haller returned, and so boldly proclaimed salvation through Christ that he roused the opposition of all who had purchased absolution from the indulgence-seller Samson. He wrote to Zwingli: "I cannot endure such unjust treatment; I am resolved to resign my pulpit, retire to Basle and study under the learned Wittembach."

"I too feel discouraged," replied Zwingli, "when unjustly assailed, but Christ rouses my conscience by his terrors and his promises. He alarms me by saying: 'Whosoever will be ashamed of me before men, of him will I be ashamed before my Father.' He strengthens me by adding: 'Whosoever shall con-

fess me before men, him will I also confess before my Father.'
Oh, my dear Berthold, take courage. Our names are written in
imperishable characters in the annals of the citizens on high. Oh
that your fierce bears* would hear the doctrine of Christ; then
they would grow tame. Be gentle with them, lest they turn
round furiously and rend you in pieces."

"My soul is awakened," answered Haller. "I must preach
the gospel. Jesus Christ must be restored to this city, whence
he has been so long exiled." He raised the new standard and
bore it bravely into the conflict. His voice called forth a kind of
force which was employed in almost all countries at the outset
of the Reformation. It was that of satire and ridicule, so generally popular in that age, but not always attended with good
results. We may furnish a specimen by noticing what was done
in this way at Berne, for it enters largely into religious history.

Nicholas Manuel, a distinguished layman, holding high offices
of State, was gifted with keen wit and wielded a scathing pen.
As a poet he won distinction. His soul took fire when Samson
was swindling the people by selling indulgences. He sharpened
his pen and wrote a drama, representing the covetousness, pomp
and arrogance of the pope and his clergy. It was called "The
Eaters of the Dead," and was to be acted by some young persons
in the Rue de la Croix on the day when the clergy began their
Lent. This was Shrove Tuesday, eight days before the people
began their Lenten season. For some weeks nothing was so
much talked of in Berne as the coming exhibition. At the time
the citizens crowded to see it. The play opens. First appears
the pope in glittering robes, sitting on a throne, with courtiers,

---

* The old word *Bern* means a bear. The city still retains its fondness
for tame bears and their effigies. They are the "lions" of the place.

cardinals, guards and a motley array of priests around him. Behind them are nobles, laymen and beggars. A funeral procession moves in, bearing the corpse of a wealthy farmer. Two of his relatives walk slowly in front of the coffin, which is laid at the feet of the pope. Then the acting begins:

FIRST RELATIVE (*in a sorrowful tone*).

Noble army of the saints!
Hear, oh hear our sad complaints.
Our cousin's dead: the yawning tomb
Must take him now in life's first bloom.

SECOND RELATIVE.

No cost to monk or priest we'll spare;
We've a hundred crowns for mass and prayer,
To save from purgatory's fire
The soul of this departed sire.

THE SEXTON (*to a priest*).

A trifle to drink, sir priest, I crave;
A farmer stout goes to his grave.

PRIEST MORE-AND-MORE.

But one! I only thirst the more.
One dead! I would 'twere half a score.
The more, the merrier then live we;
Death is the best of games for me.

＊　　＊　　＊　　＊　　＊　　＊

CARDINAL HIGH-PRIDE.

On Christian blood doth Rome grow fat;
Hence my rich robe and my red hat.
You see my honours and my wealth;
We get them from the dead by stealth.

BISHOP WOLF'S-THROAT.

In papal laws I'll firmly live and die;
My robes are silken and my purse is full;
The tournament and chase are my delight.
In former times when yet the Church was young,
We bishops dressed as simple villagers;
We priests were shepherds—now the peers of kings,
And yet at times a shepherd's life I love.

A VOICE.

You love a shepherd's life! Indeed!

BISHOP WOLF'S-THROAT.

Ay, at the shearing time. Shepherds and wolves are we:
The people are the sheep, and if they feed us not,
They fall unpitied by our ruthless fangs. . . .
Scandals! I heed them not; they fill my purse.
The smallest profit never comes amiss. . . .

THE POPE.

Now doth the faithless world at last believe
That an ambitious priest can ope or shut
At will the gates of heaven. Preach faithfully
The ordinances of the conclave's choice.
Now we are kings, the laymen a dull throng:
Wave but the gospel standard in the air,
And we are lost. To offer up the mass,
Or fee the priest, the gospel teacheth not.
Did we obey its precepts, we should live,
Alas! in poverty, and meanly die.
Ah! then farewell to richly-harnessed steeds
And sumptuous chariots. . . . .
No! firmly will I guard Saint Peter's rights,
And rash intruders with my thunders blast.

Such was the drift of Manuel's keen satire. The papal clergy felt its sting, for it painted them in living colours. The people were excited either with anger or with delight. Many were their jests as they went home. Some did more than laugh; they felt the solemn lesson, for they had been unmercifully plundered by paying for masses and funeral rites. They wanted a relief from such impositions, and asked if they could really find it in the gospel. They began to speak against papal tyranny, and in favour of Christian liberty.

Not long after this play a more real comedy was acted at Berne. It had been announced by the priests that on a certain day the skull of St. Anne, who was called the mother of Mary, would be brought to the city. The famous knight, Albert of Stein, had gone to bring it from Lyons. The clergy, council and citizens were waiting at the gate to receive it. They pressed together, when the knight appeared, carrying the holy relic wrapped in silk, and exhibited for their adoration. The bishop of Lausanne humbly bent the knee as it passed before him. It was borne in procession to the church of the Dominicans. The bells rang loudly, the train filled the church, and the skull of "the grandmother of Christ" was solemnly placed on the altar already consecrated to it. Some unusual offerings must be made by the people for this amazing privilege. The priests were looking for a harvest. What numbers it would draw from Haller's preaching! What large sums would be paid for the intercessions of St. Anne! But just then all the blooming fruit was blasted. A letter came from the abbot of the convent at Lyons, informing the more honest ones that the monks had sold the knight a profane skull taken from the common graveyard. The mystery was cleared up, the charm was broken, the arrant rogues were exposed, the rage for superstition declined, the people opened their eyes, and the satires of the poet Manuel were seen to be founded in fact. The priests were truly living upon revenues laid upon the dead.

A strong party was forming around Haller, both in the Church and in the State. In it was Bartholomew May, who had been compelled to bow to Samson and retract his words against the base trafficker. Above all was the family of the Wattevilles. James Watteville had been for years at the head of the republic, had read the writings of Luther and Zwingli, and had often conversed about the gospel with John Haller, the pastor of Anseltingen, whom he had protected from his persecutors. His son Nicholas had been educated as the child of his pride. The priests had spared no efforts to bind him to the interests of Rome. They knew that he would have means and influence at his command. It seemed as if everything would keep him from a knowledge of the gospel, but the Lord leads his chosen ones to the truth. He was drawn to Haller, and read Zwingli's letters to him. His admiration for the Zurich Reformer was inexpressible.

Nicholas became the provost of the chapter of canons in the city, and hence one of "My lords of Berne." He had talent, wealth, the power of noble blood, a genial spirit and sound common sense, all on his side. He gave all to the service of the heavenly Master. The pope offered him tempting honours, but he chose the persecuted cause of the once suffering and despised Nazarene. Haller often called him "our bishop of Berne," a title not misapplied. Thus, with Nicholas at the head of the Church and his father at the head of the State, there seemed to be hope for the young republic. But there was another party still very powerful on the side of Rome.

The two petitions of Einsidlen came to Haller; he approved

of them, but did not sign them, because he was not a native
Swiss. He went forward expounding the gospel after the manner of Zwingli. A vast audience gathered to hear him in the
cathedral. The word of God had more power than the satires
of the poet Manuel. The papal party was aroused. Haller was
summoned to the town-hall, as the apostles were before the
Jewish council. The people escorted this meek man to the door,
saw him enter into the presence of men who might burn him,
and remained on the square in front, doubtless praying for their
pastor. The councillors were divided in their opinions. "It is
a matter that concerns the bishop," said certain influential
members: "we must send him before our bishop of Lausanne." Haller's friends trembled at these words, and begged
him to get away as soon as possible. He left the hall. The
people surrounded him, went with him to his house, armed
citizens collected to defend it, determined that their bodies
should be a wall which only violence could surmount, if any
attempt was made to seize their beloved pastor. God blessed
such enthusiasm. The council dared not touch him.
The bishop shrank from ordering his arrest. John Haller was
saved.

The monk Sebastian Meyer, who had raised many a laugh at
"the Turk" of the bishop of Constance, had not been looking
out his window unconcerned. He could relish the stinging sarcasms of the poet Manuel, and yet feel that such were not the
best weapons of truth. He nobly defended Haller. He refuted
the hackneyed charge that "the disciples of the gospel teach a
new doctrine, and that the old is the true one." Said he, "To
have been a thousand years wrong will not make us right for a
single hour; or else the pagans should have kept to their creed.
If the most ancient doctrines ought to be preferred, fifteen hun-

dred years are more than five hundred, and the gospel is older than the decrees of the pope.''

The finger of God traces a channel for the streams of influence. It was Zwingli who confirmed Haller in Berne. It was Haller who persuaded the noble William Farel to begin the powerful work in French Switzerland, where this Alpine Elijah was backed up tremendously by '' My lords of Berne,'' while he filled the whole country with his doctrines. It was Farel who fixed at Geneva the man Calvin, called of God to project anew '' the grandest form of the grandest faith in earth or heaven.'' It was Calvin who reformed the Reformation, laboured more vigorously than any other man for the unity of the entire forces of Protestantism, and left behind him a more extended influence upon the nations which now enjoy the purest Christian liberty. A rill from the Tockenburg mountains was thus poured into the stream of modern civilization.

CHAPTER XIII.

MYCONIUS IN TROUBLE.

(1520–1522.)

WE left Oswald Myconius at Lucerne. This city was chiefly given to popery and foreign military service. Only a few of its leading men would listen to the voice of our patriotic Reformer when raised against the mercenaries or in favour of the truth. Myconius taught the youth what he dared of the good Word, and urged the canons Xyloctect and Kilchmeyer to preach the doctrines of salvation. The schoolmaster stood like a heroic commander on board of a ship, striving to enter a port, in spite of a furious storm, which will yet baffle all efforts and drive it to another haven.

In no other city was there a more stubborn resistance to the entrance of the revived doctrines than in warlike Lucerne. When Luther's writings reached the people, some read them and were struck with horror. It seemed to them that a demon had invented them; they flung the books aside in utter detestation. They started rumours that if any one began to study them, his room was filled with devils whose eyes burned with vengeance. Oswald heard of these visions, and knew that the real Satan was in the lying priests, who invented the absurd stories to frighten the people. But he was cautious; he never spoke of Luther, except to his intimate friends. It was enough to announce the simple gospel of Christ.

148

The papists took advantage of this moderation. Loud voices were heard crying out, "We must burn Luther and our schoolmaster."

"I am assailed by my adversary like a ship in a hurricane at sea," said Myconius to one of his friends. Early in 1520 he was suddenly called before the council. "You are enjoined," they said sharply, "never to read Luther's works to your pupils, never to mention him before them, and never even to think of him." This was claiming a wide jurisdiction. Nothing short of death could prevent Oswald from having his own thoughts. Shortly after this a priest declaimed from the pulpit against heresy. The hearers were moved; all eyes were turned upon the schoolmaster, for he must be the heretic. Oswald sat calmly in his place, letting the people stare to their satisfaction. On leaving the church with his friend Xyloctect, he met one of the councilmen whose fire had not yet cooled, and who said angrily: "Well, you disciples of Luther, why don't you defend your master?" They made no reply, but Myconius wrote of his fears to Zwingli: "I live among savage wolves; yet I have this consolation, that most of them have lost their teeth. They would bite if they could; as they cannot, they merely howl." The great Shepherd had said that he sent his disciples forth as sheep among wolves.

The people raised an uproar and blamed the innocent for the excitement. The senate met to fan the flames. "He is a Lutheran," said one of the councillors. "He is a teacher of novelties;" "He is a seducer of youth," cried others. "Let him appear—bring him in," said they all. The poor schoolmaster was summoned, only to hear fresh threats and prohibitions. His gentle spirit was wounded and almost crushed. His excellent wife could only offer her tears as a balm of comfort.

" Every one is against me," he wrote to Zwingli. " If Christ were not with me, I should long ago have fallen beneath their blows." From Constance, the bishop's stronghold, came a letter from Doctor Sebastian Hofmeister, saying: " What matters it whether Lucerne will keep you or not? The earth is the Lord's. Every country is the home of the brave. Even were we the vilest of men, our cause is just, for we teach the gospel of Christ."

Hofmeister came to Lucerne, boldly preached, but was forced to leave the city. Oswald's sorrows gained upon him. The damp climate affected him, a fever preyed upon him, the physicians declared that he must leave the place or die. He wrote to his great friend at Zurich: " Nowhere do I more desire to be than near you, and nowhere less than in Lucerne. My malady, they say, is the penalty of my iniquity. Alas! whatever I say or do, turns to poison with them. There is One in heaven on whom all my hopes repose."

Nearly two centuries before a fire had laid the greater part of Lucerne in ashes on the evening before the Feast of the Annunciation. In memory of it a great festival was still observed, when a sermon was delivered by some celebrated preacher. This year Conrad Smith, the commander of the Johannites at Kuessnacht, was to preach on the occasion. The son of a peasant, he had won distinction by his extraordinary talents. An immense congregation from city and country assembled in the church, all eager to hear an eloquent sermon in Latin, which would be all jargon to most of the listeners. They supposed that he would defend images and all the old papal rites. But what amazement was on their faces when the commander spoke in German, and all could understand him as he told them of God's love in sending his Son to save them, and that Jesus was the only Saviour!

"God forbid," he exclaimed before the astonished people, "that we should acknowledge for our head a chief so full of sin as the bishop of Rome, and reject Christ! If the pope gives us the food of the gospel, let us consider him our pastor, but not our chief: if he refuses it, let us not acknowledge him at all!"

"What a man!" said Oswald, whose joy could not be restrained. "What a sermon! How full of the spirit of Christ!" The effect was general. The former agitation was followed by a solemn silence throughout the city. But this was merely transient. The priests busied themselves in reviving the opposition. One of them committed an outrage upon a foolish woman, and afterward beat her husband so that he died, but this was not thought to be so bad as for the good canon Xyloctect to be lawfully married. The case of this lewd priest was one of the grievances which prompted the men at Einsidlen to send forth the two petitions.

Oswald was at dinner, on the 22d of July, 1522, and the canon Kilchmeyer was at his table, along with some other friends. Einsidlen was no doubt upon their lips. A signal was heard; a young messenger from Zurich stood at the door. He put into the hands of Myconius the two famous petitions, and a letter from Zwingli, asking him to circulate the papers. "It is my advice," added the Reformer, "that this should be done quietly, gradually, and not all at once; for we must learn to give up everything—even one's wife*—for Christ's sake." In these papers there was a feast for the men at Oswald's table. They knew not what a fearful shell had thus been sent into Lucerne, which would soon explode.

"May God prosper this beginning," said Myconius, turning

---

* Zwingli was recently married at this time.

his eyes to heaven. "From this very hour this prayer should be
the constant occupation of our hearts." The guests could join
in the supplication. The young messenger told them of the attacks constantly made upon Zwingli. The schoolmaster wrote
him, "You have conquered not only in one contest, nor in two,
but in three, and the fourth is beginning.* Your struggles impart unflinching courage to all who have devoted themselves to
Jesus Christ."

The two petitions passed about for signatures, perhaps too
rapidly. But these men felt that the crisis had come; only by a
vigorous effort could the fortress of popery be carried. Most
men shook their heads and refused their names; a few signed
the petitions. The monks whispered, the priests murmured, the
people became more violent against the truth. Lucerne had
sent some soldiers into the foreign service, and they had been
terribly beaten at Bicocca. It was a time of mourning throughout Switzerland; the blood of the slaughtered Swiss had put
gold into the hands of the living mercenaries. Zwingli had
raised his voice against these foreign wars. The men of Schwytz
had listened to him, and sworn to abstain from every foreign
alliance for twenty-five years. But Lucerne hated Zwingli's
patriotism more than the wars that butchered her sons. Her
citizens were wild with war. The pope must be defended; the
voice from Einsidlen must be silenced. Oswald was cast down
in spirit. The whole land seemed given over to delusion. He
said: "From the Swiss we can expect nothing which concerns
the glory of Christ."

The canon Xyloctect had feared for the safety of himself and
his wife, who was a daughter of one of the noble families. He

---

* See Chapter x.

had shed tears of regret when he refused to go to Einsidlen and sign the petitions. The canon Kilchmeyer was bolder, although he had everything to fear. He wrote to Zwingli: "Sentence threatens me, but I wait with courage." As his pen was tracing these words, an officer entered his room and summoned him to appear on the morrow before the council. He took his pen and added: "If they throw me into prison, I shall claim your help; but it will be easier to transport a rock from our Alps than to remove me a finger's breadth from the word of Jesus Christ." The respect due to his father's family, and the purpose to make the storm burst fully upon Oswald, saved the canon.

No modern man had done more for Lucerne than Oswald Myconius. He had introduced the new yet ancient literature into his native city; he had drawn students from all quarters to his lectures; he had sacrificed his own comforts; he had left Zurich and Zwingli; he had lost his health, and had laboured for the highest good of the citizens. His wife was infirm, his child was young, and he had no other house. If Lucerne should drive him thence, where could he find a refuge? But the fact that he would be a wanderer only incited his enemies; they would have their revenge. He had not yet signed the petitions, lest he should thus sign away his last hope, but this made no difference; he must be the victim. An old and valiant warrior, named Hertenstein, proposed the dismissal of the schoolmaster, and thus hoped to drive from the canton his Greek, his Latin and his gospel. He carried the motion. As he left the council he met Berguer, the Zurich deputy, and said, ironically: "We send you back your schoolmaster; prepare a comfortable lodging for him." The courageous deputy replied: "We will not let him sleep in the open air." This was promising more than he could perform.

Oswald knew that he was banished for the only crime of being "Luther's disciple." He thought of his wife, his son and himself, feeble, sickly, poor, driven forth he knew not where, with not a shelter in all stormy Switzerland offered to him. Then, if ever, are friends needed. He wrote to Zwingli: "Here is your poor Myconius, banished by the council of Lucerne. Whither shall I go? I know not. Assailed yourself by furious storms, how can you shelter me? In my tribulation I cry to that God who is my chief hope. Ever rich, ever kind, he does not permit any who call upon him to turn away unheard. May he provide for all our wants!"

Glorious faith! We in these soft days would not know when confidence in Jehovah becomes sublime, were it not for the record of men who have been in the extremity of want. There was one man in Switzerland who never knew when to give up, and who always imparted courage to those whose spirits flagged. "This is my advice," said Zwingli. "Appear before the council and make an address worthy of yourself and of Christ; that is to say, one calculated to melt their hard hearts. Deny that you are Luther's disciple" [for he was not]; "confess that you are Christ's. Let your pupils surround you and also speak; and if this does not succeed, then come to your friend—come to Zwingli, and look upon our city as your home."

In a few days Oswald appeared before the council; he plied their hearts with touching words, but it was all in vain. He must leave his country—his native Lucerne. The people cried out upon him, in order to prejudice the whole land against him. "Nothing remains for me," he said, "but to beg my bread from door to door." The "first man in Switzerland who had combined learning with a love to the gospel, the Reformer of Lucerne," with his sick wife and young child, must leave that ungrateful city. Of all his father's family, one sister only had received the gospel. He crossed the ancient bridge, bade farewell to the grand mountains so long familiar to his admiring eye, went weeping across his native country, and took God for his guide. The two friendly canons soon took their departure. No man was left to love or advance the truth. The gospel was exiled, and to this day Rome holds sway in Lucerne.

The convents had often been the asylum of such weary refugees. The homeless Myconius thought of Einsidlen. Thither he went and was kindly received by the abbot Geroldsek. He was comfortable, but he felt that he must be at work. Six months wore away. He visited Glaris; on his return, oppressed by the journey and the heat of the sun, he met his little boy Felix, panting to tell him the best of news. He had been invited to Zurich to superintend one of the schools. The tidings seemed too good to be true, but he prepared to depart. Geroldsek was filled with regret and with gloomy forebodings. "Alas!" said he to Oswald, "all those who confess Christ are going to Zurich; I fear that one day we shall all perish there together." The good abbot could not long remain behind; he followed the impulse of his heart, and went to dwell in the city of Zwingli, Myconius and Leo Juda. He doubtless often looked in upon the thriving school of Myconius, or sat in the Church of Our Lady, and heard him read and explain the New Testament to an attentive people, who preferred this mode of evening worship to the vespers of other times. One says that "he could instruct in a manner very intelligible and entertaining."

One of the most original of all the characters that appeared in the sixteenth century was Thomas Plater. He was a peasant boy from one of the deep valleys through which Mount Rosa sends the constant burden of her snows, as they melt into maddened streams. When nine years old he was placed under the care of a relative who was a priest. The lad was often so cruelly treated by this man that he cried (as he tells us in an autobiography) like a kid under the knife. A cousin took him with him to attend the German schools. He had a way of his own in gaining knowledge from all sources rather than books. Running from one school to another, he yet could scarcely read when at the age of eighteen. When nearly twenty-four he went to Zurich, and was one of our good Oswald's first scholars. The teacher was at first alarmed at finding students under his care who were so advanced in years. But he soon discovered that Thomas was not fearfully learned. Young Plater said to himself: "Here thou shalt learn or die."

The gospel shined into his heart, and he detested his former superstitions. One very cold morning, when he had no fuel for the school-room fire, which it was his duty to keep up, he thought to himself: "Why should you want wood while there are so many idols in the church?" There was no one in the church, although Zwingli was to preach and the bells were already summoning the people. He went in very softly, laid hold of an image of St. John that stood on the altar, and thrust it into the stove, saying: "Down with you, for in you must go." He most likely did not have the sanction of his teacher to this proceeding. We will know Thomas Plater when we meet him again.

Already had another strong and strange genius appeared, as a pilgrim in Zurich, to confer with the rising Reformer. He was Francis Lambert, born in 1487, at Avignon in France. His father ranked high in the offices of State, but the child was early devoted to the Church.

The boy saw crimes enough among the prelates to harden him,

but God had given him a tender conscience. He gazed on the begging barefoot monks as they passed by, and was eager for their smile. They worked upon his mind, and at fifteen he assumed the cowl. In the convent all went smoothly for a while, and he was anxious to grow holy as his companions. But he soon had his eyes opened. The halo of sanctity faded from the heads of the monks; he saw them in their true character, and was alarmed at their hypocrisy. He felt driven to the Bible, read, believed and resolved to teach its truths. When he became the preacher of the convent, he sought not "fat presents and well-stored tables," as did his colleagues. He went on foot through the country preaching to the poor. He almost wore his life away on one of his extended visits; a mule was given him to carry his weak frame to his poor cell where he might rest; some of the monks were angry, others railed at him, but all joined in selling the mule, putting the money in their purses, and asserting that this was the only profit of these gospel journeys.

Worse things might be told of the monks, who hated Lambert for his purity of life and his rebukes of their sins. The world seemed to him far more holy than the convent, and he thought of leaving this debauched society. But he found what his soul craved. At the fairs of Lyons, Luther's works had been sold; they passed down the Rhone and reached his cell. They were soon taken from him and burnt, but it was too late. He was saved. No more did he sleep sitting on a stool, nor wear hair-cloth, nor scourge himself, nor so nearly starve that he must sometimes faint when preaching in the churches and in the fields. In these there was no merit. He trusted now in Christ. He made up his mind to abandon popery, quit the convent and leave France.

On a July Saturday, shortly after the meeting at Einsidlen,

there appeared in the streets of Zurich a tall, spare monk, wearing the gray frock of the Cordeliers, and riding on a donkey with his feet almost touching the ground. He knew not a word of German, unless he had gathered it in crossing the Alps, but he made himself understood in Latin, and found the house of Zwingli, to whom he gave a letter from Berthold Haller. "This Franciscan father Lambert," wrote Haller, "who is no other than the apostolical preacher of the convent general of Avignon, has been teaching the Christian truth for these last five years; he has preached in Latin before our priests at Geneva, at Lausanne, before the bishop at Friburg, and at Berne, touching the Church, the priesthood, the mass, the traditions of the Romish bishops and the superstitions of the religious orders. It seems most astonishing to me to hear such things from a gray friar and a Frenchman—characters that, as you are aware, presuppose a whole sea of superstitions."

Zwingli was delighted with the account which the stranger gave of his experience, for here was another of those original Reformers who had struck out a line for himself. The Church of Our Lady was opened to the monk, and he was given a seat in front of the high altar. He delivered in it four sermons, in which he handled the errors of Rome quite in the style of Luther, except that in the last one he defended the invocation of Mary and the saints.

"Brother, thou art mistaken," exclaimed Zwingli, in an animated voice. Canons and chaplains were in an ecstasy over the prospect of a dispute between the Frenchman and the Reformer. "He has attacked you," said they to Lambert: "demand a public discussion." The monk did so, and on a given day the two champions met in the hall of the canons. Zwingli began, and for about four hours argued his points from the Bible. Then the Frenchman clasped his hands, raised them heavenward and exclaimed: "I thank thee O God, that by means of such an illustrious instrument thou hast brought me to so clear a knowledge of the truth." Then turning to the astonished assembly, he said: "Henceforth in all my tribulations I will call on God alone, and will throw aside my beads. To-morrow I shall resume my journey: I am going to Basle to see Erasmus, and thence to Wittemberg to visit Martin Luther."

The priests wished they had said nothing, for the effect upon the people was not to their mind. They were glad when he mounted his little donkey and rode away.

The next year he dared to marry—two years before Luther set at naught the celibacy of the clergy by taking a wife, as the Bible permits. He did much in sending books to France, and then felt that he must go himself. Luther urged him to labour among the German Alps. Farel called him to his native country. He was in perplexity. In Germany he might have peace and safety; in France, peril and death. He could not rest. He walked the streets of Wittemberg with downcast eyes, and his wife Christina could not calm his mind. She was willing to go anywhere and share his sufferings.

At last he kneeled and prayed that the Lord would end the struggle by choosing the lot that he would cast. He took two slips of paper; on one he wrote *France*, on the other *Switzerland*. He closed his eyes and drew the first slip—France. Again he prayed, drew the lot and it was again France. Some hours after he remembered that Gideon thrice asked for the sign on the fleece, and he prayed the third time and still drew France. From that hour he did not hesitate, and during Lent, in 1524, there appeared in Metz a doctor and ex-friar with a wife—an astonishment to the people, for a married priest had not been seen in France since the reign of popery. But the lot had not been ordered by the Lord; he was not successful; he afterward became a professor of theology at Strasburg, then at Marburg, then aided in the Reformation in Hesse, and was celebrated in many of the great discussions which agitated Europe. We will meet him again.

CHAPTER XIV.

NEW TRIUMPHS.

(1522–1523.)

THOMAS PLATER was not the first man who had used images to kindle fires. Most happy would it have been if all the advocates of reform had been as honest as he was and as free from rashness. But in the gospel army there were some of those desperate heroes, who left their ranks and made such reckless sallies against error that they injured the holy cause. They prevented the best effects of the two petitions that went forth from Einsidlen by inflaming the minds of the papal party. No sooner had Zwingli returned from that ancient hermitage than the case of certain zealots engaged his attention. To them we give a little space in order to fill up the picture of those stormy times.

A young priest, learned, hot-headed, high-tempered and ambitious, resolved to send forth a fiery blast against idolatry. All the friends of Louis Hetzer were startled when he published a little book in German, entitled "The Judgment of God as to the mode of dealing with Images." The volume produced a great sensation. The people read it and many were filled with hatred against images, but it gave them no love for the true worship. It was a firebrand cast among them, inciting rash men to acts of violence.

In the town of Stadelhofen dwelt "a worthy man, and well

read in the Scriptures," named Claus (Nicholas) Hottinger. A more honest shoemaker never kept his word. He had often passed through the gates, and just outside of them seen a crucifix richly carved and ornamented, which was highly venerated. It belonged to the miller of the town. One day, after reading Hetzer's book, he met the miller and asked: "When do you intend to throw down your idols?"

"No one compels you to worship them," was the reply.

"But do you not know that the word of God forbids us to have any graven images?"

"Well, then, if you are authorized to remove the crucifix, you may take it away whenever you choose. I give it up to you."

Nicholas thought that this was license enough, and on a September morning he marched out with a band of citizens, took down the image and sold the wood for the benefit of the poor in the hospital. This act caused a wondrous excitement. One might have thought that religion fell when the crucifix came crashing to the earth. A loud outcry was heard: "Down with these men! They are church-robbers and worthy of death. They have committed sacrilege."

"No," said Zwingli and his colleagues from their pulpits, "Hottinger and his friends are not guilty in the sight of God and worthy of death. Their act is not sacrilege. But they may be punished for having acted with violence and without the sanction of the magistrates." But before Zwingli was heard from, the "Idol-stormers" were arrested.

Similar acts were common; one of them increased the general commotion. Lawrence Meyer, a curate of St. Peter's in Zurich, was one day standing in front of the church looking at a number of poor people craving for bread and shivering in the cold. He said to a fellow-curate: "I should like to strip these wooden idols, and procure clothing for these poor members of Jesus Christ." Somebody took the hint. On Lady day, before three o'clock in the morning, the "saints" and all their ornaments suddenly disappeared. Plates, rolls, images and other symbols were gone. The council flung the curate into prison. He protested that he was innocent, and was at last set at liberty. But the people said: "What! is it these logs of wood that our Lord commanded us to clothe? Is it on account of these images that he will say to the righteous: 'I was naked and ye clothed me'"?

Zwingli was not so zealous against images as William Farel; he said that being near-sighted he did not see them, and they gave him no personal offence. But he declared plainly that "all images must be removed which call forth a superstitious veneration, because such veneration is idolatry. . . . An old man may remember the time when not the hundredth part of the images were in the churches that are now to be found in them: woe to us if we increase them! I verily believe that the whole of papal Christendom would rather have their images or idols than the word of God. For when the Word is presented, it is clearly seen that the whole papacy is a lie. Therefore they let the sufferings of Christ be painted on the walls and represented in statuary, and let poor fools hang silver and gold thereon, and kiss the stone feet, but they must not learn what the sufferings of Christ mean. Because, as soon as they have learned this lesson, they take Christ as their Redeemer, and no longer buy salvation from the papacy. Therefore, while the gospel is preached, the images ought to be removed, that men may not fall back into their former errors; for as storks return to their old nests, so men return to their old errors if the way to them be not barred."

The shoemaker was brought before the council of Zurich,

along with Conrad Grebel, a violent young man, of whom more hereafter. To make an example of these imprudent men would, perhaps, quiet the noisy priests. The venerable burgomaster Roust said to them : " We forbid you to speak against the monks and on controverted questions." At these words a loud noise was heard in the council chamber, says an old chronicler. Some thought that God was giving a sign of his displeasure. Every man looked about in wonder, but saw nothing to explain the mystery. Poor Hottinger was yet to be the victim of worse persecution.

A wiser man now drew general attention. The confederate Diet was sitting at Baden, seeking how to please the bishop of Constance by crushing the Reformer, and to hush the voice that cried aloud against the mercenaries. The two famous petitions were laid before the members of the Diet. Whereupon they must visit their wrath upon some faithful preachers. " Arrest the one nearest to us," said they : " one example will frighten the whole band." Urban Weiss, the parson of Fislisbach, lived nearest to Baden. He had already been in prison for saying that " Christians must not call on the Virgin Mary or other saints for help." He was quietly at home again, when he was seized, taken to Constance, delivered up to the bishop and thrust into jail. " It was thus that the confederates began to persecute the preachers of the gospel." The monks raved more furiously from their pulpits, and their followers offered to supply wood free of cost to burn Zwingli.

Shortly after Leo Juda went to Zurich he was one day listening to the sermon of an Augustine monk, who asserted that man is able of himself to satisfy the righteousness of God. "Reverend father," said Leo, "listen to me for a moment, and you, my dear citizens, be silent, while I speak as becomes a Christian." He then proved from Scripture the falseness of the doctrine to which they had been listening. Upon this a great disturbance arose in the church; several persons fell upon "the little priest" from Einsidlen, but he was "lion" enough to turn all this to victory.

"Let us hold a conference to settle these cases," was Zwingli's demand of the great council. It was granted. The time fixed upon was January 29, 1523. The call went forth; it was talked of through all Switzerland. The papists were vexed, and said in derision, "A Diet of vagabonds is to be held in Zurich; all the beggars from the highways will be there." This was a hard name to give to those of their own party who came at the time—such men as vicar Faber and the knight James von Anwyl. The confederate Diet did not condescend to appoint any delegates. The friends of the gospel came from all quarters. Berne sent up the champion against "the Turk," Doctor Sebastian Meyer. Citizens and country-people gathered at the place, "for with many," writes Bullinger, "there was a great wonderment what would come out of this affair." Yet there was but one deputy from the cantons regularly commissioned, and he came from a quarter least expected.

Far up north, at Schaffhausen, near the falls of the Rhine, the papists had attempted to create a terror among the Reformers. An aged man, named Galster, had found salvation in the good Bible, and told the glad news to his wife and children. Perhaps unwisely he openly attacked the relics, images, mass, priests and every sort of papal superstition. His neighbours hated him and put him in fear for his life. The old man left his house brokenhearted, and fled into the forests for safety, sustaining himself on what he could find in the cold winter. Suddenly, on the last night of the year 1520, torches flashed through the forests, the hounds bayed in all-directions, and the shouting hunters rode on in their cruel sport. The council had ordered this chase after the wretched man. The hounds seized their prey. The venerable Christian was taken before the magistrates, and, after refusing to abjure his faith, he was beheaded. A more powerful man rose up in his stead. No one dared to hunt down Doctor Sebastian Hofmeister, one of Zwingli's warmest supporters, nor waylay him as he went to the Zurich conference as the only deputy from the canton.

At the hour there met in the hall of the Great Council about six hundred persons of all parties, expecting some extraordinary proceedings. The aged warrior and burgomaster Roust presided. Zwingli sat alone at a table in the centre of the hall, with his Bible at hand, and all eyes turned upon him. The burgomaster made the opening speech, explaining that they were met to determine whether Magister Ulrich Zwingli was a heretic and a seditious man. If any one present thought him to be so, let him prove it. The chevalier Von Anwyl told how his bishop had sent him and his colleagues to inquire into "certain doctrines and preachings" which had made a noise in the diocese. No one wished for peace more than "my gracious master the bishop." *

Zwingli arose and said: "God has revealed his will to the human race. Pure and clear is this Word in itself; but in our days certain men have so darkened and defaced it that most people called Christians are wholly ignorant of the divine will. And now, when some begin to point out the truth, lo! they are cried down as corrupters of the Church and as heretics. Such an one I am regarded. For five years in this town I have preached nothing but Christ's saving message to man, and yet

---

* We condense all these speeches.

this has not justified me. I am stigmatized throughout Switzerland as a heretic, a misleader of the people, a rebel. . . . Now, then, in the name of God, here I stand."

In his hand was a little printed book containing his sixty-seven theses, which he held out, saying: "These propositions are the sum of what I have taught. I am ready to defend them. The spirit of God has compelled me to speak. He knows, too, why he has chosen me, all unworthy as I am, to be his herald. Go on, then, in God's name. Here I am to answer you."

Six hundred people were staring at Faber, who rose saying, very politely: " My esteemed brother Zwingli assures us that he has always preached the gospel in Zurich. Truly, I do not doubt that, for what true preacher would not. He means to vindicate his doctrine: I really wish he had come to Constance, where I would have testified my friendship for him. But I was not sent here to dispute, but to listen, and in case of a debate to decide what will make for peace." The assembly, in surprise, began to laugh. The bishop's vicar went on to say: "The Diet of Nuremberg has promised to call a general council within a year; we must wait until it meets."

"Is not this vast and learned assembly as good as any council?" inquired Zwingli. "There are bishops here, such as are overseers of the flock, and called bishops by the apostles. . . . As to the Nuremberg business, I have here three letters from there, none of which contain a single word about calling a general council. The pope, bishops and clergy are utterly opposed to it. Now is the time to defend the word of God in this assembly."

A deep silence followed this appeal; it was broken by the white-headed burgomaster's challenge: "If there be any one here who has anything to object to Zwingli and his doctrines, let him now speak." Not a word was said by the papists.

"In Christian love I call upon those who have accused me, and I know that there are several here," said the Reformer, "to come forward and reprove me for the love of truth. I do not wish to call upon them by name." Not a man among the Romanists opened his lips.

"Where are the men who would burn us," cried out Joner, the abbot of Cappel, "and who have already provided wood for the purpose?" This was driving the papists into a corner and provoking them with a sharp lance. But the slain hosts of Sennacherib were not more voiceless. They could make an uproar throughout the country, but they dare not venture upon an argument with a man who stood with all the defences of the Bible at his side.

Parson Wagner then rose and said: "Our gracious lord of Constance has lately issued a mandate requiring us to observe the traditions of the Church until a general council otherwise orders. But as no one comes forward to refute Zwingli's articles, I hope that henceforth we shall take them as our guide, rather than the bishop's mandate, and preach the word of God fully and purely. If these men cannot sustain the mandate by opposing Zwingli, then there must be some injustice done to the parson of Fislisbach, who we know has been imprisoned for not obeying the mandate. This much I say in my simplicity, for Urban Weiss is our brother."

Faber dropped his reserve for a moment, and replied that "the bishop must have seen the need of the mandate, as there are many foolish persons in his diocese who utter great nonsense. The parson of Fislisbach is an illiterate, unreasonable man, who says things that I would be ashamed to repeat. I have shown him from Scripture that it is right to worship the saints, and he now is willing to recant all that he has said against it. He ought to thank me for my trouble, and he will soon be set at liberty."

"No doubt God has caused this matter of invoking the saints to come up," said Zwingli, impatient to draw out the papists. "My lord vicar boasts that he has converted Urban Weiss from his errors; let him now tell us by what passages of Scripture he did it."

"I see, dear sirs," replied Faber, "that the tables are turned against me. 'The fool is easily caught in his words,' says the proverb." After a little slight skirmishing between the two champions, Faber sat down in silence. Not another word would he utter. Not one of his party would enter the lists and prove that the saints should be adored. The burgomaster challenged them in vain, and at last dismissed the assembly to dinner, with the remark to Faber: "It seems that the famous sword with which you smote the pastor of Fislisbach will not come out of its sheath to-day."

In the afternoon there was the same reserve in the Roman party. The council therefore resolved that "the Magister Ulrich Zwingli continue, as hitherto, to preach the Holy Scripture, as the Spirit of God may enable him," and that the clergy in town and country be commanded to preach nothing which they cannot prove to be the gospel. "Nor shall they, for the future, apply to each other abusive names, as heretic and the like."

"Praised be God," exclaimed Zwingli, "whose Word will rule in heaven and earth!" But Faber could not restrain his indignation, and he said: "The theses of Master Ulrich are contrary to the honour of the Church and the doctrine of Christ, and I will prove it." Zwingli pressed him to furnish the evidence.

"I will not debate with you unless it be at Paris, Cologne or Friburg," was the reply.

"Why not here?" answered Zwingli. "I will have no other judge than the gospel. Sooner than you can shake one of its words, the earth will open before you."

"The gospel!" sneered Faber, "always the gospel! Men might live in holiness, charity and peace, even if there were no gospel. You had better held your peace than to have thus defended yourself!" At these words the people rose up indignant at the conduct of the vicar and left the hall. Thus ended the first Zurich conference. A new position was gained. The council would defend "the bishop of Zurich," and the bishop of Constance might look after his mandate himself. Hundreds of people thought, "These noisy priests are afraid of the Scriptures."

A poor country parson met Zwingli and said: "You ask too much when you exhort every pastor to read the Bible, especially the New Testament. How can one who has a small living buy a Testament? I have such a small salary that I must here put in my word."

"There is, by God's grace, no priest so poor," replied the Reformer, "that he cannot buy a Testament, if he go seriously about it. He will find some pious citizen who will loan him the money or give him one."

Several persons took this hint and distributed Testaments among the poor. Among them was a son of the burgomaster, who gave one to an humble parson, saying: "I wish that you may read the divine Word with all diligence, and put more faith in the Creator of all things than in the poor weak creature, man."

An aged schoolmaster wrote out a faithful report of the conference. Faber was provoked when he read it, and he haughtily published his version of the affair. This aroused the indignation of the Zurichers. Six young men, most of them councillors, refuted Faber by a pamphlet entitled "Hawk Pluckings," a name applied to some rude game. Their biting wit stirred up the wrath of vicar Faber, and he soon became a heartless persecutor. One writer of that age says, in too strong terms: "We ought rather to call Faber a cruel judge than a doctor or a bishop. Throughout all Germany and the neighbouring countries his severity is known. Scarcely a hangman in our fatherland has executed so many as have been condemned by the unjust sentences of Faber. . . . . While the poor wretched Hans Huglin was groaning on the rack, the vicar sat there and laughed. The tortured man saw this and said: 'Oh, dear sir, why do you laugh at me? I am but an abandoned creature, not worth laughing at. Laugh over yourself, and may God forgive you; you know not what you do.' At these words the vicar, who looked at him more wickedly, grew very red; since which all the world has pitied the poor man." It is said that Faber rejoiced to see him burning at the stake.

The tactics were now changed for a little time. A new pope, Adrian VI., had charge of the papal seal, called the fisherman's ring, because St. Peter was represented on it as a fisherman. The captain of the pope's guard, a son of the burgomaster Roust, visited Zwingli along with a papal legate. They presented a letter from the pope, and were ready to offer him a mitre, crozier, cardinal's hat, or all that he dare ask, if he would only turn papist. Francis Zing of Einsidlen was also urged to use his influence. Rome offered her mightiest temptations. What he thought of all this may be learned from his own words: "A few days ago I received, both by letter and by word of mouth, great promises from the pope, which I have answered as God will in a Christian and unmoved frame of mind. It is, however, no matter of doubt that I could attain to a greatness such as not every one could reach, if the poverty of Christ were not dearer to me than the wordly pomp of the papists." Also to his old teacher Wittembach he wrote, June 15, 1523: "God grant the Swiss people a sense to understand and love his Word, for the pope is seeking anew to press his yoke upon them. To me, too, he has sent a letter under the fisherman's ring, with brilliant promises; but I despatched the messenger with an answer according to his merits, telling him in plain language that I believed the pope to be anti-Christ."

"What did the pope commission you to offer him?" inquired Myconius of Francis Zing, who replied: "*Everything except the papal chair.*" At that time Rome feared Zwingli more than Luther, for the Saxon Reformer was not then so uncompromising in regard to the ceremonies of popery. Rome cursed Luther; she courted Zwingli, and made both of them more terrible to herself. Eternal truth is not a subject for the arts of diplomacy.

The pope's messengers went straight to Constance to tell Faber how sadly he had failed. They all felt like fools, and wished that they had never gone to Zurich on such errands. In their vexation they discussed plans for crushing the Reformer. They would rouse the papal cantons against him. The Diet must force him into silence. We will see farther on some of the results of their efforts among "the five cantons." Some men at Berne resolved to make Zwingli a prisoner whenever he could be met away from Zurich. At Lucerne the people made a man of straw, fastened his name to it, dragged it to the scaffold and there burned it as a heretic. They laid hands on some Zurichers who happened to be in the city, and compelled them to witness the mock execution. If Zwingli had been in their power, they would have gloried in putting him to death. But when he heard of it, he said: "I rejoice that I have been thought worthy to suffer shame for the name of Christ! I have borne no insult with more equanimity than this."

Another conference was called for October. The bishops resolved to show their contempt by sending no delegates. Doctor Hofmeister was sent by Schaffhausen and made president; Doctor Vadian was sent by St. Gall. These pastors and their colabourers regarded themselves as true bishops. The ancient Presbyterian system began to be restored for the first time in Romish lands. We need not follow up the discussions upon matters of faith. They were listened to by nine hundred people in the great hall. The aged canon Hoffman undertook to defend the pope. He argued that simple pastors and laymen had no right to discuss such subjects. "I was thirteen years at Heidelberg," said he, "living in the house of a very great scholar, Doctor Jodocus [Gallus], a worthy and pious man, with whom I often ate and drank and led a merry life; but I always heard him say that in matters of faith we must not dispute; so you see. . . . ." All were ready to burst with laughter, and the dignified burgomaster could scarcely keep order.

It was settled at this conference that images should be put out of churches, that the saints should not be invoked, and that the mass was not to take the place of the Lord's Supper. The case of Hottinger, the shoemaker, came up, and the council was asked to set him and his companions at liberty. This was done, but Hottinger, having been the ringleader, was banished for two years from the canton.

The confederate Diet soon met at Lucerne, and forbade the

people "to preach or repeat any new or Lutheran doctrine in
public or private, or to talk of such things in taverns or over
their wine." Hottinger was one day dining at the Angel tavern
in Zurzach, on the Rhine, and said that the priests wrongly interpreted Scripture, and that man should put his trust in God
alone. The landlord, going in and out, overheard this language,
so extraordinary to him, and reported it. Hottinger did not let
many such occasions pass without delivering his honest opinions.
He was pursued, arrested and taken before the Diet at Baden.
No time was lost in condemning him to be beheaded. When
informed of the sentence he gave glory to God. "That will
do," said one of his judges; "we do not sit here to listen to sermons." On reaching the spot where he was to die, he raised
his hands to heaven, exclaiming: "Into thy hands, O my Redeemer, I commit my spirit." One minute more and he was a
martyr. Through much tribulation he entered into the kingdom
of heaven.

"Let us celebrate the Lord's Supper according to the Scriptural mode," said the Zurich ministers to each other. This
was done for the first time, probably, in all Switzerland, on the
Christmas of 1523. The next step was to banish the images
and repress the worship of the saints. Hoffman objected.
But the council decreed that he and his party must keep silent,
or be dismissed from the town and deprived of their benefices.
A few months later, twelve councillors, the three parsons and a
body of workmen went into the different churches, locked the
doors, took down the crosses, removed the images, dashed out
the paintings and restained the walls. The superstitious people wept; true believers rejoiced. Certain country churches
followed the example, burning the idols, selling the ornaments
and giving the proceeds to the poor.

The burgomaster Roust and his colleague had stood up nobly for the defence of the truth, but their work was done. At the very time this great change was working in the Church below, they departed, hopeful of rest in the Church above, and hailing with joy the triumphs of the Reformation.

CHAPTER XV.

HANS WIRTH AND HIS SONS.

(1524.)

ON the northern border of the canton of Zurich lived Hans Wirth, the deputy bailiff of Stammheim, and the patriarch of a large and happy family. His wife Hannah was revered throughout the district as an example to mothers, for she reared her many children in the fear of the Lord. The two oldest sons, Adrian and John, were young priests full of piety and courage, who preached the gospel with great fervour after the manner of Zwingli and Luther. John had the ardent zeal of one who was ready to sacrifice his life in the cause. Little did he suspect that he was soon to be a martyr.

The love for office has always been a dangerous foe to faith. A crafty man, named Amberg, had appeared to listen with delight to the gospel until he put himself forward as a politician. He wished to be one of the bailiffs of Thurgau, and he promised to root out the new doctrines if elected. Once made bailiff, he began to sound aloud his hatred of the gospel and his threats against its preachers. But where should he find a victim? There was no one in his district preaching the word with power.

The worthy Exlin* had been confirmed in the new faith, when

---

* Oechslin, or Œxlin.

Zwingli was with him at Einsidlen. He was anxious to preach the glad tidings of salvation. Going northward, he crossed the Rhine into the canton of Schaffhausen, and became pastor of Burg, not far from Stein, on the river. The Wirths were among his warmest friends. He did not dream of any danger from the noisy bailiff Amberg, for Exlin was not under his jurisdiction. But about midnight, July 7, 1524, some persons knocked at the pastor's door ; he admitted them and found himself in the hands of the bailiff's soldiers. They handled him so roughly that he thought them to be ruffians intent upon taking his life. He cried "Murder!" so loudly that his neighbours started from their sleep in affright, and soon the entire village was a scene of tumult and terror. The uproar spread to Stein. The sentinel on guard at the castle of Hohenklingen fired the alarm-gun. The bells were rung, the inhabitants were moving, the people of other villages joined them, all inquiring of one another in the darkness what was the matter, and prepared for any display of valour. Exlin was already bound as a prisoner and on the road to Frauenfield, where Amberg was waiting for his first victim.

Hans Wirth and his two eldest sons heard the noise of the tumult in Burg, and went forth like their neighbours to quell it. The father was indignant that the bailiff of Frauenfield should violate the common law by going beyond his lines and seizing an innocent man. The sons were roused against the man who had stolen away the friend whose example they had delighted to follow, dragging him off by night as a criminal. Each of them seized a halberd, and in spite of the pleadings of a mother and a tender wife, they joined the citizens of Stein in their determination to rescue their beloved pastor. Deputy-bailiff Rutiman also came, leading the men of Nussbaum. A large body of excited men from both sides of the Rhine had assembled. The two deputies, Wirth and Rutiman, were chosen as their leaders. They set out in swift pursuit of the kidnapping party: the more hardy and daring men hoped to overtake them, but they soon were obliged to halt. The river Thur could not be crossed; the ferry-boat had been removed.

The wiser men at once sent a delegation to Frauenfield, across the river, and requested the bailiff to liberate the pastor of Burg. They offered large bail. "The good man is so dear to us," said deputy Wirth, " that I would willingly give up my goods, my liberty and my life to have him set free." Contrary to custom and to all justice, Amberg refused to accept bail and free the prisoner.

In the mean time the rage of the people increased. Unhappily, the signals of alarm had called forth many of those restless men who are always keen for a riot, and who refuse to be controlled when they cannot control themselves. They turned their attention to the rich convent of Ittingen, near at hand. In it had been three monks, who, unknown to each other, had each written to Zwingli for light in their darkness. They were taking courage, and might have reformed the cloister, if it had been permitted to stand. One of them, named Hesch, did afterward labour for the truth. But these three good monks were not known to the mob. The rioters thought that the prior had been in the habit of stirring up the bailiff to measures of severity against the Reformed preachers. They could not be restrained by the deputies put in command. The doors of the monastery were burst open, and these disorderly wretches, hungry and thirsty, eager for plunder and violence, rushed in, damaging the church, breaking the furniture, burning the books, ransacking the store-rooms, entering the cellar and revelling in wine. The drunken peasants could not be managed. Hans Wirth entreated them to leave the convent; they turned and threatened him with violence. Rutiman could do nothing. John Wirth entered, but soon came back distressed at what he had seen. The poor monks trembled for their lives, and gave up all to the mob.

Post-haste went a messenger to Zurich; the grave council sent back deputies, who ordered all persons under their jurisdiction to return to their homes. They obeyed. But the Thurgovians knew no master, and still held their revels at the expense of the friars. On a sudden a fire broke out and the monastery was burned to the ground. It was reported that a boy had been wounded by a furious boar belonging to the convent, and his father was so angry that he took his revenge by kindling the flames. But the blame was to be charged to the innocent. The smoking embers of the Carthusian monastery made hot the wrath of the papal cantons against the Reformers.

The confederate Diet had already been in session, refusing Zurich a representation. The papists were thus the first to break the federal unity of the cantons. They had been taking council against the believers in the gospel. And now the report of the uprising in the north reached their ears. Five days after the burning of the convent, the deputies of the cantons met at Zug. Nothing was heard in the assembly but threats of vengeance and death. "Let us march with banners flying upon Stein and Stammheim," said they, "and put the inhabitants to the sword. Let us fall upon Zurich also, if she does not root out heresy."

"Hans Wirth, his sons and Rutiman are the ringleaders," said some. "They set fire to the convent, or at least urged others to do it." A Zurich deputy appeared to vindicate the canton, and he said: "If any one be guilty, let him be punished, not by violence, but by law." Vadian of St. Gall supported this opinion. Upon this the mayor of Lucerne, unable to restrain his fury, exclaimed, with frightful oaths and curses: "The heretic Zwingli is the father of all these insurrections; and you too, Doctor Vadian of St. Gall, favour his infamous cause and aid him in securing its triumph. You ought no longer to have a seat in the Diet."

"Order, order!" cried the president, but the stormy passions were not to be calmed by words. Vadian saw his danger. He left the hall, departed secretly from the town, and by a circuitous route took refuge in the convent of Cappel until he could safely return to his home. It was resolved by the deputies and council to order Zurich to arrest those who were accused and give them a trial.

Adrian Wirth was quietly preaching from the pulpit at home, and saying, "Never will the enemies of God be able to vanquish his friends." His father was warned of the fate impending over him, and entreated to flee with his family. "No," he replied, "I will wait for the officers, putting my trust in God." The soldiers came to his house; they expected resistance, but he calmly said to them: "My lords of Zurich might have spared themselves all this trouble; if they had sent only a child, I would have obeyed the summons." The three Wirths and their neighbour Rutiman were taken to Zurich and put in prison. For three weeks they were closely questioned, but nothing was found in their conduct worthy of punishment. Zurich was ready to set them free. But the other cantons were not satisfied. They said in the Diet: "Let them be sent to Baden, where all the confederate deputies can sit in common court and hear the case."

"Not so," replied the Zurichers. "To our canton belongs

the right to ascertain whether these men are guilty or not, and we have found no fault in them."

"Will you send them to us?" angrily asked the other cantons. "Answer yes or no, and not a word more. If not, we will fetch them by force." Two Zurich deputies mounted their horses and rode with all haste to their constituents. On their arrival the whole town was in agitation. What was to be done? War was threatening the only canton that had declared for the Reformation. It was what the papal cantons wished. They could sweep out the party that gathered around Zwingli. They could blame him for all the disturbances and for the civil war, just on the same principle that Abel was to blame for making occasion for Cain to slay him. If Abel had only offered the same sacrifice as Cain, there need have been no enmity. Thus some men still reason; thus they held in Zwingli's time. If the prisoners were not sent to Baden, the confederates would come down upon Zurich with an armed force, and she could not resist the whole power of the other cantons; but if she gave them up, it would be consenting to their death.

"What does Zwingli say?" was the question.

"Zurich ought to remain faithful to her constitution," was his reply, "and defend her own citizens; the prisoners ought not to be surrendered."

"Compromise is better than war," said those who sought a middle course. "Let us deliver them over on this one condition, that they be examined solely with regard to the affair of Ittingen, and not upon their faith." The Diet agreed to this proposal. Let this fact be noted, for it will furnish an instance of what the pledges of the papists were worth in those times.

It was a sad hour when four councillors and an armed troop started with the prisoners for Baden. "Alas! what a miserable setting out that was!" said one of the mourning citizens. The people filled the streets, crowded to the gates, and then to the churches. "God will punish us," cried Zwingli from the pulpit. "Let us pray him to impart grace to the prisoners, and make them strong in faith."

At evening the accused entered Baden, where an immense crowd was waiting for them, almost preventing their advance. Hans Wirth, who walked in front, said to his sons: "See, dear children, we are, as the apostle says, men appointed unto death, for we are made a spectacle unto the world, and to angels and to men." (1 Cor. iv. 9.) In the gaping crowd he saw his enemy Amberg, the cause of all his misfortunes. Wirth pressed near him, held out his hand, which the bailiff would gladly have spurned, and said: "There is a God in heaven who knows all things; you need not be so furious against us."

Hans Wirth was first examined, on the following day. He was put to the torture without the least respect to his age, character or office. He persisted in declaring that he was innocent of the pillage and burning of Ittingen. Witnesses sustained him, and a letter from the prior of the convent proved that he had made every effort to save it from destruction. He was then charged with having destroyed an image of St. Anne. The more innocent he appeared, the greater was the cruelty inflicted. From morning until noon he was tortured. His tears could not soften his judges. The prisoners were now examined about the abolition of the mass and images. "This is contrary to the agreement," said a Zurich deputy.

"We know what we are about," rejoined a member from Lucerne, with insolence, "and we act according to orders." The Zurich deputies refused to sit in such a faithless court, and rode home to make a report and secure help for the persecuted. But the trial went on. Nothing could be proved against Adrian Wirth, except that he had preached after the manner of Zwingli and was married, and for that he had good Bible authority, which his judges did not care to hear. John Wirth was tortured, and accused of having given the sacrament to a sick man without bell or taper. "Who taught you these heretical doctrines?" inquired his judges when he was in the severest agony. "Did Zwingli, or some other person?" He cried out in torture, "O merciful and eternal God, help and comfort me." One of his judges said, tauntingly, "Where is your Christ now? Let your Christ help you."

Adrian was put to the rack. A Bernese chevalier, who had won honours in the wars of Palestine, said to him: "Young man, tell us the truth; for if you refuse, I swear by the knighthood that I gained on the very spot where the Lord suffered martyrdom, that we will open your veins one after another. You have waylaid your old father with this accursed doctrine, and are to be the death of him, for we shall do our utmost to tear up this heresy by the roots."

"Do not storm so," replied Adrian, "but have mercy and hear the truth quietly." He was fastened to a rope, hoisted into the air and jeered for being married, for the knight pointed to the rope and said: "There, my little master, is your wedding-present for your new housewife." Rutiman was spared the torture. The victims were thrust into jail, there to pine away until the court of the cantons should meet again.

Four weeks passed. The wife of Hans Wirth went to Baden, carrying an infant in her arms, to intercede with the judges. Her advocate, Escher, said to Jerome Stocker, who had been twice bailiff of Frauenfield, "You know the deputy-bailiff Wirth, that he has always been an upright man." The reply was: "It is even as you say. I have never known a more honest, faithful officer than Wirth; in joy or in sorrow his home was open to all; his house was like an inn or a convent. If he had committed robbery or murder, I would help to spare him; but seeing that he has burned the image of St. Anne, Christ's grandmother, he must die."

"God forbid," replied Escher, "that a pious man who has burned nothing but wooden images should find less mercy than a thief or murderer. This will have a bad ending." The doors were shut. The court, made up of papists, spared Adrian on account of his mother's entreaties. But sentence of death was passed upon the other three prisoners. Hans Wirth said to Adrian in the prison: "My son, since God spares you, see that you never avenge our innocent deaths." The son burst into tears. "Brother," said John, "you know that we have faithfully preached the Word, but where the Word is, there will be the cross."

The three prisoners were led to the town-hall, through the midst of a jeering, taunting multitude, to hear their sentence. The statements made by them when under torture were read, but were so changed and falsified that Hans Wirth could not repress his indignation. "Let it pass, dear father," said John. "Anti-Christ must always resort to lies. One day the great judgment will be held, and then every falsehood will be exposed." They were handed over to the executioners. In passing a chapel the priest said to the two older men, "Fall down and call upon the saints."

"Father, be firm," said John. "Why should we kneel before wood and stone? You know there is one Mediator, the Lord Jesus."

"Assuredly, my son," replied the aged man, "and by his

grace I will remain faithful." Upon this the three went on repeating the Lord's Prayer. They reached the scaffold.

"Dearest father," said John, "henceforth you are no longer my father, nor am I your son, but we are brothers in Christ, for whose name we suffer. To day, if it be God's will, we shall go to him who is the Father of us all. Fear nothing."

"Amen," said the father; "and may the Almighty bless thee, my dear son and brother in Christ." The most of the spectators were in tears as the three martyrs knelt, and commending themselves to God, received the stroke of the axe. The people saw the marks of torture upon their bodies, and gave loud expression to their grief. Two innocent patriarchs had been beheaded, leaving behind them twenty-two children and forty-five grandchildren. At first their property was confiscated, but it was afterward partly restored when Hannah Wirth paid a large sum to the executioner who had taken away her husband's life. Adrian Wirth became a country pastor in the canton of Zurich, where he laboured forty years with success. The parson Exlin was dragged from one prison to another, cruelly treated, and finally set at liberty. He too laboured in a country parish of Zurich.

The death of the Wirths was to hasten forward the Reformation. When Hottinger was executed, Zurich suppressed images; after the Wirths had been beheaded, Zurich set to work to abolish the mass. There were many warm discussions before the council in regard to the "real presence," or transubstantiation. Am-Gruet the under-secretary of state, seemed to be the chief opponent of Zwingli, for he probably understood the subject more fully than the priests. He insisted that the words, *This is my body*, proved that the bread used in the Lord's Supper was really the body of Christ. Therefore the wafer (or *host*) was really Christ, and he was honoured in the mass by the lifting up of the host.

"The word *is* in the text means *signifies* or *represents*," said Zwingli. "This represents my body." The Great Council was convinced when Zwingli quoted such texts as these: "I am the Vine;" "The seed is the Word;" "The rock was Christ." The members wished to make broad the gulf between the Reformed Church and the papacy. They ordered the mass to be suppressed (April, 1525), and decreed that the Lord's Supper should be observed without it, according to the custom of the apostles.

Zwingli wished to find a still stronger text to prove his point. One evening he searched the Scriptures, but could not find what he sought. He went to sleep with his mind engrossed by the subject, for he wished to put Am-Gruet to silence. In a dream he seemed to be visited by some person, who said: "Why do you not quote the words in Exodus (xii. 11), "Ye shall eat it (the Lamb) in haste; it is the Lord's passover." Zwingli sprang from his bed, took up his Greek version of the Old Testament, and there found that "*is*" must mean *signifies*, for the lamb could not be the act of an angel *passing over* the houses of the Hebrews. The next day he preached from that text and won a greater victory.

CHAPTER XVI.

A LOOK WESTWARD.

(1524—1526.)

THE good work was progressing nobly in St. Gall under the direction of Doctor Vadian, the preacher, teacher and burgomaster. He lectured on the New Testament in the style of his old friend Zwingli. One of the people said: "Here in St. Gall it is not only allowed to hear the word of God, but the magistrates themselves teach and preach it." Of the troubles caused by certain fanatics we shall speak on other pages.

In the heart of the canton of St. Gall lies the little valley canton of Appenzell. One of its young men, Walter Klarer, was educated at Paris, and was doubtless one of the young Swiss who tossed up their hats with joy when they heard that Zwingli had been called to Zurich. He read the writings of the Reformers, and returning to his native valley he began to preach the gospel with all his energy. The inn-keeper Rausberg, a member of the council, a rich and pious man, opened his house to all the friends of truth. About this time a famous Captain Berweger returned from Rome, having been fighting for the popes. He began to wage war upon the evangelical Christians. But one day he remembered what wickedness he had seen in Rome, and opened his Bible to see who were in the right. He read with astonishment the words of Christ. He attended the sermons of the new preachers and embraced the gospel. When he saw the crowds which could not find room in the churches, he said, "Let the ministers preach in the fields and public places." As a great captain thus lifted the standard, the people rallied to his call, and in spite of a violent opposition, the meadows became like cathedrals, and the mountains echoed with the tidings of salvation.

Zwingli wrote to the zealous preacher, James Schurtanner: "Your zeal is a balsam of life to believers. My heart leaped for joy when we heard that the pious people of Appenzell had received the word of God. It is to be hoped that, although their canton is the last in the order of the confederacy,* it will not be the last in the faith. Christian doctrine and practice can be nowhere more easily planted than among a people unschooled in the deceitful arts of the world. Salute your faithful fellow-workers, the bishop of Gais, Bernardin, and all who hold truly to God, and pray for me with all your people."

A Zurich Christian, named James Burkli, went southwestward from his home, perhaps dining with George Binzli at Wesen, and looking in upon the native place of his good pastor Zwingli. Then crossing the Rhine and entering Flasch, the first village of the Grisons, he went into the house of the saddler, Christian Anhorn, who listened with wonder to the tidings of his guest. The villagers invited the stranger to preach to them in the church. He was not a priest, and dared not ascend the pulpit. Taking his station in front of the altar, he opened to his surprised hearers the words of the blessed life. Anhorn stood near with a troop of armed men to protect him from any sudden attack. Many of the people dared to believe. The rumour of this preaching spread far and wide, so that the church was

---

* Appenzell joined the Swiss league in 1513.

thronged on the next Sabbath. In a short time the majority of
the people demanded a reform. They wished to have the Lord's
Supper administered in the mode observed by the apostles, and
with one consent soon abolished the mass.

But the neighbouring people of Mayenfield took the alarm.
The priests were at work. On a sudden they rang their bells,
gathered the affrighted villagers, described the fearful dangers
that were threatening the Church, and then marched at the head
of the riotous crowd to Flasch. The saddler Anhorn, who was
working in his field, heard the bells at the unusual hour, suspected an attack, returned home and hid Burkli in his cellar.
The house was soon surrounded by the mob, the doors were
broken down, the house was searched, but the preacher was not
discovered. The angry persecutors left the place, but they had
not driven thence the gospel.

The parish priest of Mayenfield was John Frick, steeped to
his eyes in popery, and a man of great note among his brethren.
The new doctrines filled him with horror, especially when he saw
that the men who were turning the world up side down had come
into the quiet country of the Grisons.* "I'll go to Rome and
learn from the holy father the best way to check this heresy
from overrunning the land." To Rome he went, but the vices
of the papal court shocked his simple mind. Italy seemed full
of iniquity. He returned home a converted priest, and, joining
the party that he had sought to expel, he became the Reformer
of Mayenfield. In later years he used to say pleasantly to his
friends: "Rome made me evangelical." A friend wrote to Vadian: "Oh that you could see how the dwellers in the Rhætian

---

* The Grisons belonged to the Swiss confederacy, and has been called
Italian-Switzerland.

Alps are throwing off the yoke of the Babylonian captivity!"
This friend was James Salandronius, or Salzman, who was proclaiming the truth in Coire, the capital of the Grisons. The
schoolmaster of that town, John Comander, had written to
Zwingli saying: "Your name is known in this country to many
who approve of your doctrines, and who are weary of the way in
which Rome extorts money from the people." A host of strong
men were rising up in the Church, ready to resist the fanatics,
who would soon attempt to flood the land with their blasphemies.
But we leave them for a while, and return to Zurich by way of
the Tockenburg valleys.

When Andrew Zwingli was dying of the plague, he was able
to tell his brothers at home something of the doctrines which
Ulrich had been preaching. But they were not then alarmed
about his heresy, for he had only begun to show himself a Reformer. Still later, Ulrich wrote to them, saying, "When I hear
that you live by the labour of your hands, as your fathers did before you, I rejoice, because I see that you preserve the nobility
you derive from Adam. But when I learn that some of you, at
the risk of body and soul, serve for pay in the foreign wars, this
grieves me to the heart. I lament that out of honest peasants
and field-labourers, you make yourselves robbers and murderers
of your fellow-men, for the mercenaries are no better. God
grant that you may never do the like again, as indeed you have
promised me. You should also give heed that I do my work
faithfully, for God has called me to it. Do not believe the infamous reports which have been spread abroad concerning me.
I know very well what my good friend, my lord of Fischengen,*
our cousin, means. It is that I should go to work cautiously, lest

---

* John Meili, brother of Zwingli's mother.

great mischief befall me. May God reward the kind-hearted man for his good will. He has ever loved me as his own child, and I know he warns me in love. But be assured that no danger can approach me which I have not well weighed. . . . You are my natural brothers, but if you be not my brethren in Christ I am sorry, because then I must renounce you, yea, leaving father and mother unburied, if you attempt to draw me away from God. I shall quietly wait whatever God intends for me. Christ our Lord was put to death. May God guide you. I remain ever your brother, provided always that ye are brethren of Christ."

These brothers began to be alarmed for Ulrich, as they heard of the bold stand he had taken and how fierce was the enmity against him. They pictured to themselves the worst fate; they imagined him dragged to Constance and burned on the same spot where John Huss had been a martyr. These peasants were too proud to be called the brothers of a heretic. They wrote to him, describing their fears and anxious love.

Earnest men preached through the valleys of the Tockenburg, and met with a warm reception. Zwingli was full of joy, hoping that his kindred would accept the glad tidings. He addressed a long letter to "To an honourable council, and to the whole community of his native country of Tockenburg." The people were just on the point of deciding whether they would receive the gospel or remain in popery. After giving them much sound doctrine and advice, he says: "I should have often written to you but for two causes of hindrance: *First*, because my enemies would have immediately cried out that I was seeking human aid and consolation through you, which, God be praised, I did not need, for the pious in Zurich have not allowed any injustice to be done me. Yet when a door opened to the gospel, I take not holiday. *Secondly*, because, willing as I have ever been to preach the gospel in the place of my birth, I have always been hindered from it. Be intrepid and undismayed. Do not be misled by the strange stories told about me. Every talker may call me heretic, but I know the devil cannot make me out one with you."

This manly letter decided the victory of the gospel in the Reformer's native valley. The prophet had honour in his own country. In the same summer, 1524, the council declared that " the Word should be preached with one accord." But persecution began. Three ministers, Watteville, Doring and Farer, were accused by the abbot of St. Gall and the bishop of Coire, who had intermeddled with the affairs of his neighbours. These three men replied, quite in the spirit of Zwingli: "Convince us by the word of God and we will submit, even to the least of our Christian brethren: otherwise we will obey no man, not even the mightiest." The accusers went home wiser than they came. A circumstance shortly after occurred that roused the minds of these mountaineers.

A popular meeting was held on St. Catharine's day at Lichtensteig. The village was full of people. Two men of Schwytz, having come over on some law business, were sitting at a public table among the deputies. In conversation one of them said, " Master Ulrich Zwingli is a heretic and a thief."

" That cannot be," said the Secretary of State. "You must retract it or I will prosecute you by law." High words passed, and the noise drew general attention.

"Surely they are speaking of Master Ulrich," said George Bruggman, Zwingli's uncle, who was sitting at a distant table, as he sprang angrily from his seat.

Many others rose up, and followed him, as he sought vengeance upon the accuser. The uproar increased. The bailiff hastily assembled the council in the open market-place to prevent a pitched battle. They prevailed on Bruggman to be content with saying, "Master Ulrich is a pious, excellent, honest man, and whoever says the contrary is a liar, villain and thief." This was far from the gospel spirit, but it gave some satisfaction in those rough times.

"Remember what you have just said," replied the two Schwytzers, boiling over with rage, "and be sure we will not forget your words." They mounted their horses and rode home, to set their whole canton in motion against the Tockenburgers. But the latter, especially the men of Wildhaus, swore to stand by Zwingli to the last.

Zwingli heard the mutters of the storm and wrote to his native countrymen: "Be bold and fearless. Never mind the abuse against me. Refrain from insults, disorders and mercenary wars. Relieve the poor, protect the oppressed and trust in God." The storm passed away without annihilating the Tockenburgers. The mass was displaced by the true ordinances, and the Bible was restored to the homes of the people.

In Glaris the scholars and friends of Zwingli carried on the work with energy. Valentine Tschudi had letters from the Reformer, which aided him in advancing the kingdom of Christ. "The believer has no rest so long as he sees his brother in unbelief," said he; "therefore preach the good news."

We have taken a circuit westward and mingled in the good company of men earnest for the gospel. To understand the troubles of our Reformer and his co-labourers, we must fall in with some of the worst fanatics that ever broached their impieties. The Reformers of that age throughout Europe had two kinds of strong enemies; one, the Romanists, clamorous for the old papacy; the other, the extremists, who perverted the gospel and made the noisiest cries for liberty. These latter were called in one place Anabaptists; in another, Spiritual Libertines. There was no one great leader among them all. In each country some man arose and formed a sect of his own. We shall only notice certain of them who were most annoying to the Swiss Reformers.

When Doctor Vadian came from St. Gall to marry the daughter of the highly-esteemed Senator Grebel in Zurich, he found a guest at the wedding whom the family did not care to exhibit. This was Conrad, a brother of the bride. He was a youth of remarkable talents, violent toward all superstition, full of the most cutting satire, blustering, passionate, caustic and ill-natured. He was sent to Paris, where he sank in dissipation, protested his purity of life, and spoke ill of his neighbours. His vices rendered him unable to walk, and yet, being anxious to attend his sister's wedding, he suddenly appeared at home. The poor heart-broken father received the prodigal son with kind-ness; his tender mother shed tears and forgave. But he was still the same depraved genius, without natural affection or decent respect. Some time after Vadian had returned home his mother was recovered from the brink of the grave. Conrad wrote to his brother-in-law: "My mother has got well; she again rules the house; she sleeps, she rises, she scolds, she breakfasts, quarrels, dines, disputes, sups, and is always a trouble to us. She trots about, heaps and hoards, toils and worries herself to death, and will soon bring on a relapse." If she was such a woman as he describes, we may see some reason for his errors. But he, doubtless, wrote a slanderous sarcasm. Such was the man who would yet attempt to domineer over Zwingli and make a wreck of the Reformation.

Conrad set up for a Reformer, and wished to drive on faster

than Zwingli. Boasting himself to be somebody, he gathered about him other fanatics, and proposed to found a Church which would be more free than a pure liberty would permit. "Let us form a community of true believers," he said to Zwingli, "and have a Church in which there shall be no sin."

"We cannot make a heaven upon earth," was the reply. "Christ has taught us that the tares grow along with the wheat." Conrad hardly dared to appeal to the people; he would take a bolder course. He drew to himself certain of the most reckless men, such as William Rubli, the fallen priest; Louis Hetzer, who had thrown out his firebrand against images; Thomas Munzer, who had fled from Germany for his rash heresies,* and others more ignorant. They attempted to form a Church within the Reformed Church. At first they had no party standard. But they soon took their badge; it was *re-baptism.* All adults must be rebaptized—hence the term *anabaptist.* They declared infant baptism to be "a flagrant impiety, invented by the wicked spirit." Zwingli held public debates with them, but with no good result. They soon turned the Lord's Supper into an evening revel, rejected the ordination of preachers, said that no paid clergyman could preach the truth, recognized no authority in the State or the Church, claimed that they were free from all tithes and taxes, asserted that all property was to be held in common, and proclaimed other opinions which would defile our pages. The council put some of them in prison, and

* Thomas Munzer had been a preacher at Zwickau, where he fell in with the "Zwickau prophets," and became the leader of the Anabaptists of Germany. Banished from Saxony, he went to Waldshut and raised an insurrection among the peasants. Later events drove him into Switzerland.

banished several foreigners of their band. But this only maddened their zeal.

"Not by words alone," they cried, "but by our blood will we bear our testimony." Some of them girded themselves with cords, and with willow twigs ran through the streets, crying aloud, "Yet a few days and Zurich will be destroyed! Woe to thee, Zurich!" Fourteen men, among whom was Felix Mantz, who had sought to be professor of Hebrew, and seven women, were imprisoned and put on bread and water in the heretic's tower. Zwingli had protested against this punishment. After being there a fortnight, they loosened some planks in the floor and escaped, saying, "An angel opened the prison and led us forth."

A monk from Coire, named Blaurock, on account of his blue dress, joined the sect, and from his eloquence was called by them "a second Paul." He had travelled from place to place, rebaptizing all whom he could delude. His blasphemies were shocking; he claimed to be a second Christ, calling himself "the door," "the good shepherd," "the beginning of the baptism and of the bread of the Lord."

Conrad Grebel went to St. Gall, and there set up what he called "The Little Jerusalem," greatly to the annoyance of the excellent Vadian. To it he drew numbers from Zurich, Appenzell and other cantons. Zwingli's heart was wrung at the spread of this wickedness. He wrote a book against these errors; the council of St. Gall ordered it to be read in the churches. Once, when it was being read, a man exclaimed: "Give us the word of God, and not the word of Zwingli." Other voices were lifted: "Away with the book!" After service the fanatics raised the most foolish disorders. They skipped through the streets, danced in a ring, tumbled in the dust. Some burnt the New

Testament; others pretended to have had revelations from heaven.

In a village near to St. Gall lived John Schucker, with his five sons. They all, with their domestics, received the wild doctrines. Two sons, Thomas and Leonard, became noted in the sect. They killed a fatted calf, made a feast, and spent the night in revels and visions. The next morning, Thomas, who seems to have lost his reason, went through various ceremonies, and felt commissioned to take the life of his brother Leonard.. The family were called to the scene, where Leonard was kneeling, and with a sword he struck off his head, claiming that he was doing God's will. The bystanders recoiled with horror; the farm resounded with groans and wailings. Thomas, not half dressed, rushed barefoot and bareheaded out of the house, ran to St. Gall like a madman, entered the doors of the burgomaster Vadian, crying, "I proclaim to thee the day of the Lord!"

The frightful news spread through the town. The fanatic was seized, and after a trial was put to death. This event brought the people to their senses. The reign of this iniquity was ended in St. Gall. But it travelled on to the country of the Grisons. Three parties grew up in that region: that of the fanatics, that of the Reformers, and that of the persecuting papists.

A public disputation was held at Ilantz. The Grisons were largely represented. The vicar of the bishop sought to evade the discussion. "These debates lead to great expense," said he. "I am ready to lay down ten thousand florins in order to meet the costs: but the opposite party must do as much." This was a new trick.

"If the bishop has ten thousand florins at his disposal," cried out a rough voice in the crowd, "it is from us that he has wrung them. To give as much more to these poor priests would be too bad." The peasant spoke from a knowledge of the facts.

"We are poor people with empty purses," said Comander, the schoolmaster of Coire; "we have hardly the means to buy our bread: where can we raise ten thousand florins?" Every one laughed at the vicar's proposal and the business proceeded.

Among the spectators were Sebastian Hofmeister and James Amman of Zurich. They held in their hands the Bible in Greek and Hebrew. The vicar desired that all strangers should be excluded. "We have come" said Hofmeister, "to see that no violence is done to Scripture. Yet, rather than prevent the conference, we will retire."

"Ah," exclaimed a priest, looking at the books of the Zurichers, "if the Greek and Hebrew languages had never entered our country, there would have been fewer heresies."* Another said: "St. Jerome has translated the Bible for us; we do not want the books of the Jews." The visitors were finally permitted to remain, for the priests feared the people. Then Comander stood up and read the first of the theses which he had published: "The Christian Church is born of the word of God; it must abide by this Word, and listen to no other voice." He proved his doctrine, "setting down his foot with the firmness of an ox," says an eye-witness.

"There is too much of this!" said the vicar. He wished to adjourn the conference. Then a man arose from the crowd, tossed his arms, knitted his brows, blinked his eyes, and appeared out of his senses. He rushed toward Comander, and many thought that he was about to strike him. He was a

---

* Quite the same had been declared in the Sorbonne of Paris, not many years before.

schoolmaster of Coire. "I have written down several questions," said he; "answer them instantly."

"I am here," said Comander, "to defend my doctrines: attack them and I will discuss with you; if not, return to your place: I will answer you when I am through." The excited man returned to his seat, saying, "Very well." He bided his time. When the doctrine of the sacrament came up, he arose and argued that the bread was really the body of the Lord, for he said, "This is my body."

" My dear Berre," said Comander, "how do you understand the words, John is Elias ?"

"I understand that John was really and essentially Elias."

" Why then did John the Baptist say that he was not Elias?" The schoolmaster was silent, until at length he said: "It is true." Every one began to laugh, and the champion held his peace. Seven priests were convinced of their errors and devoted themselves to the truth. The Romish worship was abolished in many churches; complete religious liberty was proclaimed. Salandronius wrote: "The doctrines of Christ grew up everywhere in those mountains as the tender grass of spring, and the pastors were like living fountains watering those lofty valleys." In later years hundreds of refugees from Italy and Spain sought rest from persecution and found a welcome among the Grisons.*

The fanatic, Blaurock, still wrought mischief at Zurich. The council ordered his companion Mantz to be cast into the lake and drowned, as an example to the lawless and lewd sect. This did not check the shameful disorders. Blaurock was scourged and banished. As he was led out of the city, he shook his blue

---

* McCrie's Reformation in Italy, chap. vi. Presbyterian Board of Publication.

blouse and stamped the dust from his feet against that city. It seems that he went to the Tyrol, where the Romanists burned him alive. Zwingli took no part in these severities.

The father of Conrad Greble ran in debt through his generosity and his extravagance. He then was tempted to receive a foreign pension, although the penalty was death. His bribery came to light, and the aged senator gave his snow-whitè head to the block. His son Conrad had been the chief cause of all his misfortunes. He said that he could not pardon his ruined son, but he begged the authorities to do it. What was the end of Conrad does not appear.

CHAPTER XVII.

A NEW CHAMPION.

(1526.)

THE monks of St. Bridget, near Augsburg, had a good reputation for piety and for their profound and liberal studies. About the first of the year 1520 there came to their gates a man seeking a retreat for leisure, study and prayer. He asked the friars, "Can I live among you according to the word of God?" This was Œcolampadius. Six years before, Zwingli had been roused by his preaching when on a visit to Basle. He had returned to his native Weinsburg, where he was soon disgusted with the disorders and profane jests of the priests. He had been invited, in 1518, to Augsburg, as cathedral preacher, but finding that city agitated by the late debates between Luther and Dr. Eck, he refused the appointment. It was a time when he must decide whether he would remain a papist or cast his lot with the Reformers. He inclined to the side of Luther. This frankness soon raised up enemies against him. The times were in confusion, the world seemed to be shaken with moral earthquakes, the Church was in a tempest, and this mild, peace-loving man feared to expose himself to the storm. He fixed his eyes on the convent of St. Bridget, and the monks assured him that he could live among them "according to the word of God." He entered the monastery on the express condition that he should be free, if ever the service of the gospel should call him into the field.

"It was well," says D'Aubigne, "that the future Reformer of Basle should, like Luther, become acquainted with that monastic life which is the highest expression of Roman Catholicism. But here he found no repose; his friends blamed the step; and he himself openly declared that Luther was nearer the truth than his adversaries. At this time Œcolampadius was neither Reformed nor a follower of Rome; he desired a certain purified Catholicism, which is nowhere to be found in history, but the idea of which has bridged the way for many minds."

He began to point out to the monks certain errors in their books, their rules and their practice. Their anger was stirred up at once, and they exclaimed, "Heretic! apostate! you deserve to be thrown into a dungeon for the rest of your days." They forbade him to attend the public prayers—a strange way to bring back a wanderer. But human nature was not well understood in convents, nor among papists, who had so long domineered over men that they had forgotten the arts of persuasion. 'There were other dangers. Doctor Eck had an eye upon him, and was breathing out his threats.

"In three days," said the monks, "the party of Doctor Eck will be here to arrest you."

"Will you give me up to the assassins?" he inquired. The friars gave no answer; they neither wished to save him nor to destroy him. Some friends learned of his danger. At just the right hour they came to the convent with horses to carry him to a place of safety. The monks resolved to allow the departure of a brother who had brought too independent a mind into their cloister. He had been there nearly two years. "Farewell," said he, and he was free. He was saved; he began to breathe a better air.

"I have sacrificed the monk," he wrote, "and I have regained the Christian." But his flight was known everywhere; his heretical writings excited suspicion wherever he went. The people shrank back at his approach. He knew not what would become of him, until the knight Francis Sickengen opened to him the castle of Ebernburg. There he preached to Ulrich Hutten and other noble warriors, who wished to fight popery with sword and bombshells. He was not military enough in his sermons for them. But there, in a castle among illiterate warriors, this "most humble man of his age" was putting on another armor than that which glittered and clattered to no purpose.

The bookseller Cratander invited him to Basle, for booksellers had a vast influence in those times. They were generally men of high literary culture. The invitation was cheerfully accepted, and in 1522 he was greeted by his old friends in that city. There he lived simply as a man of learning, with no public occupation, until he was named as the curate of St. Martin's church. This call to a humble and obscure parish had much to do in deciding the Reformation in Basle. An attentive audience filled the church whenever he preached. His public lectures were so successful that even Erasmus wrote, "Œcolampadius triumphs among us."

Zwingli rejoiced, saying, "This mild yet firm man spreads around him the sweet savour of Christ, and all who crowd about him grow in the truth." It was often rumoured that he would be forced to leave Basle and resume his perilous pilgrimage. His friends were alarmed, but fresh victories made him more safe and calmed their fears. Luther heard of him, and talked with Melanchthon every day about the new ally. Yet Luther had some fears lest he should be too much under the power of Erasmus, who was playing the trimmer to please Rome. The Saxon Reformer wrote to him, to put him on his guard: "I much fear that Erasmus, like Moses, will die in the land of Moab, and never lead us into the land of promise."

It was during these days that William Farel, "the Bayard of the battles of God," escaped from France and found a refuge in the house of Œcolampadius. The bold, adventurous, powerful Frenchman needed schooling under the mild, even-tempered Franconian. Unlike as they were in nature, they loved each other with a love that works conformity. One imparted his fire, the other his gentleness. It was in the house of the Reformer of Basle that Farel was ordained to the work of the ministry. and he went from it to become the first Reformer in French-Switzerland, second to no other in the fervour of his spirit, the ardour of his prayers, the power of his stormy eloquence, and the boldness of his adventures in capturing the strongholds of the pope and the prince of darkness. We have traced his romantic life, and one of its most interesting periods relates to the time when he was the guest of the man who was "the light of the house."

The gentle preacher at St. Martin's had decided between Rome and the Reformation; now he must decide another question. He could see that Luther and Zwingli were the two leading Reformers of that period. He could see that they agreed in the great doctrines pertaining to Christ. But they held different views in regard to certain ordinances of the Church, especially the Lord's Supper. On no other subject were the Reformers so long in coming at the simple truth. They all rejected the Romish doctrine of transubstantiation. Luther held that the bread and wine were not changed into the real body and blood of

Christ; but yet that the body of Christ was present in the sacred symbols, and was received by the communicant. This was the doctrine of the *real presence*. Zwingli held that the bread and wine were merely symbols of the body and blood of Christ, and memorials of his death and his love. A long and earnest controversy was beginning; every man must take sides with one of the great rising parties.

On which side would Œcolampadius take his stand? He sought for light and guidance; he studied the Scriptures and agreed with Zwingli. Entering the lists, he sent forth a little book on the meaning of the Lord's words: "This is my body." He understood it to mean, *This is the symbol of my body.* It is said that this book "excited an immense sensation, not only in Basle, but in all Germany." Luther did not expect it. He was far from being pleased. But Zwingli felt that a new champion had been won to his cause.

Affairs in Switzerland were in a critical state. The Romanists were moving heaven and earth to put down the new doctrines. They cried out that the Reformers were bringing ruin upon the confederacy. "All order is destroyed in the Church," said a chief of Lucerne. "The sacraments, the mother of God and the saints are despised, and terrible calamities threaten to dissolve our praiseworthy confederation." They declared, "Berne must renounce the evangelical faith." The Bernese councils decreed that they would maintain "the ancient faith, the holy sacraments, the mother of God, the saints and the ornaments of the churches." Rome seemed to be regaining all her lost ground in the city where Haller had been so encouraged. All the married priests not born in the canton were banished; they drove from their borders all who were suspected of Lutheranism; they put every book sold by the booksellers under a rigid censorship and burned the writings of the Reformers. Haller was in danger. John Faber, the vicar, declared publicly and falsely that Haller had bound himself before the council to restore the mass and preach the doctrines of Rome. The five papal cantons were creating trouble and charging it upon Zurich and Berne, which had nestled the Reformation.

The times demanded a public discussion. The Romanists insisted upon it. They had pronounced such debates unlawful when they knew that they would be beaten, but now they hoped to win by force, and debates were lawful enough if they could be the gainers. They looked about for a champion. Doctor Eck offered himself. He feared nothing, and hoped to call forth Zwingli and finish him. "Zwingli has, no doubt, milked more cows than he has read books," said he, sneering at the shepherd of the Tockenburg. He had disputed with Luther and Carlstadt, and been richly rewarded by the pope. Also the papists were raising large sums for Eck, as money was never his aversion.

Where should the discussion be held? Zwingli wrote to the boasting Eck: "What need have you of addressing me to appoint a time and place to dispute? If you are so eager for it, come to Zurich when you choose. The gates of this city will stand open to you at all times, and I shall know how to answer you, depend upon it. If I have led my people astray, it is reasonable that I should be made to lead them back in the right path, by having it proved in their presence that I am a false teacher. Set off, then, on a journey to Zurich." The council sent messengers with a pressing invitation and a safe-conduct to Doctor Eck. "I cannot go," replied the crafty Eck; "I have made other arrangements with the Diet."

The arrangements of the confederate Diet were to draw Zwingli out of his city, where he had strong defenders, and get him into the hands of the Romanists. They sent him a safe-conduct to Baden, a small town and watering-place in Argau, and fixed the time for the conference in May, 1526. "Nay," said the Zurich council, "our Reformer shall not go to Baden, nor, as he proposes, to St. Gall, or Schaffhausen; for, by an article of the federal union, every accused person should be tried at the place of his abode. Zwingli is bound to defend himself only in Zurich."

It was most happy that Zwingli had something to restrain him. There was danger threatening him. He saw the trap and boldly replied to the Diet, "How can you ask me to throw myself into the power of my foes? Do I not know that they resolved two years ago to seize me wherever they could find me out of my canton? In Friburg they burned my writings; in Lucerne, my effigy. I well know who advise me to put myself in their hands. Is it not a common saying among them that they are not bound to hold a safe-conduct with heretics? Has not one of their chiefs said that his great desire was to hang Zwingli?" It was quite plain that if Zwingli should go to Baden, the "end of controversy" would be the death of the Reformer. "If we had him once here," said a member from Lucerne, "he should have prison-diet for the rest of his days."

"I entreat you, as you value your life," wrote his brother-in-law, Leonard Tremp, "do not go to Baden. I know that they will not respect the safe-conduct." A fanatic wrote him, "Zwingli, I warn you that your hour is come." It was said that a plan was laid to seize him, gag him, throw him into a boat, carry him to some secret place, and deal with him according to the mercy of the Diet In all this one can see the hand of Faber, who had not rested since the day that he had felt the deepest chagrin because the Reformer had refused the "brilliant promises" of the pope. Zwingli avoided the snare so clumsily set, and the council of Zurich firmly refused to let him appear at Baden.

Who then would appear against the redoubtable Doctor Eck? The mild, retiring, peaceable Œcolampadius found himself a chosen hero before he suspected it. At first "he hesitated, like a timid stag worried by furious dogs," says an old chronicle, but at last he resolved to go armed with the word of God. He went to Baden. He then wished Zwingli to share his danger, but was soon convinced that if the intrepid Swiss Reformer were in that fanatical town, the very sight of him would kindle the anger of the Romanists, and neither of them would escape death. Haller took his place with the Reformer of Basle.

The papal party had all the advantages of pomp and pretension. "All the time the conference lasted," says the chronicler Bullinger, "Eck and his friends were lodged at the Baden parsonage, faring sumptuously, living gayly and scandalously, and drinking much wine, with which the abbot of Wettingen provided them. Eck took the baths at Baden (it was said), but. . . . in wine. The evangelicals, on the contrary, made a sorry appearance, and the people laughed at them as a troop of beggars. Their way of living was in strong contrast to that of the papal champions. The landlord of *The Pike*, the inn where Œcolampadius lodged, being curious to know what the latter did in his room, reported that every time he peeped in he found him reading or praying. It must be confessed (said he) that he is a very pious heretic."

In the church appeared Eck and Faber, with a train of prelates, magistrates and doctors, robed in silk and damask, adorned with rings, chains and crosses: Eck ascended the pulpit, which was splendidly decorated, and represented the papacy. The wits heard his stentorian voice and said he would make an excellent town-crier; they noted his broad shoulders, and hinted that he looked more like a butcher than a theologian. He spoke with great violence, flinging out his galling sarcasms, and sometimes letting slip an oath. But the president never called him to order. Nicholas Manuel, the poet of Berne, said:

> " Eck stamps with his feet, and he thumps with his hands;
> He blusters, he swears and he scolds:
> Whatever the pope and the cardinals teach
> Is the faith, he declares, that he holds."

In contrast with all this bluster and parade, Œcolampadius sat below the pulpit on a rough stool; he was plainly clad, his voice was low and soft, his bearing noble and patriarchal, his spirit calm and firm, so that when he spoke his adversaries said one to another, "If that tall, sallow man were on our side, it would be our gain."

The subjects discussed for eighteen days were such as the mass, the real presence, images, saints, purgatory and the Church. Eck was forced to fall back on the fathers, the traditions and customs of the Church, but his opponents said: "Custom has no force in our Switzerland unless it be according to the constitution; and in matters of faith the Bible is our constitution." Zwingli was quite as much engaged in these discussions as if he had been at Baden. He was the great battery hidden in the distance.

Thomas Plater was acting a good part in his own original way, along with two other students, who were taking notes of all that passed. Every evening one of them set out for Zurich with the feet of an Asahel, and by daybreak the next morning was back again with Zwingli's answers and opinions. Armed sentinels were posted at all the gates of Baden, and these young couriers had to invent excuses to get through, for the guards wondered why they were so often passing to and fro. Once the ingenious Plater came with a basket on his head, the hens therein, doubtless, well shaken to make a noise. "What are you going to do?" asked the sentinel.

"I am carrying chickens to sell to the gentlemen at the baths," was the reply. Some Zurichers had given him the game that he might enact his strategy, but as to the selling of them we are not further informed. One night he rapped at Zwingli's door, and found the wearied Reformer in bed. Plater relates: "He soon appeared, however, when he heard I was there, rubbed his eyes, and said: 'Ay! ay! you are a restless lad. Here I am, who have not been in bed these six weeks, thinking that as to-morrow is Pentecost I should get a snatch of rest. What are your tidings?'"

"Doctor Eck has proposed that the five Forest Cantons (all papal) shall have power to pronounce the final judgment." This would be leaving the most unlearned, superstitious and stubborn of all the Swiss Romanists to judge the Reformed doctrines.

"Who can make those peasants understand these great matters?" said Zwingli. He sat down, wrote out his opinion, and Thomas was on the way to Baden to employ his wit upon the sentinels before they had fairly ceased yawning for daylight and breakfast. Myconius said, "Zwingli has laboured more by his meditations, his sleepless nights and the advice he has sent to Baden, than he would have done by discussing in the presence of his enemies."

All this time the Romanists were sending letters far and wide, boasting of their victory. "Docter Eck has laid low his opponents," said they; "Œcolampadius is vanquished—he has sung his recantation; the dominion of the pope will be everywhere restored." There were many in Switzerland ready to believe these false reports. Yet in Baden the people were not so credulous. They noticed that the Romish champions "talked the loudest, but argued the weakest."

The monk, Thomas Murner of Lucerne, nicknamed "the tom-cat," stepped forward at the close of the debates and read forty abusive charges against Zwingli. "I thought," said he, "that the coward would come, but he has not showed his face; I declare forty times, by all human and divine laws, that the tyrant of Zurich and all his followers are knaves, liars, perjurers, infidels, robbers, gallows-birds"—with perhaps full forty other epithets—"and that no honest man, without blushing, can keep company with them." Such was the abuse which passed among the papists as "Christian controversy." They knew that Murner was a low, ribald monk, whose coarse abuse was an honour to every man whom he reviled. But they did not check the torrent of his revolting libels. It was known that Zwingli had published a "Zurich Almanac," in which the saints were not mentioned; this monk had published an answer to it, in the shape of "The Black Calender," containing the worst specimens of low scandal, and heaping his venom upon the names of the Reformers. All this was a matter of joy to the papal party, who circulated the black almanac in the five Forest Cantons.

Only Œcolampadius and ten of his friends voted against Eck's theses; the conference decreed that as Zwingli, the chief of this pestilent doctrine, had refused to appear, and as his defenders had resisted all conviction, they were to be cast out of the pale of the "Holy Catholic Church." War was preparing against stout old Zurich, with the lion on her shield. Would the bear of Berne stand up in her defence? During some of these stormy times, certain wretches, set on by foreign intriguers, attacked the

house of the Reformer, broke the windows and loudly called for
"the red-haired Uli, the Vulture of Glaris." Zwingli roused
up and ran for his sword. This act was characteristic of the
man. He was yet to grasp the sword in defence of the cause of
liberty, religion and God.

We regret to find the once good friend, Glarean, who had
studied with Zwingli, recommended him to his native Glaris,
and written letters so warm in his praise, now turning coldly
from the Reformer. Glarean had been led away by Erasmus,
then by the Romanists. He was devoted to the ancient classics,
and loved the new movement, so far as it revived their study.
It was the Rennaissance, and not the Reformation, that won his
heart. He became a bitter enemy of many of the Reformers,
living to the age of seventy-four. He wrote several works, but
even the Romanists condemned them. In the Index Expurga-
torius, he is classed with "the authors of cursed memory, whose
works, published or yet to be published, are forbidden without
exception."

In contrast with this man, Vadian was a firm supporter of the
Reformer. He and many friends at St. Gall engaged to stand
by Zurich, even to the death. One day the dignified Vadian
and about thirty sharp-shooters came to Zurich, where a great
banquet was prepared for them by the guilds. Eight hundred
persons marched through the town, drums beating and banners
flying. Zwingli and his colleagues were among the guests. It
was a genuine Swiss demonstration; and the Reformers, warriors
and statesmen mingled together and strengthened the ties of
union in the State, whatever may have been the result in the
Church. We may be sure the affair was conducted with dignity.

CHAPTER XVIII.

ZWINGLI AT BERNE.

(1526–1528.)

THE two protestant chieftains went home from the famous Baden conference to rouse the enthusiasm of the people in the cause which they had defended. Berne and Basle were yet to be separated from Rome, and become greater centres in the Reformation.* Œcolampadius did not return to Basle without fears and anxieties. The first blows were to fall upon him, but his mild words turned the wrath of man. Men had perceived more sound than sense in the clamours of Doctor Eck, and had been impressed with the weight of his opponent's gentle language. Calmness ever becomes a good cause. Pious men received the modest Reformer with admiration. In vain did his enemies make every effort to drive him from his pulpit. He grew bolder; he preached with increasing energy, and the people had never shown such a thirst for the word. Here we leave

---

* D'Aubigne divides the history of the Swiss Reformation into three periods, in each of which there is a different centre of influence. From 1519 to 1526, the centre was Zurich, then entirely German; from 1526 to 1532, it was Berne, both German and French; in 1532, Geneva became the focus of light. In the first two periods, Zwingli is the eminent leader; in the third, Farel and Calvin are the most prominent. In the present volume we are treating of the work under Zwingli and his co-labourers.

him for a few months, giving welcome to French refugees, urging on the printers in scattering the truth, imparting wisdom to all who write for his advice, working with all his might, and waiting for happier times. It would be pleasant to dwell with him and share his peace, but we are called forth into the storms that beat in fury upon Berne.

No sooner had Haller returned from Baden to his home than the smaller council ordered him to celebrate the mass. "I appeal to the Great Council," said he, "and there I will make my reply." The people thought it their duty to defend their pastor, and hastened to the spot. Haller, in alarm, declared that he would rather leave the city than be the occasion of any disturbance. After quiet was restored, he said: "If I am required to perform mass, I must resign my office. The honour of God and his word are dearer to me than any care about what I shall eat or wherewithal I shall be clothed."

He spoke with deep emotion; the members of the council were affected; even some of his opposers burst into tears. Moderation was again stronger than rashness. Haller must be retained. But still some show of concession must be made to Rome: therefore Haller was deprived of the office of canon. He was then appointed the chief preacher, which was all the better for the holy cause of truth. It separated him the more from the papacy, and gave him greater independence. In wrath over this last movement, certain of his most violent foes took their revenge by withdrawing from the council and the city and throwing up their citizenship. "If they can stand it," we hear Nicholas Watteville saying to the Mays, the Manuels and the Weingartens, "I think we can. Disgust is not dangerous when it sends one into the wide world to vent it on the winds." Haller wrote: "Berne stumbled, but has risen up again with greater strength than ever." All Switzerland was astonished at this turn of affairs.

The news filled Zwingli with delight. Shortly after, he wrote to Haller: "Everything here below has its course. After the raw north wind come milder airs; after the scorching heat of summer, autumn pours forth its golden treasures. And now, after severe contests, our Creator has opened a way for us into the very camp of our enemies. Ought we then to lose courage? Nay, God has opened to you, and to us all, in Berne, a door, at which we can take in the dove, for a time scared away, but ever longing to return. Be thou the Noah to receive and save her."

Young Haller was not alone. The aged Francis Kolb had been driven away from Wertheimer, where he had been a faithful pastor. He had taken refuge in the Carthusian monastery at Nuremberg. Hearing that the "dove of the gospel" was again received at Berne, he went thither to preach to his compatriots, asking no other stipend than the liberty of freely preaching Jesus Christ. Though bending under the weight of years, and crowned with locks of gray, he was young in heart, full of fire and of indomitable courage.

Haller, thirty-five years of age, moved with a more measured step, spoke with gravity and was cautious of giving offence. The aged man seemed the younger of the two. Heart and hand they toiled on together.

Never has there been a great revival in the Church without disturbances from radical men, who cannot wait for truth to conquer. It was not long before certain enthusiasts went about saying, "We cannot worship in churches where there are images of the saints." They drew much people after them. The council began to frown and threaten. Haller knew there was danger, but he said, "It is our duty to drive out their errors, and not their persons. Let us employ no other weapons than the sword of the Spirit." They were persuaded to discuss with the Reformer; six of them renounced their errors, two others were banished by the magistrates.

It was not long before every parish became a field of strife. The peasants disputed with the priests about the Scriptures, and usually had the best of the argument. "If our lords of Berne," said the poor people, "grant to the pastors the liberty of preaching, why not grant to the flocks the liberty of acting." They wished to banish the mass, the images and all the relics of popery, and keep their good pastors and their Bibles. The Romanists grew violent. One of them tried abuse and threats, but the peasants were too strong for him, and made him take back his words, with a smooth, round apology to them. Another bailiff was more cunning. When the pastor at Rudersweil was preaching with earnestness one day, he led on a band of fifers and trumpeters, interrupted the sermon, and invited the village girls to quit the church for a dance. But these wiles did not hinder the reform. Shoemakers, masons, carpenters, bakers, weavers, tanners and tailors rose up and cleared many churches and convents of all the signs of popery. The excitement became intense; a conference was called. The Swiss bishops were invited, but as it was to be a debate according to the Scriptures, they had nothing to do with it. Romish doctors, too, were requested to be present.

"We have received the letter of this leper, this accursed heretic, Zwingli," said such doctors as Eck and Murner. "They want to take the Bible for their judge. . . . We will not go to Berne; we will not crawl into that obscure corner of the world; we will not combat in that gloomy cavern, that school of heretics. Let these villains come out into the open air, and contend with us on level ground." The only ground level enough for them was some little popish town where they could make a parade and bluster, to the amazement of its rustic inhabitants. So the conference was to be held without the great bishops and doctors.

Haller felt timid as he stood alone to defend the truth. He wrote to Zwingli: "We are between the hammer and the anvil. We hold the wolf by the ears, and know not how to let him go. Come and help us. The houses of Watteville, Tremp and Berthold are open to you. Come and command the battle in person." Zwingli went.* Œcolampadius wrote that he was coming, and said, "I am ready, if necessary, to sacrifice my life." Others said the same thing. Haller took courage. The discussions were similar to those which we have already noticed. One most remarkable conversion startled the people.

Zwingli went into the pulpit on Sunday, and when reciting the apostle's creed, he paused after the words, "He ascended into heaven, and sitteth on the right hand of God the Father Almighty." The Reformer then said, "This is in contradiction to the mass." Suddenly a priest, robed for the service and just about to offer the mass in one of the chapels, stopped in astonishment and listened to Zwingli, whose words electrified the

---

* It seems strange to us that Zwingli had to get permission from the senate of the canton to go to Berne for a religious synod. But in such cases the council had power over him. Safe-conducts were formally made out, and the learned men Conrad Pellican, Megander and Rudolph Collin were ordered to attend him, all at the expense of the government. The Romish Church had long claimed power over the State; the danger now was that the State would claim too much authority over the Reformed Church.

people. The priest went up to the altar, stripped off his mass-robes, threw them down, exclaiming, "Unless the mass rests on a more solid foundation, I can celebrate it no longer." The assembly was thrilled. Such a conversion, at the very foot of the altar, was soon told abroad, and had a most powerful effect upon the citizens. The mass must fall. In it lay the strength of Rome, and with it Rome must fall.

Two evenings afterward the bells were ringing in every steeple, for it was the eve of the festival in honour of St. Vincent, the patron saint of the city. People talked that night as they pleased about such feasts. On the morrow the doors were open, the tapers burning, the church filled with incense. But no one appeared; no priest to say mass, no devout persons to hear it! St. Vincent must fall. In the evening it was the custom for the canons to chant vespers with great pomp. The organist was at his post, but not one canon showed himself. The vespers must fall. The poor organist, who earned his bread by playing, turned sadly away, fearing that his craft would soon be gone. Immediately after he left the church, some rash men fell upon the organ, which they associated with nothing but superstitious rites, and broke it to pieces. Thus it went on St. Vincent's day. No more mass, no more organ, no more anthems!

The butchers'* company had a chapel of their own, which they proposed to decorate the following day. They would show their strength for Rome. They marched, carrying green branches of trees, with a foreign priest in the train and a few poor scholars. The priest performed his services, the boys sang in place of the silent organ, and the butchers felt proud of their victory. But it was soon announced that the conference had

---

* Every trade had its guild or company. Those of the bakers, carpenters, masons, &c., had declared for the reform.

convinced two or three of the papal clergy of the truth, and they had joined the Reformers. The two city councils had decreed that the mass should be abolished, and that every one might remove from the churches the ornaments he had placed there. Very soon twenty-five altars were overthrown; many images destroyed, but without disorder or bloodshed. The children went through the streets singing the downfall of the popish idols. Such bold work had not yet been done in Switzerland. Perhaps one reason was, William Farel was there.

"Should any one take away the altar of the butchers' company," cried out a fat papist, "I will take away his life." This provoked cutting replies from the scoffers: "Let the cathedral be stripped of its ornaments, and it will make a good stable. When the Oberlanders come to market, they will be happy to put up their cattle in it." "Oh what times! what manners! what misfortunes!" said the Romanists in despondency. "All this might have been prevented if our bishops had only given more time to learning and less to lewd company!"

Once more was the voice of Zwingli to be heard before he returned home. He went into the cathedral the day after the image-breaking, saw the fragments piled here and there in the aisles and porches, crossed over the "eloquent ruins," entered the pulpit, and with great emotion said: "Victory has declared for the truth, but perseverance alone can complete the triumph. Christ persevered even until death. . . . Cornelius Scipio, after the disaster at Cannæ, having learned that the surviving generals thought of abandoning Italy, entered the senate-house, although not yet of senatorial age, and, drawing his sword, constrained the affrighted chieftains to swear that they would not leave Rome to the enemy. Citizens of Berne, to you I address a similar demand; do not abandon Jesus Christ."

The effect was tremendous. Then turning to the fragments that lay near him, he continued, "Behold these idols! conquered, mute and shattered, they lie before us. These corpses must be dragged to the shambles, and the gold that you have spent upon such foolish images must henceforth be devoted to comforting the living images of God. Feeble souls, ye shed your tears over these sad idols; do you not see how they break like any other wood or stone? Look at that one, its head gone! And that one, its arms broken! If this ill-usage had been done to the saints in heaven, and if they had the power ascribed to them, would they not have been able to save themselves from being broken and maimed? Now, then, stand fast in the liberty wherewith Christ has made you free, and be not entangled again with the yoke of bondage? Fear not. That God who has enlightened you will also enlighten your confederates, and Switzerland, regenerated by the Holy Ghost, shall flourish in righteousness and peace."

The Romanists, sore with defeat, attempted to vex Zwingli and his friends on their return home by closing the gates of Bremgarten. But "my lords of Berne" had provided for Zwingli's safety. They sent two hundred armed men with him, who proceeded in brave style, lance in rest. The wiser ones of Bremgarten came to a parley; the gates were opened, and the escort passed through the town, attracting the people into the streets to learn that the Reformers were becoming a power in the world. Zwingli, without accident, re-entered Zurich, says Luther, "like a conqueror."

In this triumphant company was probably Doctor Vadian, who had presided at the conference. He went home to St. Gall and told the council how they did things at Berne. "A good example!" said they; "and shall we be far behind them?" They

removed the images from the church of St. Magnus, their patron saint; they carried a silver hand of his to the mint along
with other ornaments, and receiving the coin, they gave it to the
poor. The people were curious to know what those "ancient
mysteries" were, so long veiled from their eyes and called "holy
relics." They went to the abbey, laid hands on the shrines* and
the crosses which they had worshipped from childhood, opened
thus the chests of treasures, and lo! what? Nothing but some
resin, a few coins, old rags, paltry wooden images, a skull, a
tooth and a snail's shell! These were the relics they had been
adoring as "hidden mysteries." Rome fell in their respect as
suddenly as a meteor. A laugh of irony was raised throughout
the canton. Thus in the extreme northeast of reforming Switzerland the work of image-breaking was progressing; we shall
see how it went on in the extreme northwest on the return of
Œcolampadius to Basle.

In Berne, the citizens, young and old, nobles and peasants,
met in the great cathedral as one great family, and raising their
hands to heaven, swore to defend the councils in all that they
should undertake for the good of the State and the Church.
The councils published an edict of reform, and "threw for ever
from the necks of the Bernese the yoke of the four (Swiss)
bishops," who, they said, "know well how to shear the sheep,
but not how to feed them."

More touching was a later assembly, when the grave councillors, the citizens and their wives, the peasants and their children, met in the great cathedral, to receive the Lord's Supper

---

* "Everybody fell upon the idols. We tore them from the altar, the
walls and the pillars. They were beaten down and smashed by hammers:
you would have thought it a field of battle. What a noise! what a breaking! what an echoing in the lofty ceiling!"—*Kessler, quoted by Hottinger.*

for the first time in the scriptural manner. In their very dress they were returning to the ancient Swiss simplicity; in their solemnity they were restoring the ancient spirit of the disciples. They received from the hand of their pastor the simple bread and wine as the memorials of the Saviour's death for them. Each felt that the Lord was with them, and all rejoiced in the fulness of the light that had dawned upon their city.

In the ruder districts of this canton there were many who resisted the gospel for a long time and raised commotions on a small scale. The Romish cantons did all they could to provoke revolt and violence. Haller was again alarmed. The poet Manuel wrote a lament, which became very popular as a hymn and prayer in which he says:

> With rage our foes their hateful threats denounce,
> Because, O Lord, we love thee best of all;
> Because at sight of thee the idols fall,
> And war and bloodshed, shuddering, we renounce.

Gaspard de Flue, an unworthy grandson of the great Nicholas,* bore an ancient banner, which was followed by eight hundred men of Unterwalden, one of the most stubborn of the Romish cantons. They bore haughty heads, having in their hats pine-branches, the symbol of the old faith. They were resolved to interfere in matters of faith, in spite of the federal union. Marching westward into the canton of Berne, they increased their army, and proposed to move upon the city of Berne, and there restore the pope, the saints, the mass and all the machinery of popery. This was an attempt to make a peasants' war in Switzerland.

The Bernese roused, for the "Bear" was not oppressed with

---

* See Chapter ii.

sleep when the hunter drew nigh. "Let us perish," said some of the noble councillors, "rather than permit the interference of Unterwalden, and be exposed to the fiery violence of the peasants. Let our strength be in God and in loyalty." All the council responded with cheers. The great banner was unfurled, the town's-people grasped their arms, and the troops of the republic marched out under the valiant bailiff.

The Romanists were in haste to give advice to the warlike peasants when they saw Berne rising in her might. "You people of Unterwalden are all in the wrong," said they; "you must not fight your neighbours on account of their faith, nor trample on the ancient alliances. You must go home and behave so well that we will hear no more of this." Good advice, but why was it not given sooner? If the peasants could have been successful in restoring popery, it would have all been right; but the fearful power of Berne made a vast difference. "You will be beaten most woefully; therefore it is wrong." This was the logic. The rebels retired to the convent of Interlaken. Hearing that the Bernese were pushing on, and having their ardour chilled by the cold rains, and fearing that the snows would so cover the mountains as to prevent them from returning home, the men of Unterwalden left Interlaken during the night. Immediately the Bernese entered it, made their power known in that region, compelled the rebels to fall on their knees, confess their crimes and beg for pardon, and put to death four of the chiefs. The rebellion was over; the republic was satisfied. This was the first war in Switzerland between the Romanists and Protestants. No blood was shed on the field, but the spirit of the two parties was disclosed. The papists saw that they could not use force without meeting force. Whether the Protestants were right or not, depends on whether a Christian state is justified in repelling invaders with the sword. The Romanists of Unterwalden were the offenders; the Bernese acted in self-defence. The young republic was all the stronger for the Reformed element it contained, and it was often said, both by friends and foes, "God is become a citizen of Berne."

CHAPTER XIX.

THE UPRISING IN BASLE.

(1528–1529.)

ŒCOLAMPADIUS had often been thankful that he was not a monk, for he could now take care of his aged mother. Rome had broken the Christian ties of family and home; Protestantism restored them. The Reformer of Basle returned from the conference at Berne just in time to minister to his mother in her illness, close her eyes and lay her body in the tomb. This was not the only death that affected him.

For a long time the aged and pious bishop had tottered daily into the cathedral, supported by two servants, and with broken voice had celebrated the mass. He had been friendly to the Reformation, wishing, however, that it might not go so far as to become independent of Rome. Through him, Erasmus had come to Basle, and Œcolampadius at the time of his first preaching there. At his death there was a change. His successor, Gundelsheim, an enemy of reform, with a train of forty horses and minions, made his triumphal entry, proposing to overthrow the new order of things and restore the old. "Quite as well," thought Erasmus, who was now writing against Luther and holding Zwingli in contempt. But Œcolampadius wrote to the Zurich Reformer, "Our cause hangs on a thread."

The new and pompous bishop had not inspired such great admiration or terror among the citizens as he imagined. Deference to rank and pretension had wonderfully fallen ; respect for the people was greatly on the rise. It was the Reformation that restored the power of an enlightened people. The bishop feasted the aristocracy, courted the Romish nobles, and dreamed, as the wine touched his brain, that he would soon have the councils under his finger. The citizens had their feasts also; among their guests sat Œcolampadius and his colleagues; the gospel was talked of at the tables, and cheers were given with a zest at the mention of the good work in Zurich and Berne. In a short time the council began to lift a finger over the bishop and favour the reform. "Too many saints' days and festivals," said they, striking twenty of them out of their calender. It was on such days that Rome had enforced her superstitions. For a holiday the ignorant will believe almost anything. The better priests wished to cease from the mass : they were allowed the privilege. "It is all over with Rome," was now the cry of the people. The Reformer shook his head : he knew that the council was really trying to please both parties. "I am afraid," said he, "that by wishing to sit on two stools at once, Basle will fall to the ground."

But the news from Berne roused the people. The report of so much image-breaking, without one drop of blood, and with only a few angry parades by the butchers' company, created a sensation. ". Berne, the powerful old Berne, is reforming," said the people. "The fierce bear has come out of his den, where he has been asleep for so long. He is groping about for the warm rays of the sun. But our Basle, the city of learning, remains in darkness. It is time we were waking up !"

Five workmen of the spinners' company laid their plans for Good Friday, 1528. They kept them from the Reformer and the councils. The mass had been abolished in the church of

St. Martin, where Œcolampadius preached, but the images remained. These five men entered it and carried away all the "idols," no miracle preventing them. In a few days, thirty-four citizens thus cleared out the church of the Augustines. The council met and threw the five men into prison. The people rose and asked for them to be set at liberty. The spinners were released. In five other churches the images were suppressed. These half-way measures were not enough. The radicals wished to see a more violent movement; the Reformers desired to see a more thorough work of truth and of grace.

Eyes were turned to the great cathedral, which had stood for centuries, the chants of the mass resounding through the Gothic arches, and the statues of the saints exacting the reverence that was due to the Holy Trinity. Its lofty spire must become a monument to a revived Christianity. Within it the noisy priests called the Reformers, "heretics, knaves and profligates." In the churches sermons were preached against the abominations of the cathedral. One party reviled; the other used arguments. Everything tended to a fearful collision. But notice the difference between them in their measures. The Reformed party took the pen; the papists took the sword.

Two days before Christmas, three hundred citizens from all the companies assembled and drew up a petition to the senate or great council. They marched into the street quietly to present it. Just then a band of Romanists fully armed met them, flourished their swords and lances and endeavoured to bar the road. The burgomaster Mettinger, the leader of the papists in the senate, appeared. He haughtily refused the petition of the quiet citizens; he turned to the armed mob and begged them to disband. They returned to their homes, as did also the petitioners. Burgomaster Meyer, a strong friend of the reform, took the paper into the senate. It was ordered to be read. The purport of it was: "We address you as our well-beloved fathers, whom we are ready to obey at the cost of our goods and our lives. Take God's glory to heart; restore peace to the city, and oblige the pope's preachers to discuss freely with our ministers. If the mass be right, we want it in our churches; if it be an abomination in the sight of God, why should we retain it through love for the priests, and draw down his terrible anger upon ourselves and our children?" Thus calmly, firmly, orderly and with peaceable steps did the Reformed party make their first attempt. In all they did there was nothing violent or revolutionary. But their opponents were not satisfied; they were the first to depart from the legal course. They prepared for ruder measures, and the Reformed were incited to self-defence.

All sorts of rumours were set afloat by the papists; now the Zurichers were coming to sweep them away; again the bears of Berne were hurrying to devour them, or an Austrian army was on the march to defend them. They did this to have an excuse to collect weapons, fill their houses with stones, and raise the mob. Christmas came; the Romanists met each other armed; the priests were ready to shed blood, and make Christmas night one of terror and death. The Reformed citizens were too human not to be prompted in a wrong direction. They saw what a night was coming. They feared that the popish vespers were to be followed by the dying groans of God's people. The more violent among them ran from house to house, awoke their friends and told them where to assemble. Starting from their beds, some of them resorted to prayer as their best defence; others seized their weapons and hastened to the Gardener's Hall. They soon amounted to three thousand.

Both parties passed the night under arms. Not only a civil

war, but what is worse, "a war of hearths" might break out.
At length it was agreed that each party should send delegates to
the senate, that their rulers might decide upon their strifes. The
senate was sitting for long days. The Romish cantons sent their
deputies, who were allowed to enter the guarded gates, but it
seems that none were admitted from the Reformed cantons.
"We must satisfy both parties," said the majority of the senators. Hence half measures were adopted. To the one they said,
"You priests must preach the Word, but yet you can celebrate
your mass." To the other they said : "You preachers may proclaim the word of God, and meet once every week to consult
upon the Holy Scriptures." They also required the Reformed to
meet in the church of the Franciscans, and the papists in that
of the Dominicans, where the decrees would be read.

In the Franciscan church were soon gathered two thousand
five hundred people. The senators entered. The secretary read
the decree. "That shall not be," cried a citizen. A great
excitement prevailed. Voices cried loudly, "We will not put
up with another mass. No mass! we will die sooner."

The senate next went to the Dominican church, where all the
forces of Rome were mustered. They had dragged in every
popish foreigner, beggar, menial and minion, yet could number
only about six hundred persons, who heard the decrees, and
shouted, "We are ready to lose our lives for the mass. We
swear it." Their hands were raised as they repeated, "We
swear it! If they reject the mass, to arms! to arms!" The
senators were in the darkest perplexity.

Three days after, the two parties met in the church. Œcolampadius was in the pulpit. "Be meek," said he, "be teach-
able and obedient to the laws." As he preached the tears ran
down the cheeks of the people. The assembly offered up

prayers to God. Then they resolved to ask for a public discussion, such as had been held at Zurich and Berne, and abide by the decision. But it was soon found that the Romanists would not submit to this arrangement. Affairs grew more desperate. Again was relief sought from the senate, which met at night, moved slowly, but promised their decision on the morrow. It was the eighth of February.

The night was one of terror. Basle was in arms, her own citizens holding each other in seige. Chains were drawn across the streets, torches were lighted, old trees were covered with pitch and set on fire, six pieces of cannon were planted before the town hall, and all public places were filled with armed men. An angry word, the careless snap of a pistol, a cry of fear, a mere accident, might have brought on a battle, in which all would have blindly and madly rushed to destroy each other. All at once whispers were passed among the papal leaders. "There is no hope for us," said they. "We are in the minority." Burgomaster Mettinger, a heroic soldier who had fought at Marignan, lost all courage. In the darkness he fled to the Rhine with his son-in-law, took a small boat, and, unnoticed amid the fogs, rapidly descended the river. Other members of the council escaped to tell their alarms and their despair in quarters where they were sure of sympathy.

The Reformed citizens learned of this movement, and grew suspicious. "Beware of their secret manœuvres," they said. "Perhaps they are gone to bring in the Austrians, of whom they have boasted." This new fright brought more arms, and the sun rose upon a calm but firm army of citizens. No Austrians came. No decision was sent to them from the senate. Noon approached. The impatient people could not be restrained. They sent forty men to visit the different posts in the city. As these men were passing the cathedral, they turned into its doors. They looked about upon the symbols of popery. One of them had the curiosity to open a closet with his halberd. Out fell an image and broke into fragments on the stone pavement of the aisle. No miracle of judgment followed it. The spectators began to throw down other statues, until not an image was left unbroken. Erasmus had said with keen irony, "I am much surprised that these idols do not perform a miracle to save themselves; formerly the saints worked frequent prodigies for much smaller offences." Some priests ran to the cathedral, and the forty men retired.

But as the rumour spread, three hundred others came. They could not enter the cathedral. The priests had closed the gates, drawn the bolts, raised barricades and prepared to maintain a siege. The town's-people broke down one of the doors and rushed in. The hour of madness had come. They fell upon pictures, altars, confession-boxes and destroyed them all. The priests, who had fled into the vestry, were frightened beyond expression, and yet no attempt was made to discover or injure them. The fragments of the papal furniture were piled up in the squares and burned, doing some good in warming the crowd that gathered round the winter fires.

No report yet from the senators; in fact, they had never felt so far behind the times. The policies of one hour would not suit the next. But when they heard of the fires in front of the cathedral they rushed to the spot. They put forward their authority in quelling the tumult. It was throwing chaff against the wind. The people were already casting the idols out of all churches. They were preparing to cross the great bridge over the Rhine, enter Little Basle, and make a clean sweep of Romanism, to which its inhabitants were particularly devoted. In

fear the townsmen carried the images into their garrets to preserve them for a future day.   The citizens of Basle looked the
affrighted senators calmly in the face, and said, "What you have
not been able to effect in three years we will complete in one
hour."

No private property was injured; no priest or monk was
threatened; no man, woman, or child was intentionally harmed.
There was but one design, and that was to wipe out the insignia
of popery.   The senators now took a strange and sudden turn.
They sought to legalize the popular movement, thus changing a
revolution into a Reformation.   They learned to think promptly
and act with decision.   After an hour's deliberation, they granted
the citizens the privilege of electing the two councils; they abolished the mass and images from the whole canton, and gave a
liberty to the people which they had not dared to expect.   The
citizens, almost worn out with excitement, returned joyfully
to their homes to celebrate their new freedom.   They had
asked it first by a petition; they had gained it by a bloodless
battle.

What was left of the ruins of altars and papal machinery was
intended to be distributed among the poor for firewood on Ash
Wednesday.   But these unhappy peasants, eager for the fragments, began to quarrel about them, and fresh piles were made
in the streets and the match applied.   As the flames arose some
jester said, "These idols are really keeping their Ash Wednesday to-day."   Œcolampadius says that the friends of popery
"turned their horror-stricken eyes from the sacrilegious sight and
shed tears of blood.   Thus severely did they treat the idols, and
the mass died of grief in consequence."   A general amnesty was
published, hymns were sung in the churches, and devout thanks
rendered to God.   Everything in Basle was changed.   Œcolam-

padius had entered the city, a few years before, as a stranger, without resources or power, but now he stood forth as the Reformer whose gentle influence had secured the establishment of the truth. Even in the hours of madness, when men were doing what he disapproved, his spirit was manifest in the restraining of the people from robbery, revenge and personal injury. We do not justify all that was done by the citizens, nor do we draw the lines and set apart what we condemn. When Rome shows us an instance of a revolution in which she gained so bloodless a triumph amid intense excitement, then it will be time for us to point out the acts which we denounce in the great uprising at Basle.

Scarcely a monk, compelled to leave his nest in the convent and flee to more papal regions, could have felt more chagrin than did the old sage of Rotterdam at the result of all this commotion. His literary court would be broken up. Trimmers were no longer needed in Basle. No longer would he reign as the prince of the schools. For a long time previously he had turned his head aside when he met Œcolampadius. And now he must either compromise with his protectors or take his leave. He made up his mind, and thus wrote: "The torrent which was hidden underground has burst forth with violence and committed frightful ravages. My life is in danger. Œcolampadius possesses all the churches. People are continually bawling in my ears. I am besieged with letters, caricatures and pamphlets. It is all over; I am resolved to leave Basle. Only, shall I or shall I not depart by stealth? The one is more becoming, the other more secure."

Honour and fear cannot always be made to harmonize. Great men when affrighted can become ridiculous. Erasmus was not in such danger as he imagined, nor indeed was he so important in the eyes of the people. But he asked **that** the boatman who was to carry him down the Rhine might take him in at some unfrequented spot. The senate opposed it, and the timid philosopher was obliged to enter the boat as it lay near the bridge, on which was collected a crowd to see him off. He retreated to Friburg in Brisgau, where the Romanists seemed likely to hold sway to the end of time.

Oswald Myconius was yet to be called to Basle, along with other scholars, to fill the vacant chairs in the university. Education in that centre of influence was henceforth to be more thoroughly Christian. A confession of faith was published. Popery had fallen in spite of the secular and papal power. "The wedge of the Lord," says the Reformer, "has split the hard knot."

After the death of his mother, Œcolampadius was alone, under the weight of domestic and public cares; his house was like an inn for all fugitive Christians. His tender thoughts had already taken a happy direction. "I shall marry a Monica,* or else remain a bachelor," he had said. The daughter of a brave knight, the widow of a young scholar named Keller, seemed to meet his idea, and he married her, saying, "I look to the ordinances of God, and not to the scowling faces of men." Every such violation of priestly celibacy was a blow to Romanism.

---

* The name of Augustine's mother.

CHAPTER XX.

*ZWINGLI FACES LUTHER.**

(1529.)

A POOR monk was lying in a gloomy dungeon at Marburg at the very time when Luther was in Wittemberg preaching the free pardon of sins through Jesus Christ. Men and women were seen cautiously gathering about a solitary loophole of the prison and eagerly listening to the voice of the monk, James Limburg, who was declaring that the priests had falsified the gospel for many centuries. For having more openly preached the truth he had been cast into the dungeon. These mysterious assemblies lasted a fortnight. On a sudden the voice ceased; the people came in vain. The monk was torn from his cell and hurried away. While on the road some weeping citizens of Marburg overtook him, and hastily pulling aside the awning that covered the car in which he was borne, they asked him, " Whither are you going ?" He calmly replied, " Where God wills." He was heard of no more by his friends; it is not known what became of him. Unto this day such sudden disappearances have not been rare in the papacy. But he had done something to prepare the way for the gospel in Marburg, a town in Lower Hesse.

---

* To avoid confusion in subjects, we anticipate certain events recorded in the next chapter. The Marburg conference was held after the first treaty of Cappel.

About seven years later, when Philip Melanchthon was returning from a visit to his mother, along with some other friends, he met a brilliant train near Frankfort. The chief personage was the Prince Philip of Hesse, who had left his castle at Marburg, and started for the tournament at Heidelburg, where he would meet all the princes of Germany. One of his attendants said to him after the other company had passed them, "It is Philip Melanchthon, I think." The young prince put the spurs to his horse, rode back, and coming near the doctor, asked, "Is your name Philip?"

"It is," replied the scholar, somewhat in wonder, and prepared to alight. "Keep your seat," said the prince; "turn round and spend the night with me; there are some matters on which I wish to have a little talk with you; fear nothing."

"What can I fear from such a prince as you?" answered Melanchthon, who perhaps now remembered that Philip had visited Luther, three years before, at the Diet of Worms.

"Ah! if I were to carry you off and give you up to Campeggio [the papal legate], he would not be offended, I think." The two Philips rode on together talking. At length Melanchthon begged permission to continue his journey. Philip, landgrave of Hesse, parted from him saying, "On one condition, that when you reach home you will carefully examine the questions we have been discussing, and send me your opinions in writing." To this the learned doctor assented.

Thus was the way opened for the return of the gospel to Marburg. Philip the landgrave soon received from Melanchthon an "Abridgment of the Revived Doctrine of Christianity." The prince accepted the truth with all his earnestness of character, and, in spite of the league against it, he ordered the gospel to be preached purely and freely. "Rather would I give up my body and my life, my subjects and my states," said he, "than the word of God."

The Swiss Reformers pleased the young prince, for he thought that they took bolder ground than the Lutherans, spoke more plainly against Rome, and had more fully separated the truth from error. He heard of the French monk, Francis Lambert, whom we saw riding away from Zurich on his little donkey. The monk was poor, but happy. "Formerly," said he, "when I was a hypocrite, I lived in abundance; now I consume sparingly my daily bread with my small family; but I would rather be poor in Christ's kingdom than possess abundance of gold in the dissolute dwellings of the pope." Philip saw that Lambert was just the man he wanted, and he invited him to Marburg.

Theses were the style of the times; Lambert had his. He posted up one hundred and fifty-eight propositions on the church door. Friends and foes crowded to read them. Some would have torn them down, but for the town's-people, who gathered on the public square and began to discuss them. There came to the spot a young priest, Boniface Dornemann, whom the bishop had extolled as above Paul in learning and as pure as the Holy Virgin, and whose self-conceit had lost nothing by the flattery. Finding that he was too short to read the theses of the tall Lambert, he borrowed a stool, mounted it, and commenced reading them to a numerous audience.

"All that is deformed ought to be reformed," ran the first thesis. "The word of God alone teaches us what ought to be so, and all reform that is otherwise effected is vain." "Hem," said the young priest; "I shall not attack that." He continued:

"It belongs to the Church to judge on matters of faith. Now the Church is the congregation of those who are united by the same spirit, the same faith, the same God, the same Mediator, the same Word, by which alone they are governed, and in which alone they have life." The young priest said, "I cannot attack that proposition."

"Since the priesthood of the law has been abolished, Christ is the only immortal and eternal priest, and he does not, as men do, need a successor. Neither the bishop of Rome, nor any other person in the world, is his representative here below. . . ."

. This thesis savoured of heresy. But Dornemann said, "Certainly I shall not attack that one." The people listened with astonishment. One of them, a wag or a fanatic, tired with these remarks, said, rudely, "Get down, you knave, who cannot find a word to impugn." Then pulling away the stool, the conceited priest fell flat into the mud. None were found willing to come forward and contest the propositions. In a large assembly Prince Philip sought to call out the superior of a convent at Marburg, but it was in vain. The friars were all dumb. Then Lambert clasped his hands, exclaiming, "Blessed be the Lord God of Israel, for he hath visited and redeemed his people." The Reform spread rapidly in Hesse, a synod was organized and a constitution adopted, some of whose articles were, "Let no one believe that by a bishop we understand anything else than a simple minister of the word of God. Each church should elect its own pastor."

The ardent Philip was pained at the manner in which Luther treated Zwingli in regard to the Lord's Supper. At the Diet of Spires, where the name *Protestant* was first applied to the Reformers, he had been pained to hear the papists cry out, "You are more disunited than ourselves;" which, however, was not the fact. John Hanner of Frankfort went to the prince and entreated him to allay the strife. He said, "I was the first who took the trouble of persuading the landgrave Von Hesse to attempt a reconciliation between the contending parties, and this took place even as early as the first Diet of Spires." Philip took the matter in hand with usual energy as soon as he returned home. He now invited the two chieftains to meet him in his castle at Marburg. Luther at first declined the invitation.

Zwingli was ready to go to the end of the earth if he might win his brethren or be convinced of any error. But the council of Zurich positively refused to let him go. He decided for himself: Resolving to depart, he raised his eyes to heaven, saying, "O God, thou hast never abandoned us. Thou wilt perform thy will for thine own glory." During the night of August 31, 1529, he prepared for the journey to Marburg, without waiting for Philip's safe-conduct, or receiving one from the Zurich council. In this he showed his courage, for he well knew that his way lay through perils and enemies. The prince had not concealed the dangers. He had promised an escort from Strasburg to Hesse, and for the rest "the protection of God." Zwingli wrote a note to the councils, saying that they must not suppose that he despised their authority, for he knew their love for him opposed his going. Just then a fourth message arrived from Philip, urging him still more earnestly to come. He sent it to the burgomaster as his further apology, and left his house privately by night, lest his friends should beset him with their entreaties and his foes should lay snares to entrap him in their wiles. He did not even tell his wife Anna, lest she should be in distress. Rudolph Collin, the professor of Greek, was to attend him. They mounted their horses and rode off rapidly toward Basle.

It was discovered the next day that he had gone; his enemies were elated. "He has fled the country," they said; "he has run away with a pack of scoundrels." All sorts of stories were put afloat. "As he was crossing the river at Bruck," said some, "the boat upset and he was drowned." Others declared, "The devil appeared to him bodily and carried him off." Bullinger says, "there was no end to their stories." The council now resolved to allow him to go—since he had gone at any rate—and sent a dignified councillor and an armed man or two to overtake him and attend him to Marburg. Zwingli was surprised at his own importance, when Basle and Strasburg sent statesmen and their theologians to conduct him on the way. Œcolampadius was in the goodly company. They went along by-roads, through forests, over mountains, and at length reached Marburg, escorted by forty Hessian cavaliers.

Luther had come on from Wittemberg, in company with Melanchthon, Jonas and others, but stopped on the Hessian frontier, declaring that nothing should induce him to cross it without a safe-conduct from the prince. It was sent him, and he reached Alsfeld, where the students kneeling under the Reformer's windows chanted their pious hymns. He entered Marburg one day after the arrival of the Swiss. Both parties went to inns, but the landgrave Philip came down from his romantic castle overlooking the city, and invited them to lodge beneath its ancient Gothic arches. They went, and fared like princes. "Ah!" said the pious doctor Jonas, as he wandered through the halls of the palace, "it is not in honour of the Muses, but in honour of God and of his Christ, that we are so munificently treated in these forests of Hesse." After dinner, Œcolampadius, Hedio and Bucer went and saluted Luther in the castle-court. The strong Saxon talked affectionately with the Reformer of Basle, but he was rude toward Bucer, with whom he had once been intimate, because the good pastor of Strasburg had joined the side of Zwingli.

Philip wished the Reformers to have private interviews with each other before entering upon the public discussion, that they might have free, unreserved conversation together. But he dared not put Luther and Zwingli together in the same room for such a purpose, lest they should become farther apart than ever before. It was thought to be wisest to give each of the champions the gentle friend of the other. Hence Zwingli and Melanchthon were placed in one room, and Luther and Œcolampadius in another. The combatants were then left to struggle, two and two. We cannot but smile at the arrangement. It shows that Philip was not so shallow as to depend upon feasting the Reformers into unity. He wished them to be united by the truth. A union of mere feeling is nothing; there must be agreement in faith—a faith that "worketh by love."

In the room where Zwingli and Melanchthon were shut up together, the contest began. "It is affirmed," said Melanchthon, "that some among you speak as if Christ were not essentially God."* Zwingli replied, "I think on the Holy Trinity with the Council of Nice and the Athanasian creed." "Councils! creeds! What does all that mean?" asked Melanchthon. "Have you not continually repeated that you do not recognize any other authority than that of Scripture?" The answer of Zwingli was such that the Reformed † churches have ever since agreed with it: "We have never rejected the councils when they are based on the authority of the word of God. The first four councils are truly sacred as regards doctrine, and none of the faithful have rejected them." All this was at the basis of the

---

* We give a mere abstract of a part of the conversation.

† Those who accept Luther's views are called *Reformers;* those who adopt the views of Zwingli and Calvin are known as the *Reformed.*

discussion; the standard of authority and appeal must first be understood.

In the other room the same method of debate was followed. Luther complained because the Swiss would not admit that by baptism, simply, a man became a member of the Church. "It is true," replied Œcolampadius, "that we require faith—either an actual or a future faith. Why should we deny it? Who is a Christian but he who believes in Christ?" It was admitted that the infants of believing parents became members of the Church by baptism.

The signal was given for dinner; the four grave doctors met in the hall, and doubtless enjoyed the feast as one "where love is," though it was not "a dinner of herbs." Plans were proposed for a public debate. Luther opposed it; Zwingli insisted. It was finally arranged that the princes, nobles, deputies and theologians should be admitted. A great crowd of citizens and many visitors from the neighbouring cities were excluded. On the day fixed, Philip took his seat in the knights' hall belonging to the castle, surrounded by the nobles of his court, but so plainly dressed that none would have taken him for a prince. He did not wish to appear as a Constantine taking part in the affairs of the Church. Before him was a table where the four leading Reformers were seated. Behind them sat such men as Hedio, Bucer, Cruciger and Jonas. The eye of the good Jonas was studying the Reformer of Zurich, and he said, "Zwingli has a certain rusticity and arrogance; if he is well versed in letters (literature), it is in spite of the Muses. In Œcolampadius there is a natural goodness and amiable meekness. Hedio seems as liberal as he is kind. But Bucer possesses the cunning of a fox, that knows how to give himself an air of sense and prudence." Such was the opinion of Luther's confidant in regard to the Reformed party. He was severest on those of very moderate views. If he could have enjoyed Bucer's hospitality at his home and heard him talk, he would not have set him among the foxes.

Luther took a piece of chalk, bent over the table, and wrote upon the velvet cover four words. All eyes followed his hand, and soon read *Hoc est corpus meum*—"This is my body." He wished to have this text before him to strengthen his faith and be a sign to his opponents. After the conference was opened, Luther said, "I protest that I differ from my adversaries with regard to the doctrine of the Lord's Supper, and that I shall always differ from them. Christ has said, *This is my body*. Let them show me that a body is not a body. I reject reason, common sense, carnal arguments and mathematical proofs. God is above mathematics. We have the word of God; we must reverence and obey it."

Zwingli let the discussion proceed for some time and remained silent, for Œcolampadius was deriving an argument from such expressions as "I am the Vine," "That rock was Christ," "The lamb is the passover." He insisted that in the Supper we receive Christ spiritually—not bodily. Zwingli then showed how Christ teaches that "to eat his flesh corporeally profiteth nothing," (John vi. 63). Whence it would follow, that if we receive him only bodily in the Supper, he has given us something of no profit to us.

At this point a tall, spare man appeared to be greatly agitated. He was the Frenchman, Francis Lambert, who had once been convinced by Zwingli of his error in worshipping the saints. He had been at first on Luther's side, but in coming to the conference had said, "I desire to be a sheet of blank paper, on which the finger of God may write his truth." Now he heard Zwingli argue that the bread, in the Supper, represents Christ's body, and eating it, we receive Christ spiritually, by faith; also that "the soul is fed by the Spirit and not with the flesh, for *it is the Spirit that quickeneth*." "Yes! the Spirit, it is that which vivifies," exclaimed Lambert. He was converted to Zwingli's side. The Wittembergers shrugged their shoulders and called it "Gallic fickleness." "What!" replied Lambert, "was St. Paul fickle because he was converted from Pharisaism? And have we ourselves been fickle in abandoning the lost sects of popery?"

Yet Luther persisted in his corporeal view. *This is my body*, he repeated, pointing to his favourite words. "The devil himself shall not drive me from that. To seek to understand it is to fall away from the faith."

"But, doctor," said Zwingli, "St. John explains how Christ's body is eaten, and you will be obliged at last to leave off singing always the same song."

"You make use of unmannerly expressions," was the retort. Luther forgot that the Wittembergers had called Zwingli's argument "his old song." The Zurich Reformer, maintaining his coolness, inquired, "Whether Christ, in the sixth chapter of John, did not wish to reply to the question that had been put to him?" (Verse 52: "How can this man give us his flesh to eat?")

"Master Zwingli, you wish to stop my mouth by the arrogancy of your language. That passage has nothing to do here." Zwingli, *hastily:* "Pardon me, doctor, that passage breaks your neck." "Do not boast so much!" said Luther. "You are in Hesse, and not in Switzerland. In this country we do not break people's necks." Then turning to his friends, he added, "He uses camp terms and blood-stained words." Luther knew full well that it was a mere playful expression, for he himself had used a similar one in speaking of Carlstadt.

"In Switzerland also," replied Zwingli, calmly, "there is strict justice, and we break no man's neck without trial. That expression merely signifies that your cause is lost and hopeless."

"Doctor," said the prince to Luther, "you should not be offended at such common expressions." But rough Swiss and stubborn Saxon had clashed; oil did not quench the flames. The prince arose and led the combatants to dinner.

We thus give a specimen of the few sallies of severe words that passed in a discussion that lasted for several days, and was generally conducted "with very great courtesy," says an eyewitness. "During the colloquy no other words were heard than, 'Sir,' and 'very dear friend,' and 'your charity,' and such like. Not a word of schism or of heresy." It might have been said that Luther and Zwingli were brothers and not adversaries." So reports Brentz, but Jonas calls the conference "a very sharp contest." It is well for us to know that the Reformers were human, "of like passions with us." One cannot but see that Luther was not the gentlest of men in the world.

When again in the hall Zwingli began to cite a text from the original Greek, Luther interrupted him, saying, "Read to us in Latin or in German, not in Greek." Zwingli wittily replied in Latin, "Pardon me; for twelve years I have made use of the Greek Testament only." Then he went on to show that the body of Christ was finite like our own. It could be in only one place at a time. He ascended bodily up into heaven. "If Christ be in heaven bodily, how can he be in the bread bodily?" Luther still pointed to his text written on the velvet cover. He would listen to no argument from reason or Scripture. At length, resolved never to be convinced, he seized the velvet cover, raised it from the table, held it before the eyes of Zwingli and Œcolampadius, and exclaimed, in great earnestness, "See!

see! This is our text. You have not driven us from it, . . . and we care for none of your proofs." His great apologist Seckendorf says, "As Luther was of an intractable and imperious disposition, he did not cease from calling upon the Swiss to submit simply to his opinion."

Philip's chancellor exhorted them to come to some understanding. "I know but one means for that," said Luther; "and this is it. Let our adversaries believe as we do." "We cannot," replied the Swiss. "Well then," rejoined Luther. "I abandon you to God's judgment and pray that he will enlighten you." "We will do the same," added Œcolampadius. While these words were passing, Zwingli sat silent, motionless and deeply moved. He had given frequent proofs of the fervour of his affections; now he gave another in a different manner. "Every one saw that his eyes were swimming with tears" on account of Luther's obstinacy.*

The conference was ended. The prince declared, on his deathbed, years afterward, that he had been won over to Zwingli's views by the arguments advanced on the occasion. The discussion was one of the most important of those times, where disputations were the order of the day. It was the greatest of all held among the Reformers themselves. It was intended for uniting both parties, but the result was that it drew more clearly the lines between the Lutherans and the Reformed.

A great plague, "the sweating sickness," broke out in Marburg during those days, and created frightful ravages. Everybody was in alarm. All visitors wished to leave the city. Philip,

---

* "Luther did not come to prove and to weigh, free of prejudice, the arguments of his opponent, but from the very first to reject them."— *Ebrard on the Lord's Supper.*

toiling still for union, said, "Sirs, you cannot separate thus." He took one after another of them aside into his room; he pressed, entreated, warned, exhorted and conjured them. He thought the Reformation would be wrecked if the Reformers did not combine in one great organization. "Never did a general at the head of an army take such pains to win a battle." Zwingli, too, was earnest for union, if unity was not possible, "Let us confess our union in all things in which we agree," said he, "and as for the rest, let us remember that we are brothers. There will never be peace in the Church if we cannot differ on secondary points, while we all maintain the grand doctrine of salvation by faith."

"Yes, yes!" exclaimed the prince, "you agree! Give then a testimony of your unity." Zwingli said to the Wittemberg doctors, his friends joining with him, "There is no one on earth with whom I more desire to be united than with you."

"Acknowlege them as brothers," said the enthusiastic Philip. Their hearts were moved; they were on the eve of union. Zwingli, bursting into tears [so says Luther], approached the Saxon Reformer and held out his hand. The two families of the Reformation were about to be reconciled. But Luther rejected the hand that was offered him, saying, "You have a different spirit from ours!" The Swiss were shocked. Truly they had "a different spirit." Their hearts sank, as Luther kept on repeating the words. He himself is the man who records it.

"You do not belong to the communion of the Christian Church," said the Lutheran Brentz. "We cannot acknowledge you as brethren." Luther said the same. Thus ran the conversation for a short time, when the Swiss said, "We are conscious of having acted as if in the presence of God. Posterity will be our witness." The prince was indignant at Luther, who seemed now to be staggered. He said to his colleagues, "Let us beware of wiping our noses too roughly, lest we bring the blood." Then turning to Zwingli and Œcolampadius, he and his friends said, "We do acknowledge you as friends; we do not consider you as brothers and members of Christ's Church. But we do not exclude you from that universal charity which we owe even to our enemies."

Such a concession was a new insult to the Swiss, who said, "Let us carefully avoid all harsh and violent words and writings, and let each defend himself without railing." Luther then advanced and said to them, "We consent, and I offer you the hand of peace and charity." The Swiss rushed with great emotion toward the Wittembergers, and the shaking of hands delighted the prince. "Assuredly," said Luther, "a great part of the scandal is removed by the suppression of our fierce debates; we could not have hoped for so much. May Christ's hand remove the last obstacle that separates us. There is now a friendly concord between us, and if we persevere in prayer, brotherhood will come."

"We must let the Christian world know," said the prince, "that you agree in the articles of faith, except as to the manner of Christ's presence in the Eucharist." This had the assent of all. But who should draw up the paper? All looked at Luther. The Swiss appealed to his impartiality. He went to his room, uneasy, lost in thought and perplexed. "I will draw up the articles," said he, "but do I not know that they will never sign them?" He did not appreciate the eager desire of Zwingli and his party for union. Fifteen articles were produced. They were read. They were little more than an expansion of the so-called "Apostles' Creed," except on the Lord's Supper. In this the chief point was, "that the spiritual reception of this

body and blood is specially necessary to every true Christian."
They were signed by both parties and sent to the press.

The prince gathered all the doctors at his table on the last
day ; they shook hands and parted. Luther left with a spirit of
alarm in his heart.. "He writhed in the dust like a worm," he
tells us. He imagined that he would never see his wife and
children again. Perhaps the great cause of all this was the advance of the Turks to Vienna, where, a Turkish chronicler says,
"the balls flew through the air like a flight of small birds."
But in a few days "the shadow of God over the two worlds" as
Soliman called himself, "retreated, disappeared and vanished in
the Bosphorus."

Zwingli too went in alarm, but not at the Turks. It was at
Luther's intolerance. He said "Lutheranism will lie as heavy
upon us as popery." But he was braced up by the conviction that
the truth had won a new conquest. "The truth has so mani-
festly prevailed," said he, "that if ever any one has been defeated before all the world, it is Luther, although he constantly
exclaimed that he was invincible. . . . . Luther acts like an un-
skilful swordsman, who says, after he is disarmed, that his opponent knows not the art." This was true. Luther assumed
the air of a conqueror, when Zwingli was so in reality. The doctrine of the Swiss became more generally known and adopted in
other lands.* The great result of the Marburg conference was
not to bring out the differences between the Swiss and German

---

* Father Paul Sarpi, whose history of the council of Trent shows that
he had some sympathies with the Reformers, declared that the wide reception of Zwingli's doctrine was a manifest proof that a higher power
than that of Zwingli was concerned in it. It prepared the way for the
clearer statements on the Lord's Supper made by Calvin.

Reformers, but to exhibit their unity in the great principles of their faith. Certain men, widely separated, unknown to each other and without the least concert, had derived from the Bible the same essential doctrines of saving power. They had met; their enemies had thought they would be as far apart as the poles, and would wrangle and destroy themselves; but they found a unity in their diversity. The Romanists soon learned, to their chagrin, of this union in faith, and sought to make a complete end of the Reformation the next year at Augsburg.

Zwingli reached home in safety, and found the affairs of Switzerland in a most unhappy state. In fact, if he had been more devoted to politics than to truth, he would not have gone to Marburg, for serious trouble had been long fermenting. We now direct attention to them, for in them the earthly destiny of our Reformer was involved.

CHAPTER XXI.

TAKING THE SWORD.

(1528–1529.)

THE finger has been pointed at Zwingli in proof of the Lord's declaration, "They that take the sword shall perish with the sword." He has been blamed for the active part which he took in the political affairs of his country. He was indeed a fervent patriot; he was far more, for in his patriotism he wished to establish a Reformed State as well as a Reformed Church. He fully believed that the word of God ought to control politics as truly as religion. Every Christian must admit this, although he may not approve of the manner in which the Swiss Reformer attempted to bring all things in subjection to the word of the Lord. Perhaps his error was very great and inexcusable; if so, it furnishes a lesson that the Christian should never forget. Perhaps his error was greatly extenuated by the times, the circumstances and the apparent necessities of the case; if so, let us judge of him by the facts of history. Into all these facts we have not space to enter; some of the leading events will throw light upon the course taken by the Reformer.

There were five cantons* that fiercely and stoutly resisted the

---

* This title is given to the Romish party in Switzerland because it was led on by these cantons. The terms "Five Places," "Waldstettes," "Forest Cantons," are sometimes used. A map will show that they lie in

Reform. They were Uri, Schwytz, Unterwalden, Zug and Lucerne. They were intensely given to popery. We do not forget how Oswald Myconius had been driven out of the city of Lucerne, and Zwingli burned in effigy. These were specimens of what the five cantons were ever ready to do. Einsidlen was the only bright spot in Schwytz, and its glory was departing. Zwingli did all he could to persuade them to send deputies to the conferences and learn the truth. "We wish the new faith eternally buried," said the people of Uri. "We will have nothing to do with the new sect," replied Unterwalden. These five cantons were not all; the Romanists held great power in almost every other canton except Berne and Zurich. In some districts the people never knew what to expect; now one party, now the other had the influence. In Bremgarten, the gray-haired Dean Bullinger said to his people, "that for three and thirty years he had been their pastor, walking blindly and leading the blind. But now he had the light. Might God pardon him for his unintentional error, and henceforth enable him to guide the flock into the word of God?" For this he was deposed, but when his son Henry* became his successor, he was permitted to preach the word of God "according to its divine meaning," which he was rejoiced to do.

Such was the ground on which rose up one of the great parties which prepared for war. The vicar John Faber was all the while arousing them to resist the Reform. He sought to draw them into an alliance with Austria, the great enemy against which their fathers had fought for liberty. War was preparing

---

the very heart of Switzerland, and separate the two most powerful Protestant cantons of Zurich and Berne.

* Chapter xxvi.

by the Romanists of all Europe to crush out Protestantism.*
Was it strange that Zwingli thought of self-defence?

What was the strength of the Protestants in Switzerland?
Zurich and Berne were strongly decided for the Reform. Basle
was taking her stand with them. Schaffhausen had long "halted
between two opinions," but at last quietly removed the images,
and brought in the true ordinances of the Church. We remember how bailiff Amberg stole away parson Exlin, and how the
Wirths were burned; yet in the canton of Thurgau the Word
had its triumphs in many parishes. In Constance there were
many Protestants despite the bishop. In one town the people
flung away the statue of St. Blaise, but the poor image felt
lonely and disconsolate in its banishment; so, casting an eye
toward a more appreciative quarter, it swam across the Lake of
Constance into Wurtemburg! if we may believe the monk who
described the miracle. In St. Gall the good work had prospered
under Doctor Vadian. Nearly three-fourths of the people of
Appenzell voted for the Reform soon after Zwingli's death. In
Glaris there was a violent struggle. In one parish the pastor
was in the church waiting for the priests to come and debate with
him. To his surprise they came, marching with drums, entered
his house and broke his furniture; the pastor's friends took their
revenge by breaking to pieces the images in the church. It was
then agreed that every man might choose between the mass of
the priest and the sermon of the preacher. The town of Wesen,

---

* "Five catholic cantons entered into a solemn league, by oath, to defend Rome and suppress the cause of the Reformation. They formed a
treaty with Ferdinand (of Austria), the brother of Charles. V., for uphold-
ing the ancient worship; some of the Protestant pastors became victims
of their cruel hate, and all things portended the approach of a season of
war and bloodshed."—*Morrison's Prot. Reform.*

where Zwingli had lived with his uncle until he outgrew it, was threatened by Schwytz, which joined with Glaris in its government. The young men did not like threats; they took the images out of the churches, carried them to the head of Lake Wallenstadt, and said to them: "This road leads along the lake to Coire and Rome; this southward to Glaris; this westward to Schwytz, and the fourth northward into St. Gall. Take which you please! But if you do not move off, you shall be burnt!" The young people waited a few moments, and then flung the poor motionless images into the flames. Certain men of Schwytz saw the execution, went home and plotted schemes of vengeance upon the town of Wesen.

Zwingli could see a large field with a rich harvest upon it. A map will show how it lay in almost a circle around the five cantons. Haller could have started out upon a visit and made the circuit, dining and lodging almost every noon and night with some good parish minister, and hearing good reports from the lips of such men as Œcolampadius, Hofmeister and Vadian. When on the eastern borders he could have crossed into the country of the Grisons and found the writings of Zwingli in the hands of the peasants, or heard sermons with the true ring in them from the pulpit. The voice of the Swiss Reformer was resounding among the mountains of the Tyrol, and crossing the Rhetian Alps was heard among the lakes at Como and Locarno. Why should he not hope that Zurich might cast her gospel light completely around the five cantons, until, encircled by the brightness, they would yield to the truth? Or why not push on the work into Austria and Italy, and give Rome so much to do that she must draw off some of her forces from Switzerland? But Zwingli committed certain mistakes; perhaps we may describe them.

I. *The union of the churches* was not regarded as of sufficient importance. This would have secured more religious and spiritual effort. Missions would have been set on foot. A confession of faith would have been formed. To these matters Farel and Calvin afterward paid earnest attention. They laboured for a strong union of the churches within the range of their influence.

II. *The union of their cantons* was made the basis of strength. This brought Zwingli into politics and State affairs. D'Aubigne says, "It was the very extension of the Reform in Switzerland that exposed it to the dangers under which it sank. So long as it was concentrated at Zurich, it continued a religious matter; but when it gained Berne, Basle, Schaffhausen, St. Gall, Glaris, Appenzell and numerous bailiwicks, it formed inter-cantonal relations; and—here was the error and misfortune—while the connection should have taken place between Church and Church, it was formed between State and State. As soon as spiritual and political matters became mingled together, the latter took the upper hand."

It certainly was not an error for Zwingli to denounce national sins, as he had done from the first, and to promote that "righteousness which exalteth a nation;" he might display his patriotism along with his piety, and labour to infuse religion into politics; but State affairs should not have drawn him from the special work of religious reform. He became not only pastor but statesman—not only minister but magistrate. And yet there seemed to be a necessity for it. No one among the Swiss Protestants of his times saw so clearly the dangers that threatened the Reformed cantons. "If he retired, the vessel of the State would be left without a pilot. Besides, he was convinced that political acts alone could save the Reform. He resolved, therefore, to be at one and the same time, the man of the State and of the Church. The registers prove that, in his later years, he took part in the most important deliberations."*

The imperial town of Constance had become so Reformed that the bishop and canons had left in disgust. But the emperor threatened it. Constance wanted help to defend herself, and entered into the league. She asked Zurich to join it. Zwingli advised the movement. The alliance was formed on Christmas day, 1527. It was called "The Christian Burgher-Right." The design was to prevent "the ruin of confederate and civil unity." It was made "in the name of Jesus Christ, the eternal Son of God, our Redeemer." In this name the parties agreed "to defend and protect each other with their lives and chattels." Devising peace, they opened the way for war. The next year Berne, St. Gall, and some Swiss towns joined the co-burghery. Zwingli was greatly blamed for all this, even by many of his friends. It looked like forming a new confederation.

III. *An alliance was sought with Protestant countries.*† The five cantons had allied themselves with Austria, which they had no right to do without the consent of the whole Swiss confederation. Berne and Zurich had the right to make any alliance they chose. Zwingli thought if all Protestant cities and countries were united in one holy and powerful league against Rome, the Reformation would be strongly defended against all enemies. Philip of Hesse hailed with joy the idea of the new "Reformed Defensive Alliance," which was born at Zurich. The scheme

---

* D'Aubigne; who also says, "The political phasis of Zwingli's character is in the eyes of some persons his highest claim to glory; we do not hesitate to acknowledge it as his greatest fault."

† This alliance was not formally made until after the first war. Zwingli and Philip of Hesse consulted about it at the Marburg conference.

looked magnificent. All Protestants in one grand league against the pope! Even Francis I., King of France, might join it, for had he not read the book which Zwingli had dedicated to him? Francis was, however, the last man to read "The True and False Religion," or to ally himself very closely with the Protestants. This splendid dream would all vanish so soon as the eyes of the dreamers would be opened. But it cost Zwingli great labour, and raised up many foes.

Great was the wrath of the five cantons when it was known that the Reformed States were entering into these alliances. In their Diet sat William of Diesbach, a Bernese, and he was so keenly reproached because Berne favoured them that he retorted upon the Romanists, saying, "You may try to patch up the old faith; it cannot last much longer." He left the wrathy councillors in disgust. "They patched away with all their might," but their venomous needle drew blood. Persecution was increased. Amberg led on the papists in Thurgau. The Reformed people were fined, imprisoned, tortured, scourged and banished; their goods were confiscated; their pastors had their tongues cut out, or they were beheaded or burned. Bibles and evangelical books were taken away and cast into the flames. Refugees from Austria were given up to their mad pursuers. And still the gospel won more and more believers. The bishop of Constance wrote to the five cantons that if they did not act more vigorously, the whole country would embrace the Reform. They held a conference at Frauenfield. All persons of note in that region came to it. The papists hoped to produce a tremendous effect on the people. But some deputies from Berne and Zurich were there. They told the people how things went on in their country. They begged them to honour God and not fear the threats of the world. Their speeches made a great impression in favour of the gospel. Soon after the people called for the preaching of the word of God, caring little for the increased wrath of the five cantons.

Amberg and his friends wished to see the Austrian governor and secure help. But to go boldly, in open day, would create an uproar. Letters were exchanged; messengers passed to and fro; the plan was laid. A wedding in high rank was to come off over the Rhine at Feldkirch. The party formed, the deputies of the five cantons rode in the centre of the train, in order to escape detection, and they entered the town. Amberg met the governor and begged for help against "the enemies of our ancient faith." Even the Austrians were astonished that the free Swiss should ask the aid of their old enemy and oppressor. But some weeks afterward the alliance was formed with Austria. It ran: "Whosoever shall form new sects among the people shall be punished by death, and, if need be, with the help of Austria. In an emergency Austria shall send into Switzerland six thousand foot soldiers, four hundred horse and all the requisite artillery. If necessary, all the Reformed cantons shall be blockaded and their provisions cut off." Let this agreement be remembered; the example will prove dangerous to its framers. *The first steps to offensive war were taken by the Romish cantons.* This Austrian alliance might have been endured and war averted had it not been for the burning of a Protestant.

Parson James Keyser, called "the Locksmith of Utznach," went often from his home and family in Zurich to a little town in the district of Gaster to preach the good tidings, which were joyfully received. He had a call to the place. One day, when going through the forest to preach on the morrow, six men rushed from their hiding-place, seized him, carried him into Schwytz and delivered him up to the magistrates, saying, "The bailiffs have ordered all innovating preachers to be brought before the judges; here is one for you." Schwytz had no authority in Gaster, but Keyser was hated because he had been pastor and had preached zealously against images at Ufnau, where Ulrich Hutten died. Zurich pleaded for her minister, but her voice was not regarded. The Romanists wanted a victim, and the poor man was soon condemned to be burned alive. When told of the infamous sentence, he wept in his distress and timidity. But when walking to the stake he grew cheerful, courageous, strong in faith, and he died giving thanks to the Lord. "Go and tell them at Zurich how he thanks us!" said one of the heartless judges, with a sarcastic grin, to the Zurich deputies. This was adding insult to cruelty. The council of that canton also sent word to Zurich, saying, "If you had had the interests of your parson as much at heart as you pretend in your letter to us, you would have kept him with you, and not left him with our people. This would have been most agreeable to us, and better for him." This was still more provoking.

Zwingli now felt that the cup was full; it must overflow. Seven days after Keyser's pile flamed up as a signal for war there were other causes of excitement. The Austrians were reported to be raising an army for an invasion of Switzerland. The five cantons were swearing vengeance for the burning of their images. The council of Zurich resolved upon war. Zwingli, the pastor, the statesman, became almost the general of the army: "this triple part of the Reformer was the ruin of the Reformation and of himself." He called for energetic measures. In the streets, in the councils, in the pulpits, everywhere he preached war. He thought the gospel must be defended by the sword. Gideon and Joshua were like examples to him.

Poor people driven out of their houses in the five cantons

came to Zurich, saying, "We will be burned in our villages because we have broken up our images." Zwingli listened to their cries of sorrow, and felt the more strongly the gospel must have free course in Switzerland. "Let us be severe upon these haughty chiefs," he said to the Zurichers. "The mildness of the lamb only renders the wolf more savage. Let us propose to the five cantons to allow free preaching, to renounce their wicked alliances and to punish the mercenaries. As for the mass, images, rites and superstitions, let no one be forced to give them up. This we leave for the Bible to effect."

But it was too late to propose anything. Already were the five cantons enlisting soldiers. Zurich began to send out her men to hold important posts. The young burgomaster Roust said to the Reformer, "We do not wish you to go to the war, because the pope, the emperor, the bishops, the abbots and the Romish cantons hate you mortally. Stay with the council; we need you here."

"No," replied Zwingli, who was not willing to confide the enterprise to any one; "when my brethren expose their lives, I will not remain quietly at home. Besides, the army needs a watchful eye over it." He took down his glittering halberd, which is said to have been borne by him at Marignan, placed it on his shoulder, mounted his horse and set out for the war. The people were surprised ; they crowded into the streets to see him ; they covered the walls, towers and battlements, and among the old men, the women and children was Anna Zwingli, wondering if she was to lose another husband in battle.

The Zurich warriors were at Cappel. They sent the challenge to the army of the five cantons at Zug. Little Zug was terribly frightened, being the smallest of all the Swiss States. The war was about to begin. Captain William Toning was to lead his

Zurichers over the border and make the attack. Just then a horseman came galloping up the mountain. It was Ebli of Glaris, one of Zwingli's noblest old parishioners, and friendly to the gospel. " I have prevailed on the five cantons to halt," said he ; " I want you to do the same. For the love of God and for the safety of the confederation, I entreat you suspend your march." He shed the tears of a patriot. " In a few hours I shall be back again," he added. " I hope, with God's grace, to obtain an honorable peace, and prevent our cottages from being filled with orphans."

The advance was checked. The soldiers began to raise their tents only a little way from the sentinels or " pickets" of the other army. Zwingli sat in his tent silent, sad and fearful of some distressing news. It cannot be said that he was anxious for war. Oswald Myconius, who perhaps knew him best, said, " Zwingli was certainly an intrepid man in the midst of danger, but he always had a horror of blood, even that of his most deadly foes. The freedom of his country, the virtues of our forefathers, and, above all, the glory of Christ, were the sole end of all his designs." And yet Zwingli said, when fearing some trick or treason, "Let us not be staggered ; our destiny depends upon our courage. To-day they beg and entreat, but in a month after we have laid down our arms they will crush us. Let us stand firm in God. Before all things let us be just ; peace will come after that." The time delayed.

The soldiers were not so serious. The advanced posts on each side, were in the best of humour, as if it were but a holiday. They met, shook hands, called themselves confederates and brothers. " There will be no fighting," they would say. " A storm is passing over our heads, but we will pray to God, and he will preserve us from all harm." In the army of the five cantons there was a scarcity of food, but the Zurichers were feasting and wasting. Some young foresters, half starved, got beyond their lines one day; the Zurichers captured them, led them to the camp, loaded them with provisions, and sent them back in all good nature. On another day the hungry soldiers placed a bucket of milk on the front line, and called out that they had no bread. The Zurichers ran, cut their bread into the Zugers' milk, and then both parties sat down to pass their jokes and "eat out of the same dish—some on this side, some on that." What pleased the Zurichers was, that the others were willing to eat with "heretics," a thing which their priests had forbidden.

The most perfect order reigned in the camp at Cappel. Every day Zwingli, or the eloquent Smith, or Francis Zing, then abbot of a neighbouring convent, or some other good minister, preached to the soldiers. No oath, nor quarrel was heard. Bad company was kept at a distance. Prayers were offered before every meal. There was no playing at dice and cards. Now was heard the national song, and again the Christian hymn. There were amusements of a healthy kind, and a fair amount of drilling. Thus the Reformer seemed to impress his spirit upon the army. Affairs were not so orderly in the camp of the enemy.

Messengers of peace arrived before the war had actually begun. The slow business of negotiating went on. The terms were settled, June 26, 1559, about two weeks after the outbreak. The conditions were, that the gospel should be preached freely throughout the whole confederacy—that all alliances against it should be null and void—that the mass and images be left to the choice of the people—that the mercenaries be forbidden to take rewards from foreign princes—that the five cantons pay the expenses of the war—and that Schwytz pay a thousand florins to the children of the martyred Keyser.

The five cantons, "champing the bit that had been put into their mouths," were not willing to give up the deed of their alliance with Austria. Some Bernese deputies said to these papal chiefs, "If you do not deliver up this document, we will go in procession and tear it from your archives." It was brought, two hours after midnight. All the army was called out the next day to hear it read. The Zurichers wondered at so huge a parchment, bearing nine seals, one of them of gold. Scarcely had the reading begun when Ebli of Glaris snatched it, crying, "Enough, enough." "Read it, read it," shouted the Zurichers; "we want to learn their treason." But the peace-loving Ebli replied boldly, "I would rather be cut into a thousand pieces than permit it." Then piercing it with his knife, he cut it in pieces, and the flames soon finished it. "The paper was not Swiss," says Bullinger with sublime simplicity, "and what became of the seals I do not know." The banners were struck, the soldiers marched for their homes. But many men of the five cantons gritted their teeth and declared that they would preserve their "ancient faith," as if the truth was not more ancient than their errors.

In some of Zwingli's thoughtful hours while with the army, and while anxious for the Church, he composed a hymn, which became celebrated on the battle-fields of Switzerland, among the burghers of the cities, and even in royal palaces :

> Do thou direct thy chariot, Lord,
>> And guide us at thy will;
> Without thy aid our strength is vain
>> And useless all our skill.
> Look down upon thy saints brought low,
> And prostrate laid beneath the foe.

Beloved Pastor, who hast saved
    Our souls from death and sin :
Uplift thy voice, awake thy sheep ;
    They slumbering lie within
Thy fold ; and curb, with thy right hand,
The rage of Satan's furious band.

Send down thy peace and banish strife,
    Let bitterness depart ;
Revive the spirit of the past
    In every Switzer's heart ;
Then shall thy Church for ever sing
The praises of her heavenly King.

The treaty was favourable to the Reform, in so far as it sheathed the sword and gave time to spread abroad the gospel. But Zwingli foresaw that the sting had not been taken away from his enemies, and he said, "The peace of Cappel will have this result, that we shall not long have to fold our hands idly over our heads."

CHAPTER XXII.

THE GOSPEL WEAPONS.

(1529-1530.)

WAR was averted, the halberd was hung on the wall, and the sword of the Spirit was resumed. Zwingli laboured with voice, pen and prayer, as if his motto was, "the weapons of our warfare are not carnal, but mighty through God to the pulling down of strongholds." It is not to be supposed that he had, for one moment, entirely lost sight of his work as a minister of God, a theologian and a leader of the spiritual army,

Who battled under heaven's King, with all their might and main,
To drive the hosts of Satan far from every tower and plain,
And by the Word each heart and home, each vale and village win,
And to the Lord present a land redeemed from raging sin.

The pen of the Reformer wrought marvellously. If we were only informed of the fact that, within about two years, he wrote and published his two commentaries on Isaiah and Jeremiah, his full treatise on the Providence of God, and the two confessions of faith addressed to Francis I. and Charles V., we should admire his earnestness in study, his devotion to the truth and his zeal for the kingdom of Christ. But his labours appear astonishing when we know that he preached without ceasing, attended the Marburg conference soon after the peace of Cappel, visited the eastern cantons, presided at synods, attended to the order and discipline of the Reformed Church, and up to the very last days of his life never ceased to urge on the good work in distant lands. Besides the "care of the churches," he took on him the care of the States. Let us see what advantage was taken of the lull in the storm.

It was said of Zwingli that "his eye and his arm were everywhere." The Romanists became alarmed at the quiet work in progress. One of their chroniclers said, "A set of wretched mischief-makers burst into the five cantons, and destroyed souls by scattering abroad their songs, tracts and Testaments, telling the people that they could learn the truth from these, and that one need not believe what the priests said." The Romanists, punning upon a good man's name, said that "it was the devil (Tufel) that introduced the Reformation at Zurzack, on the Rhine." When the priest of that place was preaching one day, a man named Tufel raised his head and said, "Sir, you are heaping insults on good men, and loading the pope and the Romish saints with honour; pray, where do we find that in the Holy Scriptures?" At this serious question many smiled slyly, but the priest, surprised, at his wit's end and trembling, reviled the inquirer as the devil and said, "For this reason I will have nothing to do with thee." He ran from the pulpit as if he believed the evil one was on his track. The people recognized the bold Tufel as a messenger of God to them, broke their images, forsook the mass and accepted the gospel. In rough times we must expect rude scenes.

The convent of St. Gall, claiming a foundation by Gallus the Irish missionary, was one of the great strongholds of superstition. It was fortified by the traditions of nine centuries. At the very time when Zurich sounded the call for arms the abbot Francis was thrown into a fright. He was aged and on the brink of death. The canton was sending troops to the war or posting them quite near to the venerated monastery. The abbot had himself removed to a strong castle, lest he should witness some fearful work of pillage. The convent was entered four days afterward by the peaceable burgomaster Vadian, who informed the monks that the people intended to resume the use of the cathedral church and to remove the images. The friars begged, protested, cried for help, and thought such a change would be a most audacious sacrilege. But the Reformer of St. Gall was an unyielding rock against such wild surges of passion. They hid away their most precious goods and fled to Einsidlen.

One of these monks was Kilian Kouffi, a native of the Tockenburg. Crafty and vigorous, he was the head-steward of the convent. His first care was for a successor to the dying abbot, and he knew of no one who desired the office more than himself. Going to the castle, he had an understanding with those who waited on the aged father that they should not report his death. He expired very soon. Kilian watched the servants as they carried in the meals as usual, and with downcast eyes whispered to them about the health of the abbot. While the death was thus kept a secret from all who were likely to have other plans, the monks at Einsidlen elected Kilian as the successor. He soon proclaimed himself as the new abbot. But Zurich and Glaris, which had part of the control over the convent, would not recognize him unless he could prove by Scripture that a monkish life was in accordance with the gospel. "We are ready," they said through Zwingli, "to protect the house of God, but we require that it be consecrated anew to the Lord. We do not forget that it is our duty also to protect the people. The free Church of Christ should raise its head in the bosom of a free people."

The ministers of St. Gall published forty-two theses, in one of which they declared that convents were not "houses of God, but houses of the devil." The abbot, supported by the five cantons, replied that he could not dispute about rights which he held from kings and emperors. Thus the two natives of the Tockenburg were struggling for the abbey; one was a man born from the ranks of the people—honest, unselfish and devoted to the liberation of the Church; the other, born of a high, proud family, was shrewd, crafty, unscrupulous, ambitious of power, and devoted to Romish pomp and luxury. One claimed the abbey for the people, the other claimed the people for the abbey. A band of the soldiers of Zurich was approaching, and Kilian seized upon the treasures of the convent, fleeing with them across the Rhine into Austria. Peace came, and the cunning monk threw off his priestly robes and put on the dress of a citizen. Creeping mysteriously into Einsidlen, he suddenly raised a howl that ran through all the country. Zurich and Glaris replied by decreeing that a governor "confirmed in the evangelical faith" should preside over the district, with a council of twelve members, while the parishes should elect their own pastors. The abbot felt obliged to leave the country. Austria promised to help him, but on his return, while crossing a river near Bregentz, he fell from his horse and was drowned. Thus of the two Tockenburgers, Zwingli gained the victory through Providence. The convent was put up for sale and bought by the town of St. Gall, "except (says Bullinger) a detached building called Hell, where the monks were left who had not embraced the Reform." Lucerne sent a governor to the place. "You must swear to uphold our constitution," said the townsmen of St. Gall. "A governor has never been known," he replied, "to make oath to peasants; it is the peasants who should make oath to the governor." Such was the old idea of things. He saw that the people had free views, and he retired. The governor sent by Zurich, sound in the faith and in the new ideas, took the oath and remained. He swore to favour the word of God and protect it. The cloister was dissolved. The remaining jewels and ornaments were applied to the wants of the poor. The wrath of the five cantons rose to the highest pitch. By asking too much they had lost all, and had provoked the people into liberty. To God be the glory when wrath is turned to praise. Man's overstep gives God a footing.

Far down in the beautiful regions of Lake Como and Lake Maggiore the name of Zwingli had reached a poor monk in his cell. Egidio à Porta had opposed the wishes of his family, entered an Augustine convent, struggled for years, but found no peace in his soul. He cried to God, and his prayer was to be answered in an unexpected way. The writings of Zwingli fell under his eye. He read and was startled. He saw the folly of a monkish life and of outward works. He felt that he had been a persecutor of the truth and of Christ. Trembling with emotion, he wrote to the Reformer, "If I cannot be a Paul in all things, be thou at least an Ananias to guide my erring footsteps upon the path of peace. Fourteen years ago I let myself be led by an ignorant zeal to forsake my parents and turn monk, thinking thus to gain salvation by works. Thus I have taken much pains, not to *be* pious, and learned but to *seem* so; and in this error, oh shame! I held the office of preacher for seven years. My Christian knowledge all failed me, and I attributed nothing to faith, but everything to works. Boldly did I teach my people to trust in these, and who can reckon up the amount of poisonous error that I have cast abroad in the field of the Lord? Truly I have persecuted the Church of Christ. But in the goodness of the Lord he has willed that his servant perish not for ever; he has shaken

me thoroughly and cast me to the ground. The light of my eyes
is darkened; my lips are dumb till I have begun to cry hoarsely,
'Lord, what shall I do?' A message comes to my heart: 'Go
to Ulrich Zwingli; he will teach thee what to do.' Oh glorious
message! Thou—much more God, through thee—wilt deliver
my soul from the snare of the hunters."

"Translate the New Testament into Italian," replied Zwingli; "I will undertake to get it printed at Zurich." The monk
began the work. But he was greatly hindered; at one time he
must beg for the convent, at another repeat his "hours of devotion," and then he must accompany one of the "fathers" on his
journeys. Everything around him increased his distress. War
was desolating his country; the forces of the emperor were
marching toward Rome to sack the city; men formerly rich were
holding out their hands for alms; crowds of women were driven
to shameless degradation. He imagined that nothing but a great
political deliverance would ever bring about the religious independence of his countrymen. As the great Protestant general
Freundsberg * declared that he was marching on to destroy the
pope, the monk supposed his happy hour was coming. He
wrote again to Zwingli, begging him to stir up the powers to
humble the wicked monks, to take their treasured wealth and
give it to the dying, starving poor, and to open the way for
preaching the pure word of God. "The strength of Antichrist
is near its fall," said he with delusive hope; and added, "I trust
in God that this tree (meaning himself), planted so far from the
refreshing streams, will in time bear fruit."

Suddenly the letters stopped. The monk disappeared. No

---

* Aonio Paleario and his Friends, chapter ii.: Presbyterian Board of
Publication.

more was heard of his translation of the New Testament. No doubt the ear of Rome heard him, and her arm threw him into some dark dungeon, or treated him with even worse and shorter cruelty. He was not the first nor the last pious Christian whom she has suddenly put out of all human sight.

Zwingli did not rest with this, for he doubtless prompted a missionary movement in Northern Italy. James Werdmiller had been a zealous papist. He had kissed the pope's toe, and he knew what benefit that was by his own experience. When its blessing failed, he began to see his folly, and being won over to the gospel, he sat down at the Saviour's feet. He was a grave man, greatly respected. Zurich had the power to appoint a bailiff at Locarno on Lake Maggiore. "Go thither," said Zurich, "and bear yourself like a Christian." Werdmiller met with darkness intense, and nothing else, until he met a monk named Fontana in a convent. This man had been led to the Scrip-tures, and found what the monk of Como had sought. "As long as I live," said he, "I will preach upon the epistles of St. Paul," for these had given him greatest light. Two other monks had also struggled up to the fountain of life. Werdmiller told them of the wonderful Reformation in his country. Fontana forwarded to Zwingli a letter addressed "to all the Church of Christ in German lands."

"Remember Lazarus," he wrote, "the beggar in the gospel; remember the humble Canaanitish woman longing for the crumbs that fell from the Lord's table: hungry as David, I have recourse to the shew-bread placed on the altar. A poor traveller, de-voured by thirst, I rush to the springs of living water. Plunged in darkness, bathed in tears, we cry to you, who know the mys-teries of God, to send us by the hands of the munificent James Werdmiller all the writings of the divine Zwingli, the famous-

Luther, the skilful Melanchthon, the mild Œcolampadius, . . . the learned Lambert, the studious Leo, the vigilant Hutten and of the other illustrious doctors, if there be any more. Make haste to deliver a city of Lombardy that has not yet known the gospel of Jesus Christ. We are but three, who have combined together to fight on behalf of the truth; it was beneath the blows of a small body of men, chosen of God, and not by the thousands of Gideon, that Midian fell. Who knows if from a small spark God may not cause a great fire?" Thus three men on the banks of the Maggia hoped to reform Italy. They uttered a loud call, which has not been answered for three centuries by the Christian world.

Thus Zurich dared to extend her helping hand to lift up Italy from the ditch of Rome. The five cantons were again in wrath. "What!" said they, "is it not enough that Zwingli and Zurich infest Switzerland? They have the impudence to carry their pretended reform into Italy—even into the country of the pope." They gave vent to loud and furious threats, swearing to arrest the progress of these gospel invasions. Another enemy appeared. James de Medicis, a political adventurer, had gained possession of the fortified castle of Musso, on the northern shore of Lake Como. He threatened and harassed the inhabitants of the Gray League, a district of the Grisons, who had given a majority of votes for the Reform. His deeds of lawless violence were approved and incited by Charles V., who bestowed upon this proud chatelain the title of margrave, and sent him nine hundred Spanish troops, ready at any hour to aid the five cantons.

The Diet of Augsburg was opened in the summer of 1530, by the emperor, Charles V. Zwingli did not attend, but he had sent thither a confession of faith. Jacob Sturm wrote to him, saying, "If the Lord himself does not pity us, and stand by innocence and truth, then will our mighty and raging foes yet devour us alive. No one defends us more than the landgrave [Philip of Hesse], and even he does not venture to do it publicly, but only in narrower circles. To us, ears and access are completely closed. From an appeal in person, or from thy servants here, there is nothing to hope; should circumstances take a more favourable turn, I will send you word." Philip had taken courage enough to lay before the emperor, Zwingli's confession of faith, in which he plainly declared that he must obey God rather than men. At such a time Zwingli turned his eyes to Francis I., the bitter rival of Charles V., hoping to win from France some sort of defensive aid. He entered into correspondence with the French general Maigret, who had some leaning toward the Reform, and who held out hopes that Francis would enter into an alliance with the Swiss republics. Zwingli made his appeal, but no good came of it. Maigret was, perhaps, the only gainer by this contact with the Swiss Reformer, for he became in later years a staunch Huguenot.*

Zwingli was to have one more conference with his devoted friends. On a September day, 1530, there were gathered in his house the principal ministers of the Swiss Reformation, among whom were Œcolampadius, Capito, Myconius and Leo Juda. They drew up an address to the confederates, to be presented at the Diet at Baden, in which they said, "You are aware, gracious lords, that concord increases the power of States, and that discord overthrows them. You are yourselves a proof of

---

· * Of Zwingli's influence upon William Farel, and their correspondence in regard to beginning the good work at Geneva, we have treated in "William Farel and his Times."

the first of these truths. Setting out from a small beginning, you have arrived at a great end by having a good understanding with each other. May God prevent you from giving a striking proof of the second! . . . . We conjure you to allow the word of God to be freely preached among you, as did your ancestors. Away then with all that separates you from our cities! that is, the absence of the gospel. Then, placed in your mountains as in the centre of Christendom, you will be an example to it, as well as its protection and refuge."

"The minister's sermon is rather long," said the deputies of the five cantons when they heard the appeal. They rejected it with contempt, calling for the pope and not the Reformer. There was no hope of a reconciliation between the two great parties in Switzerland.

Œcolampadius had different views from Zwingli in regard to the mode of pushing forward the conquest of the gospel. He believed that the energy of faith, the largeness of charity and the meekness of submission would have far more power than the halberd and the musket. Let the Romanists persecute, imprison, banish, confiscate and burn, but let there be no resistance with the sword. He extolled the power of the divine word. If any man could have saved the Reformation in the cantons from the misfortunes that were impending, he was the man. "The hand of the magistrate wounds with the sword," said he, "but the hand of Christ heals. Christ has not said, If thy brother offend thee, tell it to the magistrates, *but tell it to the Church.* The State and the Church must be separate. The Church cannot work through the State." Zwingli, for a moment, approved of these views; but afterward he departed from them, honestly thinking that the sword must defend the gospel, and the State advance the Church.

The storms of December did not prevent Zwingli from making a journey through the partly Reformed cantons to the westward. His presence inspired respect and confidence. Everywhere he found the majority of the people ready to fight for the gospel if the papists thrust war upon them. He organized or presided over synods in the Tockenburg, in Thurgau and St. Gall. Large crowds listened with enthusiam to his sermons. No man was so great in their estimation. At St. Gall he preached in the cathedral to an immense congregation of people, who remembered that "forty wagon-loads" of broken wooden images had lately been borne away from their town. The citizens were overjoyed at the sight and voice of the father of the Reformation in Northern Switzerland. They gathered under his windows by night, and with songs and instruments testified their love and gratitude.

The voice of Zwingli had changed. Always patriotic, he now became too political; always bold in denouncing national sins and squaring everything by the word of God, he now preached a crusade against the papal cantons. He who had so faithfully laboured for a Reform in the Church, now seemed to throw his whole strength toward a revolution in the confederacy. His one leading idea appeared to be that the government must be reformed. Zurich had accepted the gospel, and therefore Zurich must rule. Berne and Basle would not come to his aid; he thought the curse of Meroz must fall upon them, and if Zurich must stand alone, let her go forth single-handed to the battle. He thought that new times called for new measures. Let every officer who received a pension from foreign powers be displaced, and let a pious man be appointed in his stead. Thus he preached in Zurich. His burning words passed from the Church into the streets, into the halls of the guilds, into the councils, into the fields, and far into the cantons. War was imminent.

CHAPTER XXIII.

THE LAND BLOCKADE.

(1531.)

SWIFT horsemen rode out of Zurich toward the end of April, 1531, as messengers of the council. They went to the cities which were allied to them against the encroachments of the five cantons. In delivering their messages they said, "Take care; great dangers are impending over us all. The emperor and King Ferdinand of Austria are making vast preparations; they are about to invade Switzerland with large sums of money and great armies."

There was danger. The five cantons had laid their plans and begun their work. It cannot be denied that they were the aggressors. They were enraged because of the peace of Cappel and the progress of the gospel. They did not confine themselves to threats, although the treaty of peace had required them to refrain from all abusive language, lest "by insults and calumnies discord should be again excited and greater troubles should arise." They were angry at having signed such an agreement. Their rude tongues could not be restrained. Two Zurichers, who had crept into their Diet, being in wrath because one had lost his pension and the other his convent, said all they could to rouse the papists against their native canton. It was declared in the wilder valleys that the people of Zurich were heretics, worthy of death—that there was not one of them who did not

276

commit sins against nature, and who was not a robber at the very least—that Zwingli was a thief, murderer and an arch-heretic—that Leo Juda was but the pander of Zwingli in horrible crimes—and that it was the duty of the five cantons to sweep them all from the earth. "I shall have no rest," said a pensioner, "until I have thrust my sword up to the hilt in the body of this impious wretch!" The people of the five cantons persecuted the poor Christians among them, fined them, put them into dungeons, tormented them and mercilessly expelled them from the country. The people of Schwytz grew bold and appeared at an assembly, wearing in their hats pine branches, the sign of war. No one checked them. Secret meetings were held, new alliances were sought with the pope, the emperor and the king of Austria. "Birds of a feather fly together," they said, and they entered into a union against the Reformed cantons.

The people of Valais, speaking their French, at first refused to enter into the papal alliance. They preferred neutrality. But on a sudden they thought they were summoned by a miraculous call. A sheet of paper was found upon an altar—or such was the report in their valleys. It contained the sentence that the Reformers of Zurich and Berne preached that a sin against nature was a less crime than to hear mass. Who had placed the mysterious paper on the altar if it had not fallen from heaven? It was copied, circulated and read everywhere. The Valaisans believed it to be a message from the protecting saints. They granted the support that was asked. Villainy has often played such a part in politics. The cantons were gathering, the clang of arms was heard, the winds bore terrible threats over the mountains to Zurich.

"Let us not abandon ourselves," said Zwingli, "and all will go well." At a meeting held in May at Arau, he prepared a new constitution for the confederacy. It did not meet with approval. Berne was opposed to the employment of arms. "There is no doubt," said her deputies, "that the behaviour of the five cantons with regard to the divine word fully authorizes an armed intervention; but the perils that threaten us on the side of Italy and the empire—the danger of arousing the lion from his slumber—the general want* and misery that afflict our people—the rich harvests that will soon cover our fields and which war would destroy—the great number of pious men in the five cantons whose innocent blood would flow with that of the guilty,—all these motives enjoin us to leave the sword in the scabbard."

Zurich replied, "We sacrifice the advantages we now possess if we refrain from war when forced upon us, and we give the five cantons time to arm themselves and fall upon us first. Beware lest the emperor attack us on one side, while the papal confederates attack us on the other; a just war is not in opposition to the word of God, but to refuse to defend the oppressed poor, whom the five cantons are torturing, is contrary to it. Let us beware that we do not cause these poor friends and brothers to become our enemies." Yet Berne would not begin the war.

A new measure was proposed. It will be remembered that the five cantons had once tried to cut off all supplies from the Reformed cantons. Berne now insisted that the tables be turned, and the Reformed cities close their markets against the five cantons, permitting them to receive neither corn nor wine, salt, iron nor steel, until they should allow the gospel to be preached and read among them without persecution. It was argued that

---

* A famine had prevailed at Zurich shortly before, and Strasburg had sent thither supplies of corn.

this measure would rouse the people against the pensioners, who were at the bottom of almost all the troubles. The Zurichers were at first strongly opposed to this measure. Zwingli argued that this was too slow a course. It would give the papists too much time to arm themselves, and it would only madden the enemy. He was in favour of a speedier mode of war. The Zurichers finally agreed to lay the embargo. The ancient record is that Zurich at last submitted, "reluctantly and sadly, only for the honour and pleasure of the allies."

On the next Sunday, according to an old custom, the resolution must be read in the churches. Zwingli entered the pulpit. An immense audience, greatly excited, was waiting to hear him. His soul was overburdened, his eye cast down. If then he had bowed in humiliation before God, confessed the sins of the whole people, and prayed, with patriotic heart, for his beloved Switzerland, who knows but that he, and his country, and the Reformation might have escaped the calamities that were preparing for them? Yet he saw not with the tearful eye of faith, but with the sad eye of force. He imagined that delay would ruin Zurich. After closing the book of the Prince of Peace, he took up the resolution, read it, and said: "Men of Zurich! You deny food to the five cantons, as to evil-doers; very well! let the blow follow the threat, rather than reduce poor innocent creatures to starvation. If, by not taking the offensive, you appear to believe that there is not sufficient reason for punishing the Waldstettes, while yet refusing them food, you will force them, by this line of conduct, to take up arms, to raise their hands, and to inflict punishment upon you. This is the fate that awaits you." In a military point of view this was the wiser policy.

The whole assembly was deeply moved. It was Whitsunday,

and on the very day when they were celebrating the outpouring
of the Holy Spirit, the minister of God was uttering a provoca-
tion to war! "It is a seditious discourse," said some of them.
"It is an incitement to bloodshed." Others replied, "No! it
it is the language which the safety of the State requires." All
the city was in agitation. "Zurich has too much fire," said
Berne. "Berne has too much cunning," retorted Zurich. The
gloomy prophecy of the Reformer was soon to be fulfilled.

One loud wail rose up from the inner districts. The markets
of Zurich, Berne, St. Gall, the Tockenburg and Thurgau were
closed against the five cantons. They seemed to be suddenly in
a vast desert, amid famine, pestilence and death. It was hoped
that certain free towns would send them assistance, but even such
places as Bremgarten and Wesen refused. Several wagons of
provisions were crossing the borders; they were stopped, un-
loaded, upset and turned into barricades for soldiers. " Already
a year of death had made provisions scarce in the five cantons;
already had a frightful epidemic, the *Sweating Sickness*, scattered everywhere despondency and death ; but now the hand of
man was joined to the hand of God ; the evil increased and the
poor inhabitants of these mountains beheld unheard-of calamities approach with hasty steps. No more bread for their children—no more wine to revive their exhausted strength—no more
salt for their flocks and herds! Everything failed them that
man requires for sustenance." People of neighbouring countries were moved with compassion. They concealed provisions
in bales of goods which were allowed to cross the line, and the
Bernese officers were often deceived to the advantage of the
needy. Zurich was more watchful and severe, seizing the con-
traband articles and sending them back whence they came.

The dwellers in the five cantons sought relief from saints,

shrines and papal rites. All sports, dances and amusements were forbidden. Long processions covered the roads to Einsidlen and other resorts of pilgrims. They assumed the belt, the staff and arms of their various brotherhoods, carried chaplets, repeated their *Paternosters* and sang their plaintive hymns among the mountains. They did more; they sharpened their halberds, burnished their swords, brandished their weapons toward Berne and Zurich, and said with rage, "They block up our roads, but we will open them with our right arms." Vain was the effort to introduce the bread of life among them by starvation. "If thine enemy hunger, feed him," was the command in the gospel of mercy. Certain French ambassadors went to them, saying, "If war invade Switzerland, all the society of the Helvetians will be destroyed; whichever party is the conqueror, he will be as much ruined as the other." They assured the Waldstettes that if they would allow the word of God to be freely preached, Zurich would at once raise the blockade. The reply was, "We will never permit the preaching of the Word, as the people of Zurich understand it." Thus ended other attempts at securing peace.

Zwingli now found himself in trouble. It is not surprising that the man who had been for eleven years at the head of the Church in Zurich should have fallen in the general esteem when he put himself at the head of the State. He was even represented as the author of the measure which he had opposed with all his might. The angry populace in the city charged him with being the sole cause of the civil war, and reproached him as a leveller, a destroyer of the ancient rights, a tyrant like Gessler. The wealthy were told that he courted the poor in order to gain popular power; the peasants were made to believe that this one man brought scarcity into their cabins and danger to their property. In the council mistrust and dissension increased. By his advice the number of nobles was diminished in the two councils, because of their opposition to the gospel; this gave offence to the more honourable families of the city and canton. Corn grew scarcer in Zurich; the millers and the bakers were laid under certain rules, and the people blamed the Reformer for these evils. All who hated the gospel joined with the monks and mercenaries, and the malcontents of every class were arrayed against the minister of peace who was preaching an aggressive war. One loud voice was raised against him.

Zwingli was heart-broken, for he saw that the pilot would not be able to save the ship in such a heaving sea. Not yet did he perceive that the Reformer had a different work to perform from the statesman. "Religious and political matters were united in the mind of this great man by such old and dear ties that it was impossible for him to distinguish their line of separation. The confusion had become his dominant idea; the Christian and the citizen were for him one and the same character; and hence it resulted that all the resources of the State—even cannons and arquebuses—were to be placed at the service of truth. When one peculiar idea thus seizes upon a man, we see a false conscience formed within him, which approves of many things condemned by the word of the Lord."* It had been far better for the cause that lay nearest his heart if he had preached faith, repentance and peace with all the energy and eloquence of his former years.

What could he do? A feeling of his forsaken condition took

---

* D'Aubigne. The stronger apologists of Zwingli, such as Hottinger and Christoffel, do not attempt to justify the Reformer in his political measures.

hold upon him. On the 26th of July he went before the council, in which intrigue and disunion reigned, and with deep emotion he said, "For eleven years I have been preaching the gospel among you, and I have faithfully warned you, as a father, of the dangers that would threaten the confederacy if the five cantons— that is, the crew of the pensioners—should get the upper hand. No attention has been paid to my words. The mercenaries and the foes of the gospel are elected to the council. You refuse to follow my advice, and yet you hold me responsible for all the mischief and misfortune. I therefore ask for my dismissal, and will look for some other means of supporting myself." The Reformer left the room bathed in tears.

The council heard his words with a shudder, for they began to see how they leaned upon the very man whom many of them had blamed. Their old feelings of respect and confidence were revived. They knew, as all the world must know, that he was honest in his views, patriotic in his intentions, and devoted to the gospel with his mighty heart. To lose him was to ruin Zurich. The two burgomasters were sent to persuade him from his fatal resolution. He asked for three days to consider it. For three days and three nights he sought what road to follow. Ought he to give up all for which he had so long struggled, simply to save himself? Where could he go? If among friends, they would reproach him; if among foes, they would destroy him. He groaned in prayer to God. He saw his country and the Church on the point of being beaten down by their enemies, "like corn by the hailstorm." He would rise to ward off the blow and send it back upon the foe. On the third day he appeared again in the council, heard their promise of amendment, and said: "I will stay with you and labour for the public safety *until death.*" Again he was upon his feet; the council rallied to his support; all Zurich summoned up her energies. Peace seemed to reign at headquarters.

Very secretly he set out for Bremgarten, arrived there by night, and lodged in the old parsonage of Henry Bullinger. He sent for the deputies of Berne to meet him there with the greatest secrecy, praying them, in the most solemn terms, to consider the dangers that threatened the Reform. They came. "I fear," said he, "that because of our unbelief this business will not succeed. By refusing supplies to the five cantons we have begun a work that will be fatal to us. What is to be done? If we withdraw the prohibition, they will become more insolent and haughty than ever. Enforce it? They will take the offensive, and if they succeed, you will behold our fields red with the blood of believers, the truth trampled down, the Church of Christ laid waste, all social relations overthrown, our adversaries more hardened and irritated against the gospel, and crowds of priests and monks again filling our rural districts, streets and temples. . . . . And yet," he added after a silence of deep emotion, " that also will have an end."

The Bernese were agitated by the solemn voice of the Reformer. "We see," they said, "all that is to be feared for our common cause, and we will employ every care to prevent such great disasters."* All were agreed that the blockade must not be raised unless the five cantons would first yield. But how to enforce it and still prevent actual bloodshed was the doubtful question. "Bernese promised to do their best," says Bullinger.

During the hours of this conference three of the town councillors were stationed as sentinels in front of the parsonage. It

---

* Bullinger; who says, "I who write these things was present and heard them."

was feared that some of the sympathizers with the papal cantons would hear of Zwingli's presence and attack the house.
Before daybreak the Reformer ordered his horse. Bullinger and
and a few other friends passed with him through the gates.
Three different times Zwingli gave the farewell to the young
pastor, once his pupil, and soon to be his successor. He had a
presentiment of approaching death. He could scarcely tear himself away from his friend, whom he was never to see on earth
again. He blessed him with dropping tears, as he said, ''Oh, my
dear Henry, may God protect you! Be faithful to our Lord
Jesus Christ and to his Church.'' They parted. But at that
very moment the sentinels at the gate shrank back in terror.
They declared that they saw a mysterious personage, clad in a
robe as white as snow, flitting past and plunging into the water
out of sight. Bullinger tells us that he did not see it, nor did
the other friends; he ''sought for it all around, but to no purpose.'' He returned to his house, and could not help but asso-
ciate the white spectre with Zwingli. Strange stories were told
of visions and omens of blood in other quarters during the days
of coming woe.

The people of Zurich wished the great Reformer with them,
but yet would not follow his advice. His former influence was
not regained. The very men who had demanded war were slow
to urge it forward, and were giving all the advantage of time to
the enemy. From his pulpit he said, ''I see that the most
faithful warnings cannot save you. You will not punish the pensioners of foreign princes. . . . A chain is prepared, it unrolls
link after link—soon they will bind me to it, and more than one
pious Zuricher with me. It is against me they are enraged. I
am ready. I submit to the Lord's will. . . . As for thee, O
Zurich, they will give thee thy reward; thou wilt not punish

them; they will punish thee. A hedge of thorns will bristle about thy head. But God will not the less preserve his word."

One night in August, Zwingli was in the church-yard, amid the tombs, with his friend George Miller, formerly the abbot of Wettingen, a convent that had been reformed. They were gazing at a frightful comet, whose long train of pale yellow turned toward the south. It was the famous comet of 1456 and 1531. It created a terror through all the land. The learned men of that day were not free from superstitious notions in regard to such appearances. "What may that star signify?" inquired the abbot. "It will light me," replied Zwingli, "and many an honest man in this confederacy, to our graves." "With God's grace, no!" said Miller. "God will not let such an event happen." "He will," was the reply; "he will for a confirmation of his truth. But if the rod begin at the house of God, then woe to the enemies of the gospel. Yet God will maintain his cause, although it is now so low that it seems to be in ruins. I trust the cause itself; it is right and good; but I trust the people as little as I can. Our only comfort is in God. The truth and the Church will mourn, but Christ will never forsake us." About the same time Vadian of St. Gall was on a hill, one starry night, explaining to his friends and disciples the planets and the miracles of the great Creator, when he was amazed at the appearance of this comet. It seemed to declare the anger of Jehovah. The celebrated Theophrastus said that this comet foreboded not only great bloodshed, but most especially the death of learned and illustrious men.* It is not strange that the

---

* It was held by John Bodin, one of the most learned Frenchmen of the sixteenth century, that comets were spirits that had lived innumerable ages on the earth, and at last coming near to death, celebrated their triumph

Swiss, in their distressful condition, took still greater alarm from such appearances.

Amid all this agitation Zwingli alone seemed calm and self-possessed. He had his presentiments, but he knew where were his refuge and repose. "A heart that fears God," said he, "cares not for the threats of the world. To forward the designs of God is his task. A carrier who has a long road to go must make up his mind to wear his wagon and his gear during the journey. If he carry his merchandise to the appointed spot, that is enough for him. We are the wagon and the gear of God. There is not one of the parts that is not worn, twisted, broken; but our great driver will none the less accomplish his vast designs by our means. Is it not to those who fall upon the field of battle that the noblest crown belongs? Take courage, then, amid all these dangers, through which the cause of Jesus Christ must pass. Others will enjoy on earth the fruits of our labours, while we, in heaven, shall reap our eternal reward." Thus wrote Zwingli in his commmentary on Jeremiah, a work composed the very year of his death. His trials brought him into sympathy with that patriotic prophet, who preached and wept, wept and preached again.

The Romanists were doing something else than gazing at comets and reading omens of terror. The five cantons held a Diet at Lucerne, and resolved to raise the blockade by the force of arms. The papal nuncio announced that the troops of the pope were marching upon Switzerland. All at once alarming

---

or were again brought into the firmament as shining stars. Their victory was attended with awful calamities upon cities and countries, whose rulers were taken away to appease the wrath of God. If learned scholars held such views, what would not the people entertain? See Bayle.

news ceased. The constant threat and rumour of war were not heard at Zurich. It was the calm before the storm; the silence in which the enemy laid their plans for a mysterious attack. All the passes between Zurich and the five cantons were closed, so that no spies might enter.

The friends along on the banks of the lakes Lucerne and Zug, who had promised to give the note of warning to Zurich, were shut up, like prisoners, in their mountains. All was so silent that the council revoked the order to call out the militia. It seemed as if there was treason at work among them, so blinded were they to the alarming facts. Brave old Rudolph Lavater of Kyburg had been called to command an army, but now the army was dispersed. One order was constantly off-setting another. Troops who were summoned were met on the way and sent home. Lavater, in discontent and disgust, retired to Kyburg, and flung away the sword which he had been commanded to sheathe. Zurich was deceived by the crafty men of the Waldstettes. The terrific avalanche was to slip down the icy mountains, and go crashing onward to the very gates of the city, without the least forewarning of its fall.

CHAPTER XXIV.

PERISHING WITH THE SWORD.

(1531.)

A LITTLE boy was to send one alarm to sleeping Zurich. He knew not what he was doing when his father sent him, from his home in Zug, on an errand just over the border. It was the fourth of October when he came to the monastery of Cappel in the canton of Zurich. He gave to the abbot Joner two loaves of bread, without saying a word. A councillor was present. The two Zurichers turned pale at the sight. They had an understanding with some good Zuger, to whom they had said, "If the five cantons intend marching upon the free bailiwicks, you will send your son with one loaf; but give him two loaves if they are marching upon Zurich." The two loaves were a fearful despatch. The abbot and the councillor Peyer wrote with all speed to Zurich, giving notice of their alarm. But no credit was at first attached to this report. Even Zwingli did not believe it. He thought it a "French manœuvre." He was much deceived. Four days more and Zurich would be almost ruined.

On Sunday, the eighth, a messenger appeared at the gates and demanded, in the name of the five cantons, letters of perpetual alliance. "A mere trick," said the majority. Zwingli was in the pulpit: it was his last time, and as if he saw some power requiring of him to deny his faith, he exclaimed, "No, no! never will I deny my Redeemer." At the same time a messenger arrived in haste from Mulinen, a commander of the Johanites, saying, "On last Friday the people of Lucerne planted their banner in the great square. Two men, whom I sent to Lucerne, have been thrown into prison. To-morrow morning the army of the five cantons will enter the free bailiwicks. Already the country-people are running to us in crowds."

"It is an idle story," said the councils. Nevertheless they recalled the commander-in-chief, Lavater, who sent a trusty man with some troops to reconnoitre at Cappel. The five cantons published the manifestoes. They set forth their grievances, charging the Reformers with all the discords sown in the confederacy, just as persecutors accused the apostles of "turning the world upside down." Absalom would have said the same of David. "It is not true," said they, "that we oppose the preaching of the truth and the reading of the Bible. As obedient children of the Church, we receive all that our holy mother receives. But we reject the books and the innovations of Zwingli and his companions."

In the evening of Monday the papal army entered the free bailiwicks. The soldiers went into a church, missed the images, saw the altars broken and were enraged. Then scattering through the country, they pillaged wherever they could find any one to rob. They were particularly enraged against pastors; they entered their houses, destroyed the furniture and heaped curses upon the indwellers. The main army was marching to Zug, and thence to Cappel.

The abbot of the convent, Wolfgang Joner, had heard the night before of the intended invasion. He was a just and pious man,. learned and eloquent, full of compassion toward the poor, and honoured throughout the whole country. Often had he

crossed the border, gone into the canton of Zug and fed the perishing. Now the Zugers were marching upon him with vengeance toward a convent that he had reformed. He paced his
cell, he could not sleep ; he took his pen and wrote to a friend,
"The time has come. The scourge of God appears." This
warning was sent to slumbering Zurich. In the mean time other
bearers of alarming tidings reached the city. It was time that
"the bandage should fall from the eyes of the Zurichers," but
the delusion was to endure to the end. A few of the councillors
met, and said, "The five cantons are only making a little noise
to frighten us into raising the blockade." Other trusty messengers confirmed the sad reports, and the aged banneret, John
Schweitzer, raised his feeble head, saying, "At this very moment send an advance guard to Cappel, and let the army follow
at once." But still the council did nothing. Were its members bribed into silent treason? One traitor strikes, another
prepares the way for the blow. A pastor near Cappel hasted
to Zurich, told how the poor people were crowding about the
convent, and loudly calling for men to defend them and the country; the pastor spoke with warmth, for he had witnessed mourn-
ful scenes, but the councillors turned in their arm-chairs and
wanted to be cautious and prudent. A new courier appeared ; it
was Schwytzer, landlord of the "Beech Tree" on Mount Albis.
He told how the five cantons had seized upon the town of Hitz-
kirk, and were gathering more troops at Baar. Now the council
woke up pale and terrified. The war was actually begun. The
papal cantons had struck the first blow. Yet the councillors
were at variance, making long speeches and wasting time in discussing whether the bells should be rung to call forth men for the
army. Six hundred men were sent to Cappel, but the command
was given to George Goldli, who had a brother in the army of

the five cantons. Treason, doubtless, caused all this apparent stupidity.

A fearful night fell upon the city. The thick darkness, the violent storm, the alarm-bell ringing from every steeple, the people running to arms, the clangour of weapons, trumpets and drums, the cries of women and children, and an earthquake as if nature herself was shuddering at the horrors of the morrow, all added to the excitement of the fatal night, which would be followed by a still more fatal day. Two hours after midnight troops of men were sent far to the right and left of Cappel, as if it was intended that they should not be in the way of the enemy. The better members of the council now were so alarmed that they thought of the "Christian Co-burgher Right," and resolved to appeal to the cities allied to Zurich. "As this revolt has no other origin than hatred of the word of God, we entreat you once—twice—thrice, as seriously, as loudly, as earnestly, as our ancient alliances and our co-burghery will permit us to do, that you set forth without delay. Haste! haste! haste! The danger is yours as well as ours." Such was the appeal, but it was already too late.

While this fearful night was coming on, the Zurichers encamped at Cappel, to the number of about one thousand, looked down from the heights upon Zug and its little lake. Suddenly they saw a few boats on the other side filling with men. The number increased, and soon the horn of Uri was heard, the banner was seen, the fierce warriors were landing and leaping upon the shore. There they were received with shouts and hospitality by the Zugers. On the morrow they would be invading Zurich, and she was not prepared for resistance.

At break of day on the 12th the banner of Zurich was raised before the town-house, but instead of flaunting proudly in the wind, it hung drooping upon the staff; a sad omen to many minds. General Lavater waited under it for soldiers; few rallied to the standard. At ten o'clock there were but seven hundred men under arms. Many of these were old men with more courage than strength, a few councillors who were devoted to the word of God, several ministers who were resolved to live or die with the Reform, the most patriotic of the citizens and many peasants from the neighbourhood. Without uniforms, without order and without efficient arms, these few men were impatient to be on the move. Four thousand had been expected, but there was not the least prospect that the tocsin had roused them from their homes. The oath was not administered to the seven hundred already gathered; they could not wait for the command of their chiefs; two hundred of them rushed through the gates to the field of strife. It was reported that Goldli had already engaged the enemy on the other side of Mount Albis.

A saddled horse was stamping in front of Zwingli's house; his master was within doors preparing to go with the soldiers as field-preacher, at the request of the council. His heart was broken, for Zurich was under the power of the pensioners and traitors. He knew that the five cantons had made long and thorough preparation, while Zurich was stupefied by the policy of the mercenaries. Yet he was calm as a Christian who places all confidence in God. If the Reform must perish, he was ready to perish with it. Surrounded by his weeping wife, children and friends who clung to his garments to detain him, he quitted the house in which he had passed so many days of happiness. He laid his hand upon his horse; the noble steed seemed to give an omen of the fatal day by starting back violently several paces; when the rider was in the saddle the horse refused to advance; rearing and prancing backward, he caused many in Zurich to regard it as ominous. Zwingli gave him the spur, the horse sprang forward, and the Reformer disappeared for ever from the streets of the city. Oswald Myconius was there, remaining in tears among the weeping. He could scarcely stand upright; a sword was piercing his soul. In all quarters were lamentations; every house seemed to be turned into a house of prayer. Amid this general sorrow one woman was silent; God only heard her heart break and knew how mild was her eye of faith. This was Anna Zwingli. She had seen her husband depart; her son Gerold, her brother and other relatives had gone to the field of death.

Zwingli rode on with the undrilled, distracted multitude. Sometimes he turned aside or fell back for a little while; one friend relates that he heard him praying with great fervency, committing himself, and especially the Church, to the Lord. "For a year past the gayety of the Reformer had entirely disappeared. He was grave, melancholy, easily moved, having a weight on his heart that seemed to crush it. Often would he throw himself at the feet of his Master and seek in prayer the strength that he needed. No one had ever observed in him any irritation; he had received with mildness the counsels that had been offered, and had remained tenderly attached to the men whose convictions were not the same as his own.". . . . When on the way to Cappel, "if any one spoke to him, he was found firm in faith: he did not conceal the presentiment that he should never see his family or church again." Thus advanced the forces of Zurich. It was rather the march of a funeral procession than of an army, except that all was disorder and confusion. Along every one of the ten or twelve miles came messengers urging them to hasten to the defence of their brothers. The army of the five cantons had fired their first gun; the ball had passed over the convent of Cappel; the twelve hundred Zurichers had fallen upon their knees and prayed to God for victory.

The reinforcements, with which Zwingli was riding, first heard the roar of cannon as they began to ascend Mount Albis. They were about half-way to Cappel. The road was steep and difficult. But the blood leaped afresh through their veins and they pushed on, overburdened with armour, dragging the artillery, panting, fainting, leaning against the trees for a moment to rest, and appearing to be stragglers rather than soldiers. At the famous "Beech Tree" on the top of the mountain, they halted, sat down and deliberated.

"Hasten forward!" was the shout of a courier from Cappel. Many of the Zurichers sprang to their feet.

"My good friends," said Captain Toning, "what can we do against such great forces? Let us wait here until our numbers increase, and then let us fall upon the enemy with our whole army."

"Yes, if we had an army," bitterly replied General Lavater, who, in despair of saving the republic, thought only of dying with glory. "We have only a banner, and no soldiers."

The voice of Zwingli was then heard: "How can we stay calmly on these heights while we hear the shots that are fired at our fellow-citizens? In the name of God, I will march toward my brother-warriors, prepared to die in order to save them."

"And I too," added the aged banneret, Schweitzer, who cast a withering look at Toning and said, "As for you, delay here till you are a little recovered."

"I am quite as much refreshed as you are," replied the captain, the blood reddening in his face. "You will soon see whether I cannot fight." All hastened to the fray. They plunged into the woods, and a few men bore the banner of Zurich in sight of the enemy.

Just then there was a pause in the battle. Goldli had stoutly held his ground, although he was accused of failing in some movements that might have thrown greater terror into the ranks of the foe. The chiefs of the five cantons had stopped to hold a council. They had seen the banner of Zurich coming down the mountain. They supposed that a greater force was on the way. It was now four o'clock. They were looking for a place to camp and pass the night. They were waiting to see if Zurich would send any request for peace. If at this moment any mediators had appeared, their proposals would have been accepted, unless Bullinger was mistaken. But none appeared. Neither Zwingli nor any man of Zurich dreamed of this state of affairs. On what mistakes and ignorance of men the fates of nations hang!

A skilful marksman of Uri, a brave warrior and an acute strategist, named John Jauch, destroyed all hope of peace without war. He pointed out to the chiefs of the five cantons a piece of woods, into which he proposed to lead a few volunteers and attack the army of the Protestants. "I know the Zurichers well," said Caspar Goldli, brother of George: "if you don't beat them to day, they will beat you to morrow. Take your choice."

"It is too late," said some, who did not find it quite to their conscience to wage war on a holyday, "and it was never the custom of our ancestors to shed blood on Childermas-day.* Remember the festival of the Innocents."

---

* The day kept in memory of the slaughter of the children of Bethlehem, and hence also called Innocent's-day.

"Don't talk about the Innocents of the calendar," replied Jauch, "but let us rather remember the innocents that we have left in our cottages." Yet the chiefs were disposed to take their quarters for the night. The warrior of Uri then drew his sword and cried out, "Let all true confederates follow me." Leaping hastily into his saddle, he spurred his horse into the forest, leading about three hundred men, confident of victory. There he dismounted and fell down upon his knees, "for he was a man who feared God," says the chronicler. All his followers imitated him, and together they invoked the aid of the "Holy Mother," the saints, the angels and of God whose Word they fought against. They then posted themselves behind trees, as sharp-shooters, to give the first notice of their presence to the Zurichers by the whistle of three hundred deadly balls.

How blind are men appointed to a calamitous death! The army of the Protestants had been deceived by the pause in the battle. No sentinels, no pickets, no scouts were on watchful duty. Zwingli was pained at their solemn trifling. One of them who was ill-disposed toward the Reformer, said harshly, "Well, Master Ulrich, what say you about this business? Are the radishes salt enough? Who will eat them?"

"I will," replied the chaplain, "and many a brave man now here in the hands of God."

"And I too," rejoined the man, ashamed of his untimely jest. "I will help eat them. I will risk my life for the cause." He did so, says the chronicler, and many others with him. He fell a victim.

All at once the scream of three hundred bullets was heard from the woods, and it was speedily followed by the wail of dying men. The living Zurichers fell on the ground and let the balls pass over their heads; but this was not to be long endured. Springing to their feet, they exclaimed, "Shall we allow ourselves to be butchered? Nay! Let us attack the enemy."

"Soldiers," cried Lavater, seizing a lance and rushing forward, "uphold the honour of God and of our lords, and act as brave men." There stood Zwingli, silent and collected, with halberd in hand. He was asked to speak and encourage the soldiers.

"Warriors, fear nothing," said the Reformer. "If we are this day to be defeated, our cause is still good. If we suffer, it is for God's sake. Cheer up, my noble comrades. Commend yourselves to God." The enemy was all in motion. Jauch had incited the whole army of the five cantons to the battle. In vain did the Zurichers attempt to repel them. Brave men fell while performing brilliant deeds of valour. The noblest blood of the republic was staining the soil. All seemed to depend on Captain Toning, for Goldli had taken to flight in so disgraceful a manner that he could never again live in Zurich. Lavater fought valiantly, fell into the ditch, was dragged out by a soldier and escaped. Captain Toning died for his country as he had foretold. Seven members of one council, and nineteen of the other, lay dead on the field.

Gerold Meyer, twenty-two years of age, a husband and a father, rushed into the foremost rank, and was met by a foe with the words, "Surrender, and your life will be spared." "Never!" said the son of Anna Reinhard. "It is better for me to die with honour than to yield with disgrace." He fell and expired not far from the castle of his ancestors.

History does not record a battle in which so many ministers of the word were smitten to the dust of death. The pastors had marched at the head of their flocks. Twenty-five of them perished. The abbot Joner expired in sight of his convent, and the Zugers almost shed a tear as they rushed over his body, remembering the good deeds to the poor that he had done among them. The eloquent preacher Smith, following by his parishioners, breathed his last, surrounded by forty of his dying men. The aged Geroldsek had marched bravely forth from his adopted Zurich and bathed his gray hairs in blood. Thus fell the preachers of the Reform.

Near to a pear tree, in a meadow, Zwingli stood at the post of danger, the helmet on his head, the sword at his side, the battle-axe* in his hand, and the word of courage on his lips. He did not intend to use his arms, but bore them from a Swiss custom. Early in the engagement, when stooping to console a dying man, he was struck by a stone, hurled by some vigorous forester; he fell but rose again. Again he was struck; again he fell. Thus it continued until he had risen the fourth time, when a lancer gave him a thrust and sent him reeling to the earth. "What evil is it?" he exclaimed. "They may kill the body, but they cannot kill the soul." These are said to have been his last words. Under the pear tree he was found lying, with hands clasped and eyes upturned to heaven, not yet dead. Some marauders came to him when the battle ceased, saw that his breath was not entirely gone, and they asked, "Will you confess? shall we fetch a priest?"

A shake of the head told them as eloquently as his tongue had last proclaimed in the cathedral, "No, I will not deny my Saviour."

---

* Those weapons were borne by him simply as a chaplain, according to a custom of the times. Œcolampadius testifies that Zwingli went with the army, not from choice, but at the order of the council, and with the hope of being called upon as a conciliator. There is no evidence that he struck a blow.

"If you cannot speak," they said, "at least think in thy heart of the mother of God and call upon the saints." He shook his head and still gazed heavenward. The soldiers began to curse him. "No doubt," said they, ignorant of his name, "you are one of the heretics of the city."

One of them being anxious to know who he was, and the night having come, stooped down, raised his head, turned it toward a fire that had been kindled on the spot, and then dropping it heavily, said in amazement, "I think it is Zwingli." A veteran captain, a papist and a pensioner, then came near, saying, "Zwingli! What, that vile heretic Zwingli, that rascal, that traitor!" The captain then struck the dying Christian Reformer on the throat with a sword, exclaiming, "Die, obstinate heretic!" Thus Zwingli at last perished by the sword of the mercenary.

The army of the five cantons had been victorious at all points. The Zurichers were driven into the retreats of the mountains. The night prevented them from being pursued. The hours of darkness were hours of exultation with the victors. Many a Protestant was taunted in death as his heroic leader had been. In the morning some of the Waldstetters came to the pear tree, and pushed through the crowd that had gathered around it, to bestow a kindlier gaze upon the face of the dead chieftain. "He has the look of a living rather than of a dead man," said one of them. "Such was he when he kindled the people by the fire of his eloquence." Another, who had been a canon of Zurich, could not restrain his tears. "Whatever may have been thy creed," said he, "I know, Zwingli, that thou hast been a loyal confederate. May thy soul rest with God."

Soon the drum beat for a court to be held over the "dead heretic." That lifeless body must be tried. Of course the evidence was abundant in such a tribunal. The body was condemned to be quartered for treason against the confederation, and then burnt for heresy. The executioner of Lucerne carried out the sentence. The flames were but a symbol of the insults offered to the corpse. The ashes of the Reformer were mixed with the ashes of a swine, in order that nothing might be preserved as a relic. A lawless multitude thought this too brutal, and rushing to the scene gave the ashes to the four winds of heaven. A few days afterward, Thomas Plater went over the field of battle and found Zwingli's heart unconsumed, which fact was regarded as an evidence of his faithful love to the country, surviving even death and fire.

One day—the awful twelfth of October—had worn away in Zurich. A frightful darkness hung over the city after it. Then came messengers with the dreadful tidings. Then, says Bullinger, "there arose suddenly a loud and horrible cry of lamentations and tears, bewailing and groaning." Two parties soon displayed their sentiments. The Romanists and pensioners were bold to express their sympathy with the victors. The other party, so far as it was separated from true Christians, pointed to the traitors in the city. "Before going to fight the enemy on the frontier," they said to one another, "we should deal with those who are within our walls." Then pointing to the councilrooms, they were ready to say, "Let us chop off the heads of some men who sit there in those halls, and let their blood ascend to heaven to beg for mercy on those whom they have slain." Their words betray their Romish ideas.

The greatest fury broke out against the ministers of the truth and the leading Protestants. Leo Juda had scarcely recovered from a serious illness. The mob rushed upon his house, drove him from it, pursued him, and would have slain him could they

have got him in their hands. A few worthy citizens took him
and hid him in their houses.

Anna Zwingli had heard from her door the rumble of the artillery, and offered fervent prayers to heaven. At length one
awful report after another was borne to her ears. Oswald Myconius was in the street listening to the sad accounts of the couriers. One told that Zwingli had fallen. Zwingli is dead! was
the cry. It ran through the city swift as the wind. It reached
the anxious Anna. She fell to the floor in prayer, for her husband had taught her the source of all consolation. Then came
reports that the battle had laid in the dust her son Gerold, her
son-in-law, her brother, her brother-in-law and other near relatives. Never, perhaps did a woman have a sadder report from
the field of war. Scarcely one of her kindred was left, except
widows and orphans. She closed her doors, she remained alone
with her young children and her God, seeking resignation to the
divine will.

On a sudden the alarm-bell rang. The council had finally resolved to defend Zurich vigorously, to call forth all her men and
send them to the Albis. Commanders were sent to gather up
the defeated, fugitive soldiers along the way to Cappel, and to
organize new troops. It was possible yet to retrieve the defeat
and to wipe out the disgrace by resolution and harmony. But
there was not enough of union. The army of Berne was coming. It had not been pushed forward by General Diesbach, who
was no friend to the Reformation. Lavater again appeared.
There was great activity in reorganizing the men. Regiments
came from the Grisons, from Thurgau, from the Tockenburg and
from other quarters, until the army numbered twelve thousand
men. Even children ran to arms, but the council sent them
home.

Thomas Plater was sitting on the top of Mount Albis the night after the battle. He had gone out from Zurich in the evening, meeting wounded fugitives and frightened deserters. He wished to return, but was not permitted. John Steiner was gathering up the scattered troops and defending the pass, lest the enemy should press on into Zurich. His men bivouacked around their fires, and Thomas Plater among them. He tells us that he was benumbed with the cold and was sitting near the fire with his boots off. Suddenly an alarm was given, the troops were drawn up, and while Plater was getting ready, a trumpeter, who had escaped from the battle, seized his halberd. Plater wrested it from him, put himself in the ranks, and was ready to fight as a free volunteer. Before him stood the trumpeter, without hat or shoes, and holding a pole in his hand. Such was the army of Zurich at the front.

We have not space to tell the whole story of the war. It is enough to relate some of the events and results. Captain Frey was placed in command of the Zurichers and their allies. He called loudly for a forward movement of all the troops, in all now about twenty-four thousand men. They could have defeated the forces of the enemy and sent them begging for mercy to their homes. If God had designed that the gospel should gain a victory by the sword, rather than by spiritual weapons, the Protestants might have won the field. But he intended, doubtless, to teach the Church of all time that the victorious weapons of her warfare were not carnal. He permitted dissensions in the ranks of the Reformed. Berne refused to press forward.

The Protestants were assembled at Bremgarten, the Romanists at Zug. On the night of October 23d, Captain Frey set out with four thousand men, fell upon the outposts of the enemy, drove them back and took an advanced position. His imprudent soldiers then sank into a heavy sleep. The main army of the five cantons saw it all and watched their hour. The next night they quitted their camp in profound silence, wearing white shirts over their coats, that they might recognize one another in the moonlight. Their watchword was "Mary, the mother of God." Stealing into a pine forest near the Reformed forces, they rushed upon them, crying, "Har, Har! where are these impious heretics? Har, Har!" The Protestants at first made a stubborn resistance, and many of the white shirts fell covered with blood. But soon the tide turned; the bravest, with the valiant Frey at their head, bit the dust, and the rout became general.

The aged Francis Kolb had left Berthold Haller at Berne, and came with the army as chaplain. He was provoked at the cruel negligence and cowardice of the Bernese. "Your ancestors," said he, "would have swum across the Rhine, and you—this little stream (the Sihl) stops you. They went to battle for a word, but even the gospel cannot move you. It only remains for us to commit our cause to God." Many voices were raised against the old preacher; others defended him. James May, a Bernese captain, was as indignant as the chaplain. Drawing his sword, he rushed upon the bear on the banner, thrust him through, and cried aloud, "You knave! will you not show your claws?" But the bear remained motionless, and so did the Bernese.

Italian soldiers came to the help of the five cantons, attended by several missionaries to convert the heretics. They moved toward Zurich. Great was the alarm. The pensioners threw themselves forward as peace-makers. Others said, "Above all things, preserve the gospel, and then our honour, as far as possible." A treaty was made. It granted to both parties their faith; the Protestant cantons were to have the gospel as before; the Romanists were to indulge in their popery. But there was one lamentable surrender: such towns as Wesen, Bremgarten and Mellingen, and abbeys like those of Einsidlen and St. Gall, were to be abandoned to the five cantons. Zurich and Berne preserved their faith. They held all that Zwingli had really gained; they lost what he never should have sought. The treaty was signed. The deputies of Zurich got off their horses, knelt on the ground, and called upon the name of their God. Captain Escher, an eloquent, hasty old man, turned to the Waldstettes and said: "God be praised that I can again call you my well-beloved confederates." He then shook hands with the chieftains, the terrible victors at Cappel. All wept, each offered his flask to the opposite chiefs, and parted in peace. The confederacy was saved, but not entirely reformed. The papists did not gain all that they at first imagined. The gospel was not expelled nor the Reformation crushed. The clouded sun would break forth again from behind the smoke of war. Men would hang up the brazen helmet and the sword of steel, and put on the whole armour of God.

Zwingli was dead, having fallen under the weight of his own strength, not yet forty-eight years of age. The next day after his death the anger of Zurich was aroused at the fiendish treatment of his corpse. With eyes bedimmed by tears and voices strong with indignation they said: "These men may slay and quarter and burn his body, but he lives—this invincible hero lives in eternity, and leaves behind him an immortal monument of glory that no flames can destroy. God, for whose honour he laboured, even at the price of blood, will make his memory eternal." Never was a funeral oration more eloquent and truthful. Zwingli lives. We forget his error in urging his canton to make war for the defence and extension of gospel liberty; we insist that his motive was an honest, fervent, pious patriotism, somewhat misdirected; we remember what a hero he was in the cause of God, and what a mighty work he accomplished.

It was Thomas Plater who first met Oswald Myconius after the evening of slaughter and woe. The teacher asked, " Is Master Ulrich dead?" "Alas! yes," replied Thomas. He could say no more. "Then I can live in Zurich no longer," said Oswald. The young man had eaten nothing for twenty-four hours; his teacher took him to his own house, and at the table sat down by him silent and oppressed. Then, taking him into his study, he said, "Where must I go?" The student had another sad story: the pastor of St. Alban's church at Basle had also fallen in the battle; said he, "Go to Basle, and become the minister there." They soon after went to that city.

Plater tells us another part of this history. Myconius was in-vited to preach the *Council Sermon* soon after his arrival, and it must be delivered at six in the morning. "When I entered his room on the appointed morning," says Plater, "I found him still in bed. I said, 'Father, get up; you have to preach your sermon.' 'What! is it to-day?' said Myconius, leaping out on the floor. 'What shall be my subject? Tell me.' 'I cannot.' 'But I insist.' 'Very well, then, show the cause of our disaster, and why it was inflicted upon us.' 'Jot that down on paper.' I obeyed, lent him my Testament, and he went into the pulpit. The desire to hear a new preacher drew a large audience, and so eloquent was he that all wondered. After sermon I heard Dr. Simon Grynæus say, 'Oh, Doctor Sulter, let us pray God for this man to stay with us, for he may do us much good.'" Thus Myconius became pastor, and shortly after he was called to suc-ceed Œcolampadius. He grew warmly attached to Calvin, and mild as he was, he felt a strong sympathy for Farel in his fiery zeal against every sort of Romish idolatry.

CHAPTER XXV.

WE remember Dean Bullinger and the generous welcome which he gave to all visitors in his house at Bremgarten. Strangers noticed there a child of intelligent features and studious manners, who was introduced as Henry Bullinger. He was one of the dean's sons, born in 1504. He had incurred many dangers from his earliest infancy. At one time he seemed to be dead of the plague, but when he was about to be buried some feeble signs of life restored joy to his parents' hearts. At another time, a vagabond was so delighted with him that he was carrying the child away when some neighbours recognized and rescued him. At three years of age he knew the Lord's Prayer and the Apostles' Creed, and creeping into his father's pulpit he gravely repeated, with a full voice, the articles of his faith.

When twelve years old he was sent to the grammar school of Emeric. The customs of those days seem strange to us, for, like Luther, young Bullinger was obliged to beg his bread. The students often found the rules very severe, and to show their displeasure they marched off into the woods, made a camp, gathered little children into it and set up a sort of young republic. They sent the youngest of their number, with arms in their hands, to beg or demand bread. Often they fell upon the foot-traveller, robbed him and spent the proceeds in riotous living.

Henry was preserved from such wickedness, but he sang from door to door and won his supplies, for his father wished him to live upon his own resources, and know by experience how to pity the poor.

He was sixteen years old when he opened a New Testament. "I there found all that is necessary for man's salvation," he afterward said, "and from that time I adhered to this principle, that we must follow the sacred Scriptures alone, and reject all human additions. I believe neither the Fathers nor myself, but explain scripture by scripture, without adding or taking away anything."

Zwingli was one day, in 1521, in his study poring over the Fathers when a young man entered whose face won his eye and his heart. It was Henry Bullinger, who had been studying in Germany, and was anxious to know the teacher of his native land, whose name had become familiar in Christendom. The fine-looking youth was directed in his plans and hopes, and it is said that he was, for a time, a student under Zwingli. The first visit made a powerful impression on him for good. The example of the Reformer was before his eye when he returned to his father's hearth. In due time he became a preacher, and the successor of his father at Bremgarten. We have had glimpses of him, and have quoted his chronicle.

The battle of Cappel filled the heart of Bullinger with gloom and sorrow, for the great Protestant chieftain of Switzerland had perished. The peace could give him little joy, for Bremgarten must be yielded to the papists. The banner of the Lord must be removed; the voice of the Word must cease; popery must reign; persecution would cause woe in many a family and drive humble Christians into banishment. The faithful would be as sheep among wolves. Only a few days after the treaty of peace the Swiss and Italian bands entered into those flourishing districts, which Bullinger had done so much to reform; they brandished their weapons, laid heavy fines on the people, drove the gospel ministers from their parishes, and at the point of the sword restored the mass, the idols and the altars.

This was but the beginning of woe in those towns, convents and bailiwicks which had been surrendered to the Romanists. The convent of St. Gall, of which Kilian had craftily secured the abbacy and died in trying to gain possession, was again filled with monks and insolent priests. Einsidlen, which Zwingli had converted into a sanctuary for the Word, became again the resort of superstitious pilgrims, who gave thanks to the Virgin that the chapel of "Our Lady" was restored. The people of the five cantons made a pilgrimage thither to express their gratitude for their victories.*

A strong man was needed to take the place of the fallen Zwingli. The eyes of the Reformed Zurichers were turned to Basle. Awful tidings had wrung the heart of Œcolampadius. "Alas!" he said, "that Zwingli, whom I have so long regarded as my right arm, has fallen under the blows of cruel enemies!" He was not the man to reproach the dead by saying, Would that he had taken my advice; he might have been spared. He defended the memory of his brother Reformer. "It was not," said he, "on the heads of the most guilty that the wrath of Pilate and the tower of Siloam fell. The judgment began at the

---

* "Einsidlen is the most renowned resort of pilgrims, not only in Switzerland, but for all Middle Europe. The throng every year is still 150,000, and last year (1859) it was said to reach a higher number than ever before, though in 1700 it is stated to have been 202,000, and in 1710, the incredible number of 260,000."—*Cottages of the Alps (Scribner)*.

house of God; our presumption has been punished; let us now trust in the Lord alone, and this will be an inestimable gain." A call came for him to take the position that death had vacated at Zurich, but he declined, saying, "My post is here; I must remain in Basle."

The plague was in the city; all Basle was soon plunged into mourning. "Our pastor is stricken with the pestilence," was the swift report. People of every age and rank hastened to his house. It was not the plague, but a "black carbuncle" that had fiercely attacked his life. The gentle Reformer meekly said, "Rejoice, for I am going to a place of everlasting joy." Gathering about him his family, he celebrated the love of Christ in the supper of the Lord. His wife, children, relatives and domestics "shed floods of tears." The dying man calmly said, "This supper is a sign of my real faith in Jesus Christ, my Redeemer." On the morrow he sent for his colleagues, to whom he said, looking heavenward, "My brethren, the Lord is there: he calls me away. Oh! what a black cloud is gathering on the horizon! what a tempest is approaching! Be steadfast; the Lord will preserve his own." The Church was to pass through a storm. He then reached forth his hand; the faithful ministers clasped it with veneration, and with breaking hearts turned from the peaceful scene.

On the 23d of November—about a month after the last battles of the Swiss—he called his little ones around him. The eldest was barely three years old. He took their tender little hands in his and said, "Love God, who is your Father, will you?" The mother made the promise in their name. He blessed them, and they went to their rest before he should fall asleep in Jesus on this last night of his life. The ten pastors of Basle were standing around his bed. "What is the news?"

he inquired of a friend just coming in. "Nothing," was the reply.

"Well, I will tell you something new," said the dying Reformer. His friends looked astonished as if some awful disclosure was to be made. "In a short time I shall be with the Lord Jesus."

"Does the light of the lamp trouble you?" asked one of his friends, as there were signs that his eyes grew dim. Placing his hand on his heart, he answered, "There is light enough here." The day began to break, and he repeated with feeble voice the fifty-first Psalm, "Have mercy upon me, O God, according to thy loving-kindness." The ten pastors knelt as he added, "Lord Jesus, help me!" At this moment the sun arose and greeted him who was bidding farewell to earth to rest in heaven. Œcolampadius—"the light of the house"—was gone to shine as a star in the firmament of God.

Thus the second great light of Northern Switzerland was removed. He was "in an especial degree the spiritual Christian and the biblical divine," says D'Aubigne. "The importance he attached to the study of the books of the Old Testament imprinted one of its essential characters on the Reformed Theology.* Considered as a man of action, his moderation and meekness placed him in the second rank. Had he been able to exert more of his peaceful spirit over Zwingli, great misfortunes might perhaps have been avoided. But like all men of meek disposition, his peaceful character yielded too much to the ener-

---

* He published commentaries, whose dates we note: On Isaiah (1525); Ezekiel (1527); Haggai, Zachariah, Malachi (1527); Daniel (1530). After his death there were published notes on Jeremiah, Joel, Hosea, Amos, Obadiah, Jonah and Micah.

getic will of the minister of Zurich; and thus he renounced, in part at least, the legitimate influence that he might have exercised over the Reformer of Switzerland."

Two great men were taken from the Church, and the void was felt. The chasm could not be filled. Luther was moved, melted to tears, and keen pangs came upon his mighty soul as he remembered the Marburg conference. Years after he said to Bullinger, "Their death filled me with such intense sorrow that I was near dying myself."

Young Henry Bullinger had been threatened with the scaffold, driven from his parish at Bremgarten, with his aged father, his colleague and sixty of the principal inhabitants. Their houses were pillaged by the Romanists. Three days later he was preaching in the cathedral of Zurich. "No! Zwingli is not dead," said Myconius, "or, like the phœnix, he has risen again from his ashes." The people were carried away by his warm, comforting sermons. They gave him the unanimous call, and he became the successor of Zwingli.

Young as he was—only twenty-seven—he felt as a father to the family of the deceased Reformer. He adopted the orphan children, Wilhelm, Regula and Ulrich, and reared them as their sainted father could have wished. When Ulrich grew up and preached the gospel, he married a daughter of his guardian. Bullinger became the father of six sons and five daughters, thus adding no little strength to the Reformed cause. Two of them became ministers; three daughters married ministers, one of whom was the celebrated scholar, Josias Simler. One son fought for Protestant liberty under Philip of Hesse and William Prince of Orange, and lost his life.

Forty years long did Bullinger exert a most happy influence in Zurich and in the Reformed Church. He won the title of "the second Reformer" in his native land. In six years after the death of Zwingli the Reformation was not only firmly established in the cantons where it had sprung up, but its triumphs were extended in other directions where it had not been tolerated during the life of the man whose voice had first widely proclaimed the Word in Switzerland. The spiritual weapons employed by his successors were "mighty, through God, to the pulling down of strongholds." Anna Zwingli lived to see the day when the seed sown by her husband grew up into the great harvest which he had longed to reap. She died seven years after his death, and with him sang the triumph in the home of peace.

Henry Bullinger was the true man for those quarrelsome times. Talented, gentle, wise, limiting himself to the work of the pen, the parish and the pulpit, he united the clergy, who had been severed by contentions, and drew to himself the good-will of many who had been enemies of his predecessor. His rich stores of learning, his unshaken firmness, his unwearied zeal in maintaining the great principles of Zwingli, made him a man of power. Not in principle, but in policy, did these two Zurich Reformers differ; their work was one—their names will ever be blended in harmony.

In Southern Switzerland, on the shores of Lake Leman, God had placed a man who was the light for which Geneva had long been waiting. On her shield was the motto, "I wait for the light;" she received it in John Calvin, for whom William Farel had prepared the way. An intimacy soon sprang up between the Reformers of Geneva and Zurich. Calvin visited Bullinger in 1539, and attended a synod in that city. Letters passed between them. "How I wish that we could have a single day for free communication together!" wrote Calvin. "How well we could agree!" Again he wrote, "What ought we rather, dear Bullinger, to correspond about at this time, than the preserving and confirming of brotherly kindness among ourselves by every possible means in our power? . . . Our friendship, which commenced so happily, and which rests on so solid a foundation, will continue firm and entire to the last. Between this Church and yours, although I do not see that there exists any disagreement or secret grudge, yet I might wish there was a closer relationship. Let us be free from all appearance of offence. Forgive my anxiety, for I do not doubt your prudence or your courage. But charity hath this peculiar quality, that, while hoping everything, it is meanwhile anxious. . . . Adieu, most learned and upright man. Would that you may not scruple freely also to admonish me."

Leo Juda, who had sung with Zwingli at school and in the convent of Einsidlen, was touched by the plague in 1542, and taken away to strike a golden harp and sing with him in the Father's house. He had translated the Old Testament into Latin, and written more popular works upon theology. He had lived sixty years. Bullinger wrote: "Our Church has lost in that man an inestimable treasure. As for myself, I have lost a good part of my life by the death of that much-beloved brother, and if I did not find consolation by the hope of a better life in that which is to come, and of the resurrection of the dead, I must have given way under my sorrow."

Calvin also wrote to Bullinger: "The death of our brother Leo, as there was good reason why it should be lamented by all good men, so also has it sorely afflicted me. For he had always evinced toward myself personally a singular affection, and when I dwell upon the loss the Church has sustained in the death of this man, it is impossible not to be deeply grieved. With us, also, the past year has been more than usually fatal; for it

carried off both Grynæus and Capito, and many other distinguished men, together with Leo. Wherefore we ought all the
more assiduously to sow the good seed, that the Church may not
remain utterly destitute."

One of the most brilliant men of that age was Vadian of St.
Gall, so long the intimate friend of Zwingli. He seemed to be
equally at home in poetry, eloquence, medicine, mathematics
and scriptural theology. He was the model of all burgomasters,
having been elected to that office eleven times. On a summer
day in 1545 he broke the seal of a letter from Calvin, and
blushed as he read the praises of a candid pen : "Before I knew
you personally, my dear Vadian, I always loved and respected
you; for you had become known to me by your excellent writings,
in which both a wonderful candour, rare among the learned men
of the present day, and a pious zeal of no common character, as
well as your solid erudition, shine forth. But when at Basle, many
testified of your astonishing love to me, and when, in receiving
me, you yourself gave such abundant proofs of it, how could it
be otherwise than that there should be some acccession to my
former feelings toward you ? . . . . Add to this, that I saw that
your friendship would be no small honour to me." Six years
later Calvin wrote to Viret: " I have now again experienced a
fresh wound from the death of Vadian, whose labour, although
of wide influence and calculated to be felt throughout the entire
Church, was nevertheless of especial use in the State, and of
great importance among the Swiss and Grisons. I feel my heart
almost like to break when I think of the great loss the Church
of God has sustained in the death of Bucer." The Vadian
library is still one of the treasures of St. Gall.

Thus the good, the great men were passing into their rest.
Oswald Myconius, labouring zealously at Basle, was preaching

in the cathedral, when he was struck by apoplexy, in his sixty-fourth year. He never rallied. The plague carried him off in 1552, and his prudent wife soon followed him.

The seventy-nine letters* of Calvin to Bullinger prove their affection and union of spirit. They prove also that Calvin held a powerful influence in the churches of German Switzerland. One subject greatly interested them in 1555. We heard the cry of the pious monks of Locarno for the bread of life. Zwingli's hand was reached forth to the believers in that Italian city. Their number increased.

The church which they formed had a brief yet bright career under the preaching of Beccaria, who had read the Bible and struggled up to the true cross. It was an object of deep hatred by the pope. The five cantons, having some authority over Locarno, troubled the church by every sort of intrigue and threat. The pastor was driven into exile. At length a forgery was perpetrated, without a parallel in the annals of treachery. The town-clerk was a native of Uri, the land of Tell. He forged a document which purported to be a pledge to remain for ever firm in the Romish faith, and to be signed by the senators and citizens. It claimed to be somewhat ancient. It was laid away until the forgery would be difficult to detect. It was then laid before the five cantons as a genuine agreement with them to uphold the Romish doctrines, and to punish with death any persons who refused the mass. They set about enforcing it with glad zeal. A severe persecution was waged against the little Locarnese church. In the winter its members were driven from their homes. Zurich offered them a refuge. On a mem-

---

* Calvin's Letters: Presbyterian Board of Publication. There are also seven letters to Myconius.

orable day two hundred men, with their wives and children, left their native town. The story of their banishment and their march through the canton of the Grisons is a most touching one. Two hundred and twenty of them reached Zurich. Those exiles were the ancestors of many of the chief families still in that city, having aided in raising the place of their refuge, in manufactures, wealth and celebrity, above the other cities of Switzerland.

Bullinger wrote: "The church of Locarno has been assembled by the magistrates of our city. The church of St. Peter has been granted to them. Bernard Ochino [the banished Italian Reformer] has been called to be the pastor of the exiled church. The men who have come to us are honourable. Our townsmen love and cherish them."

Calvin replied, in effect: "In this remarkable office of humanity, which your senate has displayed toward exiled brethren, there is a bright example of piety. The world may forget it, but in God's sight it will never cease to be remembered. To me it is not doubtful that some rare blessing of God awaits your city. Because to those who are in distress neither your counsels nor your consolations have ever failed, I offer you my most heartfelt thanks." Geneva and Zurich became refuge-cities for the persecuted Christians of all Europe.

Bullinger lived to mourn the death of Calvin, and to wail with the whole Protestant world over the horrible massacres of St. Bartholomew's day in France. Bayle says, "He died like a good Christian, the 17th of September, 1575. He is the author of a great many books, for besides those which have been printed, and which amount to ten volumes, he wrote several others that are preserved in manuscript."

With tearful reverence must he have sometimes stood by the pear tree where his predecessor fell, and remembered how gloomy was the vision after that sad event. **He had** then written to Myconius, "We will never come together again. No one trusts his neighbour any longer. Surely, surely, we live in the last times. It is all over with the confederacy." But he had lived to see the skies grow bright, and the land rejoice under the smile of the Lord. He had seen that war is not the work of the Church, that the halberd is for the soldier, and that the minister of Christ must employ the hammer of the Word, which breaketh the flinty rock in pieces. Not the strong mind of man, but the mighty spirit of God can govern the Church, and bring the world to a pure faith in Jesus Christ.

Zwingli's pear tree has fallen. A rock has been placed over the spot, engraved with a suitable inscription to his memory. Like that rock is the Reformation, wrought by Zwingli and the men who followed him or laboured in the same age, preaching, as he did at Einsidlen, that "Christ alone saves, and he saves everywhere." It too is inscribed with the memorials of his name, his life and his deeds. It tells us that a peasant's child of the Tockenburg became a hero in the cause of God, and that Ulrich Zwingli holds a first rank among the illustrious Reformers of the sixteenth century.

Our work is not complete without a fuller statement concerning Zwingli's character and theology. If his life were not an exhibition of great principles, it might not deserve to be kept before the Church. His general character " has never been subjected to any very serious or formidable assaults. He was in a great measure free from those weaknesses and infirmities which have afforded materials for charges, in some degree true, and to a much greater extent only plausible, against both Luther and

Melanchthon. He usually spoke and acted with calmness, prudence and discretion, and at the same time with the greatest vigour, intrepidity and consistency. He gave the most satistory evidence of being thoroughly devoted to God's service and of acting under the influence of genuine Christian principle; and his character was peculiarly fitted in many respects, to call forth at once esteem and affection. . . .

"Zwingli was not endowed with the fire and energy, with the vigorous and lively imagination, or with the graphic power of Luther; but his understanding, upon the whole, was sounder and his mental faculties were better regulated and more correctly balanced. He had not been led, either by the course of his studies or by his spiritual experience, to give such prominence as Luther did to any particular departments or aspects of divine truth. He ranged somewhat more freely over the whole field of Scripture for truths to bring out and enforce ; and over the whole field of Popery for errors to expose and assail. . . . Considering the whole circumstances in which Zwingli was placed, the opportunities he enjoyed, the occupations in which he was involved, and the extent to which he formed his views from his own personal independent study of the sacred Scriptures, he may be fairly said to have proved himself quite equal to any of the Reformers in the possession of the power of accurately discovering divine truth, and establishing it upon satisfactory scriptural grounds. . . . His mental constitution gave him a very decided aversion to the unintelligible and mystical, and made him lean toward what was clear, definite and practical."

Thus wrote the late Principal Cunningham,* who admits that, upon certain points of doctrine, Zwingli's precise views are not

---

* The Reformers and the Theology of the Reformation ; Essay v.

easily determined. No doubt they have been often misrepresented, even by those who have endeavoured honestly to state them. Perhaps no one has more thoroughly examined them than the author just quoted ; therefore he may lessen our labour. He says of Zwingli : "His theology upon almost all topics of importance, derived from his own independent study of the word of God, was the same as that which Luther derived from the same sacred and infallible source." Yet at the Marburg conference, he was obliged to satisfy the German Reformers that he fully believed in the divinity of Christ! Such was the suspicion against the man who had preached that "Christ is everywhere, and he alone saves." It was a token of what was coming. The later, cooler judgment has been quite recently expressed by Archdeacon Hardwick : "Notwithstanding all the heavy charges brought against him, then and afterward, it seems impossible to convict him of departure from the central verities of Christianity, such as the Incarnation, the Atonement, the Personality of the Holy Spirit, and other tenets of that class."

One point made by certain writers against the orthodoxy of Zwingli is, that he altogether denied original sin. He did use some terms out of their ordinary meaning. He seemed disposed to limit the word sin, or *peccatum*, to an actual personal violation of God's law ; in this sense sin would not pertain to the nature, but only to the conduct. He seemed to regard the cause of such ill conduct as a disease (*morbus*) rather than as a sin. Hence the supposition that he denied the natural depravity of man, but he did teach "the great scriptural doctrine that all men do, in point of fact, bring into the world with them a depravity of nature, a diseased moral constitution, which certainly and in every instance leads them to incur the guilt of actual transgressions of God's law, and which, but for the interposition of divine grace, would certainly involve them in everlasting misery."*

Zwingli himself declares : " To attain the knowledge of man is as difficult as it is (according to a proverb) to take the cuttle-fish. For, as that animal is said to conceal itself from its pursuers by a black fluid which it casts around itself, so man, when the effort is made to search into his character, shrouds himself in such thick clouds of darkness and hypocrisy that no created eye can detect him. And so the prophet affirms : ' The heart is deceitful above all things and desperately wicked ; who can know it?' For instance, if you assert that the prophet here declares the heart of man to be depraved, that heart immediately devises the evasions, that *depraved* here means only *propense* to depravity, and that the declaration does not apply to *all ;* meaning to assume that it is itself free from depravity, and to prove it from its constancy in the defence of injured human nature ! Indeed the resources of self-love are so inexhaustible that few, or rather none, can arrive at a full knowledge of themselves. God therefore alone, who made man, can give the right knowledge of man. . . . Adam being dead (in sin) they who spring from him must be the same. . . . False theologues, satisfying themselves with admitting that man is *prone* to evil, yet attribute to him a sound power of discriminating good and evil, and of freely applying himself to either the one or the other of them ; but this is only to twist a rope of sand, or to convert Belial into an angel."†

Very striking is this passage in Zwingli's *True and False Religion :* " Had Adam felt that he had anything remaining after his fall, which might gain the favour of his Maker, he would not have fled to hide himself ; but his case appeared to himself so

---

* Cunningham, *Reformers,* etc.   † De Verâ et Falsâ Religione.

desperate that we do not read even of his recourse to prayer.
He dared not at all appear before God. But here is displayed
the mercy of the Most High, who recalls the fugitive, even when
he is passing over as a traitor to the camp of the enemy, and not
even offering a prayer for pardon: who receives him to his mercy,
and, as far as justice will permit, restores him to a happy state.
Here the Almighty exhibited a splendid example of what he
would do for the whole race of Adam; sparing him and treating
him with kindness, even when he deserved only punishment."
He teaches that men "can work no good thing" of themselves,
so morally "diseased and corrupted are they become." He declares that the law "cannot render man righteous and pious; it
only shows him what he ought to be. We must all therefore
despair of our own righteousness."

This might be enough to prove that he did not deviate quite
so far from sound doctrine in his views about the salvation of
certain heathen as has been charged. True, he did intimate, as
some of "the fathers" had done, a hope that some of the more
wise and virtuous heathen were saved. He imagined that in
some way the atonement might be applied to them, and the Holy
Ghost imparted. But his writings prove that he held that none
could be saved "by framing their lives according to the light of
nature and the law of the religion they profess."* He taught
that men were saved, if saved at all, only on the ground of
Christ's atonement and by the Holy Spirit.

Zwingli passed away before "the peculiarities of the Calvinistic system" came to be discussed in connection with the name
of the Genevan Reformer. Mosheim says that the doctrine of
election was "unknown to Zwingli," in the form afterward "in-

---

* Westminster Confession, ch. x.

culcated by Calvin." Milner very cautiously says : " On a careful perusal of Zwingli's voluminous writings, I am convinced that certain peculiar sentiments, afterward maintained by Calvin, concerning the absolute decrees of God, made no part of the theology of the Swiss Reformer." But Scott, in his "Continuation of Milner," has ranked Zwingli with the leading Reformers on this very ground. He asks, "Why, then, is all the odium of these obnoxious doctrines to be accumulated upon the devoted head of Calvin, who had never yet been heard of in public life ?" Zwingli would have been willing to share in the supposed "odium." He tells us that in his earlier life, when studying the schoolmen, he held to the view that God elects some men to eternal life, because he foresees that they will repent, believe and persevere in holiness. But he tells us, also, that he rejected this view, because it makes men the authors of their own salvation.

"The question may still be asked," writes Dr. Cunningham, "whether Zwingli agreed with Calvin in those peculiar doctrines with which his name is usually associated? . . . . We have no hesitation in saying, what is equally true of Luther, that, although Zwingli was not led to dwell upon the exposition, illustration and defence of these doctrines so fully as Calvin, and, although he has not perhaps given any formal deliverance on the irresistibility of grace and the perseverance of the saints, . . . yet in regard to the universal foreordination and efficacious providence of God, and in regard to election and reprobation, he was as Calvinistic as Calvin himself." Of course the truth of Zwingli's theology does not depend upon its agreement with that of Calvin ; the correctness of the theology of both is to be proved or disproved by the Holy Scriptures.

A general opinion is that Zwingli held low and defective views of the sacraments, especially that of the Lord's Supper. He was not quite free from the charge. He is represented as teaching that "the sacraments are just naked and bare signs or symbols," and that the reception of them is a mere commemoration of what Christ has done for sinners ; or a public profession of their faith, and a pledge to live a Christian life. Against this view the later Reformers zealously contended. John Knox in the original Scottish Confession (1560) declared, "We utterly condemn the vanity of those who affirm sacraments to be nothing else but naked and bare signs." Zwingli's views are not so clearly expressed. He was aiming to deny that the sacraments "confer grace;" that in themselves they have a saving or sanctifying power. Insisting upon a part of the truth, he may not have grasped the whole truth, that "the sacraments are signs and seals on the part of God as well as of men ;" that they are means of grace. When Calvin and Bullinger brought the churches of Geneva and Zurich to the higher ground taken in the " *Consensus Tigurinus,*" the former declared his conviction that "if Zwingli and Œcolampadius, those most excellent and illustrious servants of Christ, were now alive, they would not change a word of it."

This may suffice. If Zwingli was somewhat erratic in giving way to his patriotism and his Protestanism so far as to take the sword, he was not a mere adventurer in theology, nor an enthusiast in opinions which have ceased to command respect or belief. His were, in the main, the great doctrines by which the Reformed Church won her triumphs. In general, his theology was that which has always been derived from the most earnest, piercing and prayerful study of the Holy Scriptures.